PLATE 1

LARCH AT WALCOT
Aged 124 years. Height of tallest tree 145 feet. Average volume
77 cubic feet

Photograph by M.C.DUCHESNE. *From the* QUARTERLY JOURNAL OF FORESTRY

FORESTRY FOR WOODMEN

By

C. O. HANSON, I.S.O., M.B.E., F.R.E.F.S.

Formerly Deputy Conservator of Forests, Indian
Forest Department. Instructor, the Crown School
of Forestry for Woodmen, Royal Forest of Dean.
Divisional Officer, Timber Supply Department.
Divisional Officer, Forestry Commission.

THIRD EDITION

OXFORD UNIVERSITY PRESS

OXFORD UNIVERSITY PRESS
AMEN HOUSE, E.C. 4
London Edinburgh Glasgow New York
Toronto Melbourne Capetown Bombay
Calcutta Madras
HUMPHREY MILFORD
PUBLISHER TO THE UNIVERSITY

FIRST EDITION 1911
SECOND EDITION 1921
THIRD EDITION 1934

Reprinted photographically in Great Britain in 1942
by LOWE & BRYDONE, PRINTERS, LTD., LONDON, from
sheets of the third edition

PREFACE

THIS book is, by permission, based on Schlich's *Manual of Forestry*. It has been written to supply a cheap book on scientific forestry for foresters and woodmen, few of whom can afford the more expensive works, and was at first drawn up for the use of the School of Forestry for Working Men in the Forest of Dean. I am greatly indebted to Sir William Schlich, K.C.I.E., F.R.S., Professor of Forestry in the University of Oxford, and to the late Mr. W. R. Fisher, under whom I studied the subject while at Cooper's Hill College, for giving me permission to make use of the *Manual of Forestry* and to reproduce some of the illustrations from that work. I have also referred in Chapter I to Gifford Pinchot's *A Primer of Forestry*, and to Bridges's and Dicks's *Plant Study*; I have occasionally referred to Nisbet's *The Forester*, Forbes's *English Estate Forestry*, Simpson's *The New Forestry* and *The Estate Nursery*. The part on hedges is indebted to Malden's *Hedges and Hedgemaking*. Most of the photographs were taken by myself; some are by Mr. R. C. Milward or Mr. M. C. Duchesne, who have kindly allowed me to reproduce them. The other illustrations are from Schlich's *Manual*. My thanks are due to Mr. E. P. Popert, Consulting Forester to the Commissioners of Woods and Forests, and to Mr. A. G. Hobart-Hampden, Agent to the Earl of Buckinghamshire, both retired Conservators of the Indian Forest Department, for reading through the manuscript and for much valuable advice and help in its preparation, and to Professor J. Bretland Farmer for revising the botanical part of the book.

C. O. H.

LATIMER LODGE, CINDERFORD,
1911.

PREFACE TO SECOND EDITION

THE reception given to this little work has been very gratifying, and the book appears to have been found useful not only by 'Woodmen', but also by foresters, forestry students, land agents, and the owners of woods. During the ten years since the book was first published much has happened to increase the interest taken in forestry. The woods of the country have been ruthlessly felled to provide timber during the war, and in consequence the Forestry Act has been passed and the Forestry Commission appointed to deal with afforestation. I have therefore brought out this second edition to provide a simple handbook for those who will now, in increasing numbers, be dealing with forestry.

In order to retain the character of the book and to be able to keep it at a moderate price, I have not much altered the original chapters, except to bring them up to date in accordance with experience gained during the last ten years, and to revise planting distances and costs of operations, the latter having, of course, increased very much. I have added a chapter on the Forestry Act and Forestry Commission, and also one on the Afforestation of Waste Lands. I hope that the book will continue to be of service to all 'Woodmen' or persons interested in forestry. It is, however, only meant to be an elementary book, and it is hoped that those interested and who are in charge of woods will study the more detailed works, especially Schlich's *Manual of Forestry*.

C. O. H.

8 THE CLOSE, EXETER,
    1921.

PREFACE TO THIRD EDITION

IN this edition I have made no change in the general form of the book. There are, however, many alterations in detail to bring the book up to date in accordance with further experience gained during the last twelve years; and the chapters on planting, nursery management, insects, and fungi have been partly re-written. A new and enlarged index has been prepared. All reference to the cost of operations has been expunged as it has been found that figures given are so soon out of date.

My thanks are due to Mr. Fraser Story and Mr. G. B. Ryle, both of the Forestry Commission, and to Mr. W. E. Hiley, of Dartington Hall Ltd., for reading through the book and for giving me many excellent suggestions regarding alterations and additions required. I am also greatly indebted to the Forestry Commission for financial assistance to enable this edition to be published.

C. O. H.

WARBOROUGH, OXFORD,
  July 1933.

CONTENTS

		PAGE
I.	THE LIFE HISTORY OF A TREE	9
II.	TREE GROWTH IN RELATION TO CLIMATE AND SOIL	19
III.	PURE AND MIXED WOODS	37
IV.	NURSERY MANAGEMENT	48
V.	SOWING AND PLANTING IN THE FOREST	60
VI.	TENDING OF WOODS	73
VII.	METHODS OF TREATMENT (including natural regeneration)	83
VIII.	PROTECTION OF WOODS AGAINST DESTRUCTIVE ANIMALS, BIRDS, AND INSECTS	106
IX.	PROTECTION OF WOODS AGAINST WEEDS AND FUNGI	123
X.	PROTECTION OF WOODS AGAINST FROST, DROUGHT, STORMS, AND FIRES	136
XI.	SYLVICULTURAL NOTES ON BROAD-LEAVED TREES	146
XII.	SYLVICULTURAL NOTES ON CONIFERS	162
XIII.	FENCING AND DRAINING	175
XIV.	FELLING AND MEASUREMENT OF TIMBER	185
XV.	WORKING PLANS	201
XVI.	THE FORESTRY ACT AND FORESTRY COMMISSION	213
XVII.	THE AFFORESTATION OF WASTE LANDS	221
XVIII.	THE USES OF BRITISH TIMBER	228
	INDEX	231

LIST OF ILLUSTRATIONS

FIG.   PAGE

1. The cockchafer 113
2. The pine-weevil 114
3. The pine-beetle 116
4. The oak-leaf roller moth 117
5. The larch miner moth 118
6. Pine sawfly caterpillars 119
7. The spruce-gall aphis 121
8. The larch aphis 121
9. The honey fungus 127
10. The conifer heart rot fungus 129
11. Pine blister 130
12. The larch canker 132
13. Canker caused by *Nectria ditissima* . . . 134
14. Weise's hypsometer 193
15. Friedrich's calliper 196

PLATE

I. Larch at Walcot . . . . *Frontispiece*
II. Oak and beech aged 18 years, in alternate lines   *facing p.*   42
III. Oak aged 37 years, with natural beech underwood   ,,   44
IV. Oak aged 50 years, height 43 feet . .   ,,   46
V. Oak aged 95 years, height 40 feet . .   ,,   78
VI. Natural regeneration of oak aged about 8 years   ,,   92
VII. Beech aged 18 years, at 4 ft. by 4 ft. . .   ,,   148
VIII. Hornbeam aged 18 years, at 4 ft. by 4 ft. .   ,,   152
IX. Oak and larch with coppiced beech . .   ,,   154
X. Douglas fir aged 16 years, at 4 ft. by 4 ft. .   ,,   164
XI. Larch aged 18 years, at 4 ft. by 4 ft.. .   ,,   166
XII. Mature spruce at Walcot . . .   ,,   172
XIII. Survey Plan . . . . .   *page* 220

CHAPTER I

THE LIFE HISTORY OF A TREE

SYLVICULTURE means the cultivation of trees in masses such as are found in woods or forests, and is not the same as arboriculture, which means the cultivation of single trees as they occur in parks and gardens. The object of arboriculture is usually to produce a beautiful tree which will be an ornament to the place where it grows. The object of forestry or sylviculture is usually to produce the largest amount of the best quality of timber which it is possible to grow on a given area of land.

Before commencing the study of forestry it is necessary to know something about the life history of the trees which make up the forest. A tree is a woody plant growing up from the ground usually with a single stem. It consists of three parts. First, the *root*, which grows downwards into the earth to a depth of 3 or 4 feet, and binds the tree to the soil; it takes in water and certain mineral matters which are dissolved in it, and which are needed by the tree in its growth. Second, the *stem*, *trunk*, or *bole*, which supports the crown, and through which the water and its dissolved matters go up from the roots to the leaves. Third, the *crown*, consisting of branches, twigs, buds, leaves, and flowers. In the leaves all the food material is worked up and, as it were, digested.

The bole is the most important part to the woodman, as almost the whole value lies in this part of the tree; nevertheless to get the bole into a proper shape the woodman devotes most of his attention to the crown, because its size and shape are more easily regulated and, as will be seen later, by manipulating the crown the woodman can cause the bole to grow into the shape he desires.

In a forest the crowns of the trees form a cover over the ground, and this cover is called the leaf-canopy.

The food of a tree. The youngest roots are covered with fine root hairs which take in water, and minerals (including compounds containing nitrogen) dissolved in it, from the soil. The water passes up the stem into the leaves, and these take in from the air carbon dioxide gas, which dissolves in the water contained in the leaves of the plant. The leaves, and often other parts of the tree, contain a green coloured matter called *chlorophyll*, which has the remarkable power of being able to cause the elements provided by water and carbon dioxide to become united into complex carbon compounds which form a large part of the actual food of the tree. The principal substances thus formed are known as carbohydrates, and of them sugar is the most important. There are several different kinds of sugar, but sugar of some sort is the chief body to arise in consequence of the activity of chlorophyll. Sunlight, a suitable temperature, and the presence of a trace of iron salt are all essential for the process; indeed, chlorophyll itself is not formed unless at least these three conditions are complied with. It does not, however, need so bright a light for its own production as is demanded for the synthesis (or formation) of the sugars. The latter process, being dependent on light, is generally spoken of as *photosynthesis*, and it is one of the most important of the activities of green plants.

When sugar is produced in a leaf faster than it can be removed to other parts of the plant, of course its concentration in the cell sap rises. If this were allowed to go on, its further production would soon be arrested. But this stoppage is prevented by the fact that when the concentration reaches a certain point, new activities of the protoplasm of the living cell are awakened, and the formation of insoluble starch at the expense of the sugar begins. As the starch is insoluble the action of photosynthesis can continue unchecked, seeing that the concentration of the sugar will not rise beyond the critical point. Sugars, as they arise, are also continually passing away from the leaf to other parts of the tree, there to be used up, along with other materials, in the formation of new living substance, wood and other materials, as well as to supply the chemical energy needed for vital processes. The sugar thus translocated may also accumulate in other parts of the tree, and, by stimulating the production of starch in those regions, e.g. in the medullary rays or silver grain of the wood, provide reserve stores of carbohydrate to be drawn on as occasion may arise When the photosynthetic activity of the leaf ceases, e.g. at night time, the starch formerly produced in the leaves is reconverted, by special ferments, into sugar, which thus continues to replace that which is being still withdrawn from the leaves till all the starch may be finally removed from them. This explains why it is that towards the end of a summer's day the leaves may be full of starch, but next morning may contain little or none.

It must be clearly understood that starch, as such, is of no direct use as a food—it must first be changed into a soluble sugar before it can be employed in the life processes of the plant. The sugar is the utilizable floating capital, the starch the bank reserve, of the plant.

The water from the roots passes upwards to the leaves in the outer layers of the wood, and the sugary sap travels from the leaves to the parts where it is required in the inner layers of the bark. Hence if a tree is 'girdled' by having a ring cut out of it all round the stem, through the bark and outer layers of the wood, it will be killed, as no water can then pass upwards. As a rule, European species are killed by merely cutting through the bark, as the sugary sap cannot then pass downwards to nourish the parts below the ring.

The carbon dioxide gas taken in by the leaves is made up of two elements, carbon and oxygen. The leaves keep the carbon and return most of the oxygen to the air, and, as oxygen is the gas we require when we breathe, this process purifies the air from our point of view.

How the tree breathes. All plants, like animals, breathe in air, keeping the oxygen and exhaling the carbon dioxide gas. This process, which is called *respiration*, is the exact opposite to that

of photosynthesis. The difference between the two processes is
as follows:

Photosynthesis.	*Respiration.*
1. Is a feeding process.	1. Is a breathing process.
2. Carbon dioxide gas is retained.	2. Oxygen is retained.
3. Oxygen is returned to the air.	3. Carbon dioxide gas is returned
4. Purifies the air.	to the air.
5. Only takes place in green parts.	4. Fouls the air.
6. Only takes place in sunlight.	5. Takes place in all parts.
	6. Goes on day and night.

Curious as it may seem, these two processes go on together,
but whereas respiration goes on always in all the living parts of
the tree, photosynthesis only takes place in green parts and in
the day time. During the day photosynthesis is the more active
process, and more oxygen is returned to the air than is retained.
At night respiration alone is going on. Plants therefore, on the
balance, purify the air in the day, and foul it at night, but on
the whole the purifying action is much greater than the other.

Under a microscope little openings can be seen through the
skin of a leaf, especially on the under surface. These are called
stomata, and it is through them that the leaves take in and give
out gases. On the bark of the hazel and cherry long slit-like
openings are seen; these are also used for breathing purposes,
and are called *lenticels*. They exist on all trees, but are not easily
seen on rough barked ones.

Transpiration. Very small quantities of mineral matters are
contained in the water coming up from the roots, and a large
volume of water must therefore pass through the tree in order
that it may obtain a sufficient supply of mineral matters. The
excess water is evaporated into the air through the stomata,
leaving the mineral matter behind. This evaporation from the
leaf surface is called *transpiration*. On a hot day transpiration is
rapid, and if at the same time the soil is dry and the roots do not
get enough water, the leaves fade. A great deal of power must
be required to force the water from the roots up to the top of a
tall tree: what this power is cannot be explained exactly, but it

is known that there is a considerable pumping action by the roots and also a sucking action due to transpiration from the leaves, and these two forces, especially the latter, may be perhaps the main factors in producing the flow of water up the stem.

The growth of a tree. The tree forms sugar in the way described, and from it, together with the mineral matter, makes new wood and other material. The wood consists of cells which formerly contained protoplasm, the living substance of which plants and animals are essentially composed. Concentric layers of these cells are laid on in the form of a thin coat over the whole tree between the older wood and the bark. The new twigs grow in length by a kind of stretching out from the buds; this stretching only goes on in the first year of the life of the twigs and then ceases, buds being formed from which the next year's twigs shoot out. The older twigs, the branches, and the stem grow in thickness only, and do not increase in length; they grow thicker because new wood is laid on over them each year. Between the wood and the bark there is a very thin layer of living cells called the *cambium*; this, obtaining nourishment from the sugary sap, increases and grows in thickness, its inner layers giving rise to wood, and its outer layers to bark, while between these two there yet always remains a thin layer of cambium. The multiplication of cells inwards which turn into wood is greater than that outwards which turn into bark, and thus the layer of wood formed is much thicker than the layer of bark. In this way each year a new layer of wood is added to the outside of the older wood, and a new layer of bark to the inner side of the old bark. The result of this is that the outer bark gets stretched until it can stretch no more, and then it cracks or peels. Before this stage is reached, however, another layer of cells in the bark is formed, called *cork cambium*, and this continuously forms cork on the outer side. The whole tree is thus encased in cork, which prevents water getting into the tree when the outer bark cracks. After a time this layer of cork in its turn gets stretched and cracks, and the process is repeated, a new cork cambium being formed behind the old one and making another layer of cork.

The structure of bark is thus very complicated. What is ordinarily called bark consists of two parts. All that is outside of the latest formed cork is dead matter, because no water or food supply can get to it from the interior of the tree. This is the true bark which serves to protect the tree from outside dangers. It may remain for a long period or it may strip off in patches or rings. All between the cambium and the cork cambium is the inner bark, or *bast*. This remains alive, and through it the food material passes from the leaves to any part of the tree.

The structure of wood. All wood is made up of very small tubes and cells. In the latest formed wood the tubes act as pipes through which the water flows up the tree. In this part the wood is usually soft and light in colour, and it is known as the *sap-wood*.

In the centre of the tree the pipes are blocked up and are no longer used for the transit of water. They are, in fact, dead, and they usually become hard and tough. This is the *heart-wood*, which serves to give strength to the stem. The heart-wood is not necessary for any vital action, and the tree can live without it, as is shown by the fact that hollow trees can live to a great age.

These pipes and cells are of many shapes, and are arranged in many different ways in the several species.

On cutting across the stem of a tree we see the *annual rings*. These are formed in the following way: In the spring when the leaves sprout there is a great demand for water, and the pipes and cells which are then formed have thin walls and large openings. Later on in summer there is not so much want of water, and smaller openings will do; at the same time the bark begins to press on the wood, so that the cell walls must be capable of resisting this pressure; therefore, in summer the pipes have thick walls and small openings. In winter growth stops, and it begins again next spring with the pipes with large openings. These being formed next to the thick-walled ones give the appearance of a ring on a cross section.

These rings are well defined and easily seen in the timber of conifers. In that of broad-leaved trees, though the general manner of formation of the rings is the same, there are slight differences in detail which result in the rings being rather less sharply marked.

Usually one ring is formed each year, so that the age of the tree is known by counting the rings on a section cut at the bottom of a stem. Under certain circumstances, however, such as when the leaves are destroyed by caterpillars in early summer, followed by a second flush, two rings may be formed in a year.

Flowering plants are divided into three great classes: dicotyledons, which have two seed leaves; monocotyledons, which have one seed leaf; and gymnosperms, which differ in many important respects from the other two, though for timber purposes they may be compared with dicotyledons inasmuch as their wood is also characterized by annual rings. The structure of the stem of a monocotyledon is entirely different, but need not be noticed here, as no monocotyledon is of importance in British forestry.

Running across the annual rings, on a section of oak, from the centre of the tree to the bark, are seen some thin lines. These are the *medullary rays* which cause the silver grain when cut in a certain direction. They vary in breadth in the different species, being difficult to see in coniferous timber. Seasoning cracks usually follow these rays.

The rays consist chiefly of soft cells, which keep up a connexion through the harder timber from the pith (the central part of the tree) to the bark, and they are used by the tree, in addition to other parts, as store-houses for any excess of starch, and are possibly concerned in the series of changes whereby sap-wood is ultimately converted into heart-wood.

Reproduction. There is a natural provision for a future generation by the means of seeds. All species have male and female organs, though not necessarily on the same tree, the seeds being produced by the females after fertilization by the males. These reproductive organs are called *flowers*, whether conspicuous or not. To understand the structure of a flower it is as well to examine a simple one like that of a buttercup. On the under-side of a buttercup we find five greenish-yellow floral leaves; these are the *sepals*, whose duty it is to protect the inner parts of the flower while in the bud stage. The five sepals together are called the *calyx*. Inside these we find five bright yellow *petals*, and, if one is examined carefully, a small honey gland or *nectary* will be found at the base of the upper surface. These petals, which are together called the *corolla*, serve to attract insects. Within these petals we find a large number of stalked *stamens*, each of which has a yellow swollen head. This head, which is called the *anther*, contains a very large number of yellow grains called *pollen* grains, each of which contains the male fertilizing substance. The stamens are therefore sometimes called the male organs of the plant. In the very centre of the flower we find a large number of small bottle-shaped *carpels*, which together form the *pistil*. As the carpels of the buttercup are very small it is best to examine a young pea-pod, which is a single carpel of the pea-plant in a rather later stage; it will be seen that the carpel is a hollow body containing *ovules* which after fertilization grow and become seeds. The carpel is therefore, on the analogy of the stamen, the female organ. The hollow part of the carpel is called the *ovary*. At the outer end of the carpel we find a thin projection with its end feathery. This feathery portion is called the *stigma*, and the stalk-like projection from the ovary is called the *style*. The carpel thus consists of the ovary which bears ovules; the stigma which is feathery or sticky and which catches and holds the pollen grains; and the style which holds the stigma in position, connects the ovary with it, and provides for the passage of pollen tubes to the ovules. In some plants several carpels are joined together to form a single ovary; in this case there are often as many separate stigmas as there are carpels in the united ovary.

The pollen from a ripe stamen is carried by insects from flower to flower and in course of time it touches a ripe stigma, to which it sticks. The pollen grain then throws out a tube which grows down the style into the ovary and finally reaches an ovule into which the contents of the pollen tube are emptied. Fertilization is thus completed and the ovule now grows into a seed and the ovary into a *fruit*.

The flowers of trees vary in many details from that of a butter-cup, but the general process of fertilization is similar. In some cases the pollen is blown about by the wind, and is not carried by an insect. In this case the flower often has no petals, and is frequently inconspicuous. Some trees (e.g. lime) have both stamens and pistils in one flower. Others (e.g. hazel and oak) have them in different flowers on the same tree; in the hazel the familiar catkins are a collection of male flowers containing stamens only; the females are small, bud-like, and inconspicuous till fertilization takes place, when they grow into nuts. Species which have separate male and female flowers on the same tree are called *monoecious* species. In willows, poplars, and juniper, the male and female flowers are on different trees, some trees having male flowers only and others having females only; these species are said to be *dioecious*.

The seeds of many trees are aided in their dispersal by means of wings (e.g. Scots pine and other conifers), or by hairs (e.g. poplars and willows). In sycamore, Norway maple, ash, elm, and birch, the fruit is winged. Seeds aided in this way are able to travel farther than those with no such provision, with the result that we find young plants of such species coming up at a great distance from the mother tree, whereas young oaks or other plants whose seeds are heavy will not be found naturally reproduced at any distance from the mature tree, unless carried and dropped by squirrels or birds. The seeds of alder and wil-lows are often conveyed by running water.

Besides reproduction by seeds, most of the broad-leaved trees are able to spring up again by means of stool shoots after the tree has been cut down, or by suckers from the roots. This power varies in the different species, and on it depends the production of coppice woods. Some conifers, for example, *Sequoia sempervirens*, have the power of sending up coppice shoots, but the power is so weak with most conifers that it may be neglected for all practical purposes.

The terms 'broad-leaved tree' and 'conifer' or 'coniferous tree' will often be used to distinguish between two classes of our forest trees. For our purposes a broad-leaved tree may be defined as a species whose leaves are more or less broad and flat, and whose foliage is usually deciduous, the leaves falling off in autumn, leaving the tree leafless in winter. *Quercus Ilex* affords a good example of an evergreen broad-leaved tree, and several broad-leaved shrubs such as holly and privet are also evergreen. A conifer may be defined as a species whose leaves are needle-shaped, or a good deal longer than they are broad, and which, with the exception of yew, juniper, and a few other species, bear cones. British grown conifers are all evergreen, with the exception of larch and *Taxodium distichum*, the swamp cypress.

Broad-leaved trees are often called *hardwoods*, while conifers are called *softwoods*, but this is not a good distinction as some broad-leaved trees have a soft timber.

CHAPTER II

TREE GROWTH IN RELATION TO CLIMATE AND SOIL

It is very important to decide correctly what species should be planted on any given spot, as if a wrong one is chosen, no matter how carefully the wood is afterwards treated, the final result will be disappointing. Many species will do fairly well while young on soils and situations where they will never grow into large timber, and it is often only after twenty or thirty years that they become unhealthy and fall off in growth. There is then nothing to do but to fell the wood long before the trees reach a paying size and to start again with another species. If only poles are required the choice is not so difficult, but when large timber is wanted it is essential to choose those species which will be satisfied with the local conditions of climate and soil. The various requirements of the different species are discussed in this chapter, and, by careful attention to all the points referred to, a woodman should be able to decide what is best to plant.

The following list gives the species which are likely to be found in British woods and plantations. Of these the really important species most likely to be planted are spruce, Sitka spruce, larch, Japanese larch, Douglas fir, Scots pine, Corsican pine, sycamore, ash, pedunculate oak, sessile oak, beech, and Spanish chestnut.

It is almost impossible to raise plantations of silver fir or Weymouth pine owing to various diseases, and these species have practically gone out of cultivation. The elms are chiefly hedge-row trees, and the other species are of minor importance except under special circumstances.

The scientific names given in this edition are those decided upon by the Empire Forestry Association, and are in some cases different from those given in previous editions.

Natural order.	*Name.*	*Scientific name.*
Aceraceae	Norway maple	Acer platanoides
,,	Sycamore	Acer Pseudo-platanus
Oleaceae	Ash	Fraxinus excelsior
Ulmaceae	Common elm	Ulmus campestris
,,	Wych elm	Ulmus glabra (U. montana)
Betulaceae	Birch	Betula pendula and B. pubescens (B. alba)
,,	Common alder	Alnus glutinosa
,,	White or grey alder	Alnus incana
Cupuliferae	English or pedunculate oak	Quercus Robur (Q. pedunculata)
,,	Sessile or Durmast oak	Quercus sessiliflora
,,	Beech	Fagus sylvatica
,,	Hornbeam	Carpinus Betulus
,,	Sweet or Spanish chestnut	Castanea sativa
Salicaceae	White or Huntingdon willow	Salix alba
,,	Crack willow	Salix fragilis
,,	Aspen	Populus tremula
,,	Black Italian poplar	Populus serotina
Papilionaceae	False acacia or locust	Robinia pseudacacia
Coniferae	Norway or common spruce	Picea Abies (P. excelsa)
,,	Sitka spruce	Picea sitchensis
,,	Larch	Larix decidua (L. europaea)
,,	Japanese larch	Larix Kaempferi (L. leptolepis)
,,	Silver fir	Abies alba (A. pectinata)
,,	Douglas fir	Pseudotsuga taxifolia (P. Douglasii)
,,	Scots pine	Pinus sylvestris
,,	Austrian pine	Pinus nigra var. austriaca (P. austriaca)
,,	Corsican pine	Pinus nigra var. calabrica (P. Laricio)
,,	Weymouth pine	Pinus Strobus
,,	Red cedar	Thuya plicata

Note: Where two scientific names are given in the above list the first of them, in each case, is the one approved by the International Botanical Congress, 1930, and may therefore be accepted as correct according to international rules. The names previously sanctioned are also given however—in brackets—as they are still in common use. Additional species are referred to in Chapters XI and XII.

In determining which of these species should be grown in any given spot the following points require consideration:

1. The objects of the owner.
2. The species which have done well on the spot or near by.
3. The latitude, elevation above the sea, and aspect.
4. The danger of, or freedom from, frost.
5. The exposure to winds.
6. The light available.
7. The soil.

1. *The objects of the owner.* In many cases the wood will be grown with a special object in view, and this will often narrow the choice considerably if the soil and climate suit the species desired. If the wood is near a factory requiring a particular species it would probably pay to grow it; for instance, near a chair factory beech may be desirable; near a wood-pulp factory for the manufacture of paper, spruce, or some other quick-growing soft-wooded tree would probably be chosen, as the market for the future timber is assured. Near mines, where pit props have a ready sale, the larches and possibly Douglas fir, the pines or spruces, may be the best species to plant. If there is no such special object in view the woodman's aim should be to grow the greatest volume of the best quality of the most valuable timber. At present, the most paying trees to plant are probably larch, Japanese larch, ash, Douglas fir, Scots or Corsican pines, Sitka spruce, and black Italian poplar.

2. *Species which have done well on the spot or near by.* In deciding what species are likely to do well the examination of neighbouring woods is of the first importance. If a species has already succeeded near by, it may be accepted as fairly certain that the various factors of soil and situation suit that species, and that it will be safe to grow it. But in judging from existing woods it is important to remember that mature woods only are a sufficient guide. A flourishing young wood will only show that the soil and climate suit that species up to its present age or a

little beyond, and does not prove that it will continue to grow well up to maturity; a flourishing mature wood, however, may be accepted as a good indication that a new crop of the same species will succeed if properly managed. If, however, the existing woods are in poor condition it must not be at once concluded that the species is unsuitable. The past management must be taken into consideration, as the poor growth may be due to bad treatment and not to unsuitability of soil or climate. As an example the Forest of Dean may be mentioned. Over large areas the present crop of oak is poor, the trees are short in bole and much branched, and at first sight it might be assumed that the soil and climate are not suitable for oak. Nevertheless, this is not so; the previous crop consisted of fine tall oak, which produced much-prized timber. The poor condition of the present crop is due to different treatment, the woods having been thinned heavily in order to produce knees and crooks for the use of the Navy, in the days when the ships were built of oak. This sort of timber is now valueless.

3. *Latitude, elevation, and aspect.* These factors of the situation must be considered together, as upon them depends the temperature of the local climate. Some trees require warm situations, whilst others will flourish in cold, breezy places; and in deciding what species to plant these factors are perhaps more important than any others. However good the soil may be, no species will grow to timber size if the climate is unsuited to it, while if the climate is good a somewhat poor soil will often grow good timber.

Generally, we may say that the nearer one is to the south of England the warmer is the climate, while as one proceeds towards the north of Scotland it gradually becomes colder. As, however, the local climate, due to its latitude, is modified very considerably by its elevation and aspect, no general rule can be laid down regarding the species to plant in any county, but roughly we may say that oak, chestnut, common elm, ash, beech, Austrian pine, and Corsican pine succeed best in the south of England but, generally speaking, larch, spruce, Scots pine, wych elm, and birch grow at least equally well in Scotland.

Regarding elevation, the higher up a mountain we go the colder it gets, so that we should only plant hardy species on high elevations. Below 1,000 feet above sea-level, all our forest trees will do well if not too much exposed to high winds, if the other factors of the climate and the soil are suitable. It is only when we wish to plant land above 1,000 feet that we must take elevation into consideration. It is generally considered that forests will not pay above 1,000 feet, but if properly treated, and grown densely, it is likely that several species would produce paying timber at a greater elevation (provided that they are near a possible market), at any rate where the site is sheltered by adjacent higher land.

When planting above 1,000 feet it is best to use Corsican pine, larch, Japanese larch, spruce, Sitka spruce, sycamore, and birch, which are more likely to succeed than other species.

Turning now to aspect, south and west aspects are warm, and they are exposed to strong winds and heavy rain, but as the sun shines strongly on them the soil dries rapidly. North and east aspects are cool and the winds are less strong but are drier and colder than those from south or west; the soil remains moist for a good time after rain; vegetation is later in awakening in spring, and owing to this plants escape to a great extent from severe damage by late frosts. Moreover, thaws are more rapid on warm aspects than on north and east ones, and rapid thaws do more harm to plants than slow ones.

It is obvious that these differences in the climate of the various aspects must have their effect on the growth of trees, and we find in practice that, other conditions being equal, some species do better on certain aspects than on others.

The aspect most suited to a species may vary in different parts of the country, because much depends on the latitude and elevation. Thus a tree which does best on a north aspect in the south of England will possibly prefer a south aspect in the north of Scotland, and one which does well on a north aspect at a low elevation may do best on a south aspect at a high elevation.

As a general rule the following aspects are best for the various species, more especially in the Midlands and south of England:

North and *east* aspects are the best for ash, beech, larch, Japanese larch, Douglas fir, hornbeam, silver fir, and spruce.

South and *west* aspects are best for oak, chestnut, elm, maple, sycamore, false acacia, Austrian pine, and Corsican pine.

The following species will do well on any aspect: Alder, aspen, birch, hazel, and Scots pine.

When the land to be planted varies in its aspect it will be well as far as possible to plant each species on the aspect which suits it best. This is especially important with the larch, which is apt to get much diseased; it should be grown on cold north and east aspects, where its bursting into bud will be rather delayed, and where the climate more nearly approaches that of its natural home in the Alps.

4. *The danger of, or freedom from, frosts.* Frosts which occur in winter seldom do great damage to our indigenous trees, though they may kill exotic plants. Early frosts, or those occurring in early autumn, do a certain amount of harm by killing the young unripened shoots, but they seldom kill young trees outright. It is the late spring frost which does the greatest damage and which must be guarded against. Frosts occurring in May or June are very dangerous, while those coming in April are bad but do not do so much harm, as vegetation is not so far advanced.

The effects of frost may be recognized by the frozen plants, or parts of plants, becoming soft and flexible; they usually turn brown, hang downwards, and wilt.

Species which burst into leaf late in spring do not suffer so much as those which do so earlier, as there is then less chance of a bad frost; at the same time the young plants of almost all species will suffer considerably if a frost occurs just as the buds are bursting.

The date when a species bursts into leaf depends on the elevation and aspect, and it is therefore impossible to say that a species is hardy or tender in every circumstance. On a north aspect at a high elevation a species may break out into leaf so much later than under opposite conditions that it may escape from a frost which does great damage to the same species growing on a south aspect at a lower elevation.

Taking all things into consideration we may group the species as follows:

Very frost-tender: Ash, false acacia, sweet chestnut, beech, silver fir.

Moderately hardy: Oak, Douglas fir, maple, sycamore, spruce, Sitka spruce, larch, Japanese larch.

Hardy: Lime, elm, aspen, willows, birch, hornbeam, alder, Corsican pine, Austrian pine, Weymouth pine, Scots pine, red cedar.

Of the three varieties of the Douglas fir, the green or Pacific variety appears to suffer most from early frost, and the Colorado and Fraser River varieties from late frosts.

This list may be taken as fairly accurate in most cases, and a little careful observation will easily enable a woodman to modify it according to the local conditions of his own woods.

Of other species, black walnut, hickories, and Turkey oak are all frost-tender; while American ash, Lawson's cypress, Wellingtonia and Nordmann's fir are hardy.

Danger is greatest while the plants are young. A single night of frost while seeds are sprouting may kill a whole bed of seedlings; the danger continues during the first four or five years of life, and is then gradually reduced as the plants grow taller; it is not at an end till they have grown above the local frost zone, the height of which varies according to the shape of the ground. In damp, deep, narrow valleys forming what are called 'frost holes', quite tall trees may have their foliage destroyed by a bad frost. Woods on hill-sides and high land suffer least. Frosts are worse on north-east, east, south-east, and south aspects, than on north or west ones, and are worse on wet clayey soils than on lighter ones.

In all places where frosts are known to be bad, care should be taken to plant frost-hardy species, of which perhaps the pines, spruce, and hornbeam are the best, the last especially being able to resist severe frosts. Larch, though hardy, is very liable to suffer from diseases in such places, and should not be planted except as a temporary shelter for other trees. The choice of species is greatly enlarged if there is an existing wood on the spot, as the new crop can be planted under the shelter of the old wood, which will considerably reduce the danger. In this case the effect of the shade thrown by the older crop must be carefully considered, as pointed out a few pages farther on, and the over-head cover must be reduced to the degree which will suit the species to be planted. It is not only directly under the shade of the older trees that the frost is reduced; in fact, a very thin overwood of scattered trees will very materially reduce the damage done to young trees planted under and between them.

If no older crop exists, and it is desired to plant a tender species, it will be necessary to start operations by planting a thin wood of birch or larch, and to introduce the new crop when these are tall enough to give some shelter. The birch or larch should be cut out when the young crop is well established and out of danger.

Put shortly, the following measures may be taken to protect plants from frost:

(a) *In a forest nursery.*

    1. Form nurseries on north and north-west aspects.
    2. Do not sow seed before the first of May, and cover it well.

3. Cover the seed beds with dead leaves or moss in autumn, or with branches of trees in spring, or place mats over the seed beds, on short supports, when a bad frost is expected.

(b) *In the forest*.
1. Drain wet places before planting.
2. Plant tender species under a light shelter wood.
3. Use large plants 2 to 3 feet high.
4. When about to plant in a frosty place lift the plants from the nursery early and heel them in, as this delays their sprouting.

5. *Exposure to winds*. In places exposed to *cold* or *dry* winds it is necessary to plant a shelter belt of evergreen trees which will protect the young woods behind them. This should be completed some years in advance of the main crop and should be at least 40 to 50 feet wide, the trees being planted rather far apart on the outside edge, so as to encourage them to branch right down to the ground. The outer rows may be planted about 6 feet apart, and should be kept in an open condition, the inner rows being 4 feet apart. Spruce, Austrian pine, Corsican pine, and *Cupressus macrocarpa* make good belts, and one of these species may be chosen according to the soil. Spruce, although a shallow rooted tree, is fairly wind-firm if grown from the commencement in a thoroughly open position, as it throws out long roots to a considerable distance, and gets a good hold on the ground. When planting a shelter-belt at the same time as the main crop Sitka spruce is best as it is a rapid grower.

Where the woods are exposed to *strong* westerly or south-westerly gales a belt of existing weather-beaten trees should be left standing, or, if no wood already exists, a shelter belt should be formed consisting chiefly of broad-leaved trees, as these are less liable to be blown down than conifers. Both sycamore and beech are good for this purpose, and conifers may be mixed with them in the back rows to thicken the belt.

Along the sea coast, where the winds carry salt spray,

sycamore, Norway maple, beech, white poplar, birch, cluster pine, and Austrian pine are the best species, and a broad belt of these will, when once formed, efficiently protect young woods planted behind their shelter.

6. *The light available.* In order that the chlorophyll in the leaves may be able to make food material, it is essential that they should have sunlight, and it is a matter of first importance for a woodman to understand thoroughly the effect of light and shade on the growth of the different species. A tree which does not receive enough light languishes and eventually dies. Moreover, any individual branch which is too much shaded will die. This fact is taken advantage of by the woodman to make his trees grow into the desired form. If, for instance, an oak wood is planted closely, say at 2 feet apart, after a few years it will enter into the thicket stage, and become densely crowded. In this state a struggle for existence is set up in which each tree is striving to outgrow its neighbour in order to obtain light. This causes the trees to grow rapidly in height, while at the same time the branches are killed off by the heavy shade of the surrounding trees, and we thus get trees which are tall and clear of branches. If, on the other hand, we plant the oaks far apart there is no struggle for existence, as each tree has plenty of light, and it develops a large crown and large side branches.

The woodman, as explained in Chapter VI, regulates the amount of light given to any tree by making thinnings, and causes that tree to grow into the shape desired.

The actual amount of light which must be given to a tree depends on the species. Some must have their heads fully out to the light, and will not stand any overhead shade at all. Such species are called *light-demanders*. Others will bear a considerable amount of shade and are called *shade-bearers*. Others occupy an intermediate position, demanding light on poor soils and situations, but bearing a fair amount of shade under favourable conditions. These trees may be termed *moderate shade-bearers*.

The following list shows the species in the order in which they demand light:

Light-demanders.
1. Larch, Japanese larch, birch.
2. Scots pine, poplars, willows, false acacia, Corsican pine.
3. Oak, ash, sweet chestnut.
4. Elm, alder, Austrian pine.

Moderate shade-bearers.
5. Lime, Weymouth pine, Norway maple, sycamore, hazel, Douglas fir, spruce, Sitka spruce.

Shade-bearers.
6. Hornbeam, red cedar.
7. Silver fir.
8. Beech.

In a general way it may be said that the light-demanders will bear no shade at all, and must be planted fully in the open, except that when coppiced the broad-leaved light-demanders will usually bear temporarily a light shade thrown by an overwood of light-demanders. The shade-bearers may usually be planted under a cover of light-demanders, which only shade the ground slightly, especially if the leaf-canopy is at some height above the ground.

The actual amount of shade which any species will stand must be learnt by experience—not a difficult matter if the woodman keeps his eyes open while walking through the woods. When planting under the cover of existing woods the foregoing list must be borne in mind. Under a cover at all dense, silver fir, beech, or hornbeam must be chosen. In the openings where there is no direct overhead cover but some side shade, spruce, Sitka spruce, Douglas fir, and sycamore will probably succeed.

It must be understood that all the shade-bearers will grow much faster in the light, but they will remain alive and grow, more or less slowly, under cover, and when at any future time they obtain more light they will then shoot up and fill up any blanks in the leaf-canopy.

In early youth beech and silver fir might be termed *shade-demanding*, as they must have shelter, being frost-tender species. Ash and sycamore seedlings will also bear shade for the first four or five years, and oak to a lesser degree.

This question of light and shade has not been properly understood by British woodmen, and in a large number of cases unsuitable species have been planted under the shade of standing trees, with the result that the plantation has failed.

When considering whether any particular species, not mentioned in this list, is light-demanding or shade-bearing, a useful broad rule is that a tree with a light thin crown is usually a light-demander, while one with a dense crown is a shade-bearer.

7. *The soil.* The character of the soil is not so important as that of the climate, nevertheless trees make certain demands upon the soil which it must be capable of fulfilling; thus it must give space for the roots to grow so that the tree may obtain a good hold upon the ground, and it must give moisture and nourishing substances in sufficient quantities.

For practical purposes soils may be divided into *clays* which contain over 60 per cent. of pure clay; *sands* which contain over 75 per cent. of pure sand; *loams* formed of clay and sand in fairly equal quantities; *limy or calcareous soils* containing over 10 per cent. of carbonate of lime; and *peats* which consist chiefly of vegetable matter with very little mineral earth. These soils merge one into another and thus we get such soils as loamy sands, sandy loams, loamy clays, loamy limes, &c. *Marls* are limy soils with over 30 per cent. of clay, the lime being equally admixed throughout each particle of soil.

With regard to the *mineral composition* of a soil, the minerals most necessary for the growth of forest trees are potash, lime, magnesia, iron, sulphur, and phosphorus, and fortunately almost every soil contains these minerals in sufficient quantity to support tree growth, though possibly there may not be enough water to hold them in solution, in which condition alone can they be absorbed by the roots. A crop of trees, provided the humus or layer of leaf-mould formed by the decaying leaves is not removed, requires a far smaller quantity of minerals than a field crop. The fact that agricultural crops are annually removed totally, except in some cases the roots, means the relatively rapid exhaustion of the mineral matters in the soil. This does not apply in the case of a wood, where each year a considerable quantity is returned to the soil in the fallen leaves and only a very small proportion is retained in the timber, to be finally removed when the timber is felled. As a consequence a soil can support a continuous succession of forest crops without any necessity for manuring, and, as another consequence, we find that soils which are too poor for agricultural crops can, as a rule, be profitably employed for afforestation. Conifers require smaller quantities of mineral matters than broad-leaved trees, and should therefore be preferred for planting up minerally poor soils.

Turning now from the mineral character to the physical properties of the soil we find these are of far greater importance, and that a soil which has a sufficient depth, a suitable degree of porosity, and a proper amount of moisture, may be accepted as a good forest soil whatever the mineral composition.

With regard to *depth* we may say that 4 feet of soil, including the subsoil so far as it is well broken up, is sufficient for the good growth of all our forest trees. A deep soil is always more favourable than a shallow one, as in it the roots can obtain a good hold, and have a larger space in which to search out and obtain supplies of water and mineral matters. Moreover, a deep soil is less likely to become dry in dry weather or to become swampy after a heavy rainfall. A deep soil has a great effect upon the height growth of trees, so much so that a fair estimate of the depth of the soil may be made by looking upwards to see the height of the trees.

The different species are content with varying depths of soil according to the nature of their root system; the spruce, for instance, having roots which spread out laterally and remain close to the surface, will grow to a good size on shallow soil; while the oak, which has a deep burrowing root system, will not grow to fine proportions except on a deep soil.

The chief species may be arranged as follows with regard to the depth of soil they require. The depths given are necessary for the species to grow to large size, but they will produce good timber of medium size on shallower soils.

Species which will grow on shallow soils, about 1 foot to 18 inches in depth: Spruce, mountain pine, birch, aspen, mountain ash.

Species which require moderate depth, from 18 inches to 2 feet: Austrian pine, Corsican pine, Weymouth pine, beech, hornbeam, black poplar, willows, alder, Sitka spruce.

Species which require greater depth, from 2 to 3 feet: Scots pine, elms, Norway maple, sycamore, white poplar, Douglas fir, red cedar.

Species which require the greatest depth, over 3 feet: Silver fir, larch, Japanese larch, ash, lime, sweet chestnut, and oaks.

Regarding the degree of *porosity* of a soil neither a very loose soil nor a very heavy one is favourable. In a loose soil the roots cannot obtain a good hold on the ground, and the trees are apt to be blown down; such soils do not retain moisture, and soon dry up. In a very heavy soil the roots cannot penetrate easily, air cannot get in, nor can water percolate, and the surface is apt to be swampy. The best soils are those of middling consistency, such as a good loam, or a limy soil with a good layer of humus. On such a soil most species will do well, while, as a rule, we should plant broad-leaved trees on soils which are decidedly heavy, and pines on very light soils.

The *moisture* contained in a soil is of first importance. If the ground is very wet and swampy air cannot get in and the roots decay, while if the soil is very dry the trees get insufficient moisture and there is not enough water to dissolve the mineral matters. The most favourable soil is one which is fresh all the year round, but more especially in the growing season. Such a soil will suit almost all species. The different species can be classified as follows with regard to the moisture they demand:

Species which demand a wet soil. (In summer water runs off in drops from such a soil on the application of a little pressure): Common alder.

Species which like a moist soil. (In summer such a soil does not become dry for more than 1 inch below the surface): ash, poplar, willow, hornbeam, elm, lime, pedunculate oak.

Species which like a fresh soil. (In summer such a soil does not become dry for more than 6 inches below the surface): Silver fir, spruce, Sitka spruce, larch, Japanese larch, beech, sessile oak, Norway maple, sycamore, Weymouth pine, sweet chestnut, Douglas fir. (Spruce and Sitka spruce will succeed sufficiently well on a wet soil.)

Species which will do well on a dry soil. (Such a soil becomes dry to a depth of 12 inches within a week after heavy rain): Corsican pine, Austrian pine, Scots pine, birch, false acacia.

Stagnant water is unfavourable to all species.

A woodman can do much to regulate the amount of water in a soil by draining parts which are too wet, and by keeping a good cover of trees over soils which are too dry.

Taking all the different factors of the soil into consideration it is best to choose oak, beech, chestnut, Sitka spruce, or spruce for *stiff clay soils*; Scots pine, Corsican pine, Austrian pine, Weymouth pine, false acacia, or birch, for *dry sandy soils*; while, if the soil is *sandy, but moist,* sycamore, chestnut, and spruce may be added to this list, and on pure sands on the sea coast Corsican pine and, in warm climates, cluster pine will succeed. Beech is decidedly the best species for *chalky* or *limy* soils, and with it may be mixed oak, sycamore, ash, elms, and larch to increase the revenue; if such a soil is too dry and shallow for beech, then Corsican and Austrian pines are the best species to grow; Douglas fir and chestnut should not be attempted on limy soils, as they do not grow to large size on such soils. On *peats,* alder, birch, mountain ash, white poplar, sallow, Sitka spruce, and spruce will do well provided that the peat is first thoroughly drained and especially if the plants are raised on turfs or mounds. On *loams* and *sandy loams* most species will succeed and grow to a large size, and naturally the most valuable should be chosen.

Species which will accommodate themselves to various soils and which will do fairly well on poor soils are called *accommodating* trees; such are Austrian pine, Corsican pine, Scots pine, Japanese larch, birch, poplar, false acacia, mountain pine, white alder, and red cedar.

Species which must have a good soil to produce large size timber are called *exacting* trees; such are chestnut, oak, sycamore, ash, and elm. Intermediate between the two classes are certain species which do not require the best class of soil, and yet which will not grow in the poorest soils. These may be called *moderately exacting* trees; this class includes spruce, Sitka spruce, larch, alder, lime, hazel, hornbeam, Norway maple, and Douglas fir. Whenever the soil to be planted does not appear exactly suitable to any particular species, it will be safest to plant one or more of the accommodating trees, as the risk of failure is then reduced to a minimum.

It must always be the first aim of a woodman to improve the physical properties of the soil and to maintain its fertility. Fortunately there is a simple way of doing this by encouraging a heavy fall of leaves to form humus, and by preserving this when formed. By keeping a dense cover overhead, a heavy fall of leaves will be obtained which will slowly decompose into an excellent leaf mould; on the other hand, if sun and air are let into the woods by overthinning, the humus will decompose rapidly, and will disappear, with the result that the soil will gradually deteriorate. Humus improves the soil in many ways. It acts as a manure, returning to the soil much of the mineral matter taken out of it, and, in addition, provides a large amount of vegetable matter which, on decomposing, forms carbon dioxide gas, ammonia, and humic acid, and thus the fertility of the soil is improved. The acid is dissolved in rain-water, and acts on the minerals in the soil, making them soluble and therefore useful to the trees. Humus also acts like a sponge, retaining moisture, which gradually finds its way into the soil and is available for the roots of the trees. It also improves the degree of porosity, making a stiff soil looser and a loose soil heavier. It adds in the course of years a good deal to the depth. Finally, it acts like a blanket and keeps the soil warmer in cold weather and cooler in hot weather than a bare soil.

The humus of all species, however, is not equally good. During youth, while in the thicket stage, all species form a good humus and improve the soil, but when the woods begin to open out, between the twentieth and thirtieth years, certain species have only a light cover and their leaves do not form sufficient humus. As a general rule shade-bearing species are soil improvers, while under a cover of light-demanding trees the soil gradually deteriorates, owing to the fact that the cover is broken and sun and air get into the ground and the humus disappears.

Beech is the greatest soil improver, because it has a dense cover and throws a heavy crop of leaves which decay slowly and form the best kind of humus. Hornbeam, silver fir, spruce, and Douglas fir are also good soil improvers; chestnut, sycamore, maple, and hazel are moderately good; while oak, ash, larch, birch, poplars, willows, and elm are all species under which, when grown pure, the soil will gradually deteriorate. Of the pines, Weymouth pine gives the best humus, whilst Scots, Austrian, and Corsican pines improve the soil for some thirty or forty years; after that age they usually open out, and the soil begins to deteriorate.

It is owing to the great soil improving qualities of the beech that the woodman will be often recommended to grow this tree together with the more valuable species. Although in many places beech timber is not of very great value, yet a place should be found for it in every wood, as other and more valuable species will grow better in mixture with beech than without it, as they get the advantage of the humus and improved soil, while, in addition, they grow cleaner timber owing to the heavy cover of the beech, which kills off the branches. This is easily observed in any oak and beech wood; where the oak has been grown densely surrounded with beech it will almost always be found to be taller, cleaner, and of better shape than when it has been grown pure; if a wood of pure oak has reached the age of about a hundred years the soil will almost always be found to have deteriorated under it, while humus is conspicuous by its absence; the oaks will also almost certainly be very branched.

A good rough method of determining the quality of the soil is to dig holes here and there throughout the area to a depth of 4 feet or to rock if found at lesser depth. One side should be made vertical, and on this the thickness of humus and of the different layers can be measured. To determine the degree of porosity place a little soil in a test tube with three times its bulk of water. Shake well and allow it to settle. The rough grains of sand and gravel fall to the bottom, and then the fine grains of sand; the clay comes down in a fine state of division and forms a layer above the sand, while humus or vegetable matter floats on the surface. From the proportion of sand and clay the degree of porosity can be determined sufficiently accurately for all practical purposes, the more sand there is the more porous being the soil. To decide whether much lime is present pour a few drops of dilute hydrochloric acid on to a little soil; if there is a distinct effervescence lime is present.

CHAPTER III

PURE AND MIXED WOODS

WHEN species suitable for the soil and situation have been chosen it is necessary to decide whether the plantation shall be pure or mixed. A pure wood is one where a single species is grown, while if there are two or more species the wood is a mixed one.

Opinions differ to a certain extent as to whether pure or mixed woods are the best, but, as a general rule, *over a large area* it is best, in theory, to have mixed woods, for the following reasons:

1. Over a large area the soil and climate probably vary, and if the whole is planted up with one species the growth will be unequal. If, on the other hand, a mixed wood is planted, each spot can be stocked with the species which appears likely to do best, and therefore every part of the forest will be utilized to the utmost extent, and the financial returns are likely to be better than if the whole area contained one species only.

2. Better timber of the valuable light-demanders like ash, larch, and oak can be produced if these species are grown mixed with shade-bearing trees, like beech, than if grown pure, because they obtain the benefits of the humus thrown by the shade-bearer, and because their branches are naturally pruned.

Moreover, a larger out-turn per acre is usually obtained from such a mixture, as the light which filters through the crowns of the light-demanders is utilized by the shade-bearers.

3. If a light-demander is grown pure, the soil will, after a time, deteriorate. This must be prevented by growing the light-demanders mixed with shade-bearing soil-improving trees. In certain circumstances it is, however, legitimate to plant the light-demanders pure, afterwards underplanting with a shade-bearer. Such a wood is a mixed one for the greater part of its life.

4. By mixing different species together the damage done by wind, fire, frost, insects, and fungi is usually reduced. Thus,

by mixing a firm-rooted species like Scots pine with a shallow-rooted one like spruce the danger from storms is minimized; an additional advantage of such a mixture is that each species draws its nourishment from different layers of the soil, which is, therefore, utilized to the fullest extent. Conifers are less exposed to danger from fire when mixed with broad-leaved trees. Frost-tender species like beech escape damage by frost when planted under, or between, hardy, light-foliaged species like oak or birch. Insects are less dangerous in mixed woods as they usually attack only one species, and the isolation of the stems and crowns by other species retards the progress of the insect pest. Some fungi, such as the Honey fungus, are likely to be less serious as the damage would probably be confined to only certain species of the mixed crop.

5. Mistakes made in the selection of species can be more easily put right, as unsuitable species can be removed in the thinnings without leaving the ground bare.

6. The demands of the market may be better met from mixed than from pure woods. If there is only one species in a wood and the demand for that species, for some reason, is reduced, there is nothing to sell, except at a sacrifice. Too much stress, however, should not be laid on this, as if one has a large quantity of well-grown timber of any species one can usually obtain a good price for it.

7. Mixed woods are usually more beautiful than pure ones, and are also better for sport.

In practice, however, we find that mixed woods are very difficult to manage, especially if there are more than two species on any one spot. One species will almost always grow faster than, and tend to kill out, the other. Thinnings are very difficult to carry out as often it is the tallest and heaviest trees which have to be removed. For these reasons the author personally prefers to plant pure woods on all small areas, and to form a mixed wood on large areas by planting a series of pure woods in groups. This is explained more fully on page 41.

The advantages of a mixed wood will only be realized if the following conditions are attended to:

1. The soil and climate must be suitable for all the species chosen.

2. The mixture must be such that the fertility of the soil is preserved or improved.

This practically means that the soil-improving species must appear in every wood, and that light-demanders must be mixed with shade-bearers.

3. The mixture must be so arranged that one species does not outgrow and kill the others, thus establishing a pure wood.

In this connexion the rate of growth in height of the various species, more especially in youth, is of great importance. Assuming favourable conditions, the species may be arranged as follows, commencing with the fastest growing species:

1. Douglas fir (Pacific variety), Japanese larch, Sitka spruce, black Italian poplar.
2. Larch, sweet chestnut, red cedar, birch.
3. Aspen, alder, Norway maple, sycamore, ash, lime, elm, beech.
4. Weymouth pine, Corsican pine.
5. Scots pine, Austrian pine.
6. Oak.
7. Hornbeam.
8. Spruce, Douglas fir (Colorado variety).
9. Silver fir.

The rates of growth, however, vary considerably in different situations, and local rates of growth may be quite at variance with this list, so the woodman should be guided by his local experience.

Some species like larch, Douglas fir, Weymouth pine, Scots pine, and birch continue their fast growth until they have completed their principal height growth; others, like hornbeam, remain slow growers through life; but after the first twenty years spruce, silver fir, beech, and oak increase their rate of growth, and soon catch up and pass ash, Norway maple, and sycamore, which do not then grow so fast.

Trees usually grow in height all through their life, but a time comes when the rate of growth decidedly diminishes, and it is this period at which we say that the principal height-growth ceases. This occurs with Scots pine at about the sixtieth year, with spruce at about the seventieth, and with oak and beech between the eightieth and ninetieth years. The crowns of broad-leaved trees become rounded off at this period.

The rate of height-growth must be well considered when planting a mixture of two or more species, as upon it depends the management of the mixture.

There are three usual forms of mixture: by single trees when each tree is surrounded by another species; by alternate lines where one line consists of one species, and the next line of another; and by groups where each species is planted pure in a small group surrounded by groups of other species.

A mixture by single trees is difficult to manage, and is only possible where all the species grow more or less at the same rate. This is, however, very seldom found to be the case in practice, as usually one species grows faster than the other and the wood tends to become a pure one as the slow growers are overshadowed by the fast growers. Whenever such a mixture has been formed the woodman must very carefully watch the growth of the various species and by the judicious use of the axe must prevent the extinction of one species by another.

A modification of this system, when one species is planted singly at some distance apart into a plantation of another species, is, however, excellent in certain cases. For instance, where larch is to be grown in places where it is liable to disease, it is an excellent plan to plant it singly here and there at about 15 feet apart into a plantation of another species of which the best is beech. Each larch then grows completely isolated from other larches for some years.

In the same way, ash, oak, elm, sycamore, poplars, and all fast growing, light-demanding, broad-leaved trees may be scattered singly in beech woods to increase the revenue, or in woods of evergreen conifers, care being taken in the thinnings to prevent the beech or evergreen conifer from topping the single tree. It is perfectly useless to plant spruce, Douglas fir, or any evergreen conifer singly into a wood of larch or of a light-demanding, broad-leaved tree, as its branches will not be naturally pruned and its timber will never be of good quality. Such trees may, however, be mixed singly into beech woods, as in this case the side branches will die off.

As the tree to be planted singly will usually be the most valuable species, as many should be planted in the acre as is possible. When it is one, like oak or ash, which is not very liable to disease, it can be put in, say, at 12 feet apart, but with larch 15 to 20 feet apart is safest.

Mixtures in alternate lines may be made when the species are of about the same height-growth or when the slow grower will bear the shade thrown by the fast grower. The future management of a wood arranged in this way is comparatively easy and the slow grower does not get easily suppressed as the light shines down the lines between the tops of the taller species; but, on the other hand, if the fast grower forms cover over the slow grower the advantages of isolation are lost. If this is likely to be the case, as it usually is with larch and beech, it is better to plant, say, three or four lines of the slow grower and then one or two lines of the fast grower. As a general rule not more than two species should be intimately mixed together on any one spot, as otherwise difficulties may arise later on owing to the different rates of height growth.

When the species to be grown vary considerably in height-growth it is best to separate them by planting in groups of one species only. The groups may vary in size from a few square yards up to an acre or so according to circumstances. No group consisting of a light-demander should be large enough to become practically a pure wood. The size and shape of the group may depend on the nature of the soil, but no hard and fast rule can be laid down about this. In natural woods the different species are usually found in irregular patches and groups, and it is this arrangement that the woodman should try to imitate, always trying to get as intimate a mixture as he can without risk of one species ousting the other. For instance, where it is decided to plant oak and beech, if it is known that, in the locality to be planted, the oak grows faster than the beech, the two species may be planted in alternate lines, because there will be no fear of the oak being suppressed and the beech will grow very well in the shade thrown by the oaks, and the intimate mixture obtained will be excellent. If, however, the beech is the faster grower, as it often is on certain soils, the two species should be put into separate groups, each group of oak being surrounded with beech. By doing this, only the outer oaks will be suppressed, while those in the centre of each group will grow into fine trees. If the groups of oak are fairly small to start with, the number of trees in each group being gradually reduced in the thinnings, a fairly intimate mixture of oak and beech will finally be obtained.

By planting in groups, any number of species may be grown in a wood, each in a separate group, and the wood as a whole will have the character and advantages of a mixed wood. In the author's opinion, the formation of mixed woods by groups is the best method, while to facilitate future sale of the timber, as far as possible the various groups in a block of forest should consist of species which mature at the same time. Thus groups of larch, Sitka spruce, spruce, Douglas fir, and Scots pine could be grown in one block, the whole to be felled at say sixty or seventy years of age.

Mixtures may be of three types, according to whether they are mixtures of shade-bearers only, of light-demanders and shade-bearers, or of light-demanders only.

Of mixtures of two shade-bearers only, silver fir and spruce; silver fir and beech; and spruce and beech are the best, but they

PLATE 11

Oak   Beech

OAK AND BEECH PLANTED IN ALTERNATE LINES
Aged 18 years. Oak 28 feet high and up to $20\frac{1}{2}$ inches girth.
Beech have been topped as they outgrew the oak. In the
background pure oak with brambles beneath. Coopers Hill

are not species which are sufficiently valuable to plant on a large scale alone, though they can be used for filling in gaps in existing woods. Douglas fir and Sitka spruce is a good mixture, choosing the wetter places for the latter.

Mixtures of light-demanders with shade-bearers are of more interest to the woodman. These mixtures can be, in certain cases, formed at once by planting in alternate lines when it is certain that the light-demander is the quickest grower. Thus larch and beech (preferably at least one-quarter should be beech), and ash and beech are good; oak and beech can be mixed thus in localities where oak is the faster grower. Neither larch and spruce, nor ash and spruce, are good in this form, nor is oak and spruce, as the spruce takes up so much moisture from the soil that the oak goes 'stagheaded' (or dies at the top). Larch or Japanese larch and Douglas fir is a good mixture, but is best formed by groups, as in alternate lines the Douglas fir will probably outgrow the larch and will not get properly clear of branches. The pines can be mixed with beech or spruce with good results, provided the shade-bearers are given some help at first by planting three or four lines to one line of the pines.

Where the light-demander is likely to be outgrown, the mixture may be by groups, or, especially with oak, the light-demander may first be planted pure, the shade-bearer being underplanted later on, thus forming an uneven-aged wood. In the majority of cases beech is the best species to use for this under crop, the action of which may be explained as follows: If a pure wood is planted of some light-demanding species like oak, larch, or ash, after a certain time, depending on the species, the wood begins to open out and forms only a thin canopy which is no longer able to protect the soil. If the wood is then left alone the soil deteriorates, the humus decomposes too rapidly and disappears, and a rank growth of weeds soon covers the soil; moreover, the trees form large crowns, and if this state of affairs is allowed to continue the timber will not be of first-class quality.

Oak woods begin to thin out when between thirty and fifty years of age; and larch between the fifteenth and twenty-fifth years, the actual time being indicated on the ground by the appearance of brambles and other weeds. When this happens a fairly heavy thinning should be made, cutting out all dead and dying trees and very badly shaped ones, so as to allow more light to reach the ground. Then the wood should be underplanted with beech, though one of the Abies or red cedar or western hemlock may also prove suitable for this purpose. Under no circumstances should any light-demanding species be used for the underwood.

The underwood will grow, slowly it is true, and will in course of time form a thicket under the overwood. From this time on it will throw a heavy fall of leaves to the ground which will form humus, and this will act as a manure to the valuable trees forming the overwood and will cause them to grow rapidly in volume. The soil will be well protected in every way. Individual trees in the underwood, wherever they get enough light, will grow and fill up blanks in the overwood, thus keeping the cover dense and the area fully stocked, and the wood gets the advantages of a mixture. As the trees in the underwood grow upwards they will shade and kill off any small branches formed on the stems of the overwood and will thus improve their value—causing them to form clean timber and also to become more cylindrical.

Underplanting may therefore with advantage be carried out in woods of light-demanders, as soon as the latter are no longer capable of protecting the soil by themselves. Care should, however, be taken to see that the existing crop is worth underplanting; for instance, open oak woods are seldom worth underplanting if these have been left till they are sixty or seventy years old, as the oaks are then too old to respond to the improved character of the soil. Put shortly, only valuable species, sound and of good shape, and young enough to respond to the treatment, should be underplanted, as to underplant badly growing woods is a

PLATE III

OAK AGED 37 YEARS WITH NATURAL BEECH UNDERWOOD. Height 47 feet, number 248, volume 1162 cubic feet per acre. Photograph taken on a ride side; in the interior the oaks are clean of side branches. Bradley Hill, Dean Forest. *Photograph by* R. C. MILWARD

waste of money and it is more profitable to cut them and to replant the area.

As a rule one does not expect to obtain fine timber from the underwood itself. A certain amount of produce will be obtained from it, but we look chiefly to the improved value of the over-wood to repay us for the cost of forming the underwood. The fairly heavy thinning made at the time of underplanting will, however, often produce enough to pay the cost of the operation, especially if the wood contains larch which have been grown as nurses and which must be removed for the benefit of the permanent species. One case where underplanting is of special value is that of a larch wood between fifteen and thirty years of age, where the trees are badly attacked by the larch disease. In a wood of this type the best thing to do is to make a heavy thinning, cutting out all, or the larger portion, of the diseased stems, leaving only the tallest and most healthy trees; then the area is filled up with whatever kind of shade-bearing species appears to be most suitable.

In the course of time an underwood thus formed will catch up the overwood and from that time onwards the crowns of the two species are fairly intimately mixed.

For one important reason underplanting is not popular in Great Britain and it is seldom carried out. Owing to the almost invariable presence of rabbits it would be necessary to fence the area for the second time when underplanting is to be done, and rabbits within the fence must then be exterminated. This is costly, and therefore underplanting is avoided.

It is not usually good to mix light-demanders only, without any shade-bearers, as the soil deteriorates under them, and one species very often outgrows and suppresses the other. Such mixtures as the following are often found in existing woods:

Oak with ash, elm, or sweet chestnut.
Oak with alder or birch.
Oak with Scots pine or larch.
Scots pine with birch.

Scots pine with larch.

Scots pine with sweet chestnut.

Any intimate mixture of such species should, however, be avoided, as they almost always lead to difficulties.

Oak has often been planted in alternate lines with conifers, the latter being *nurses* to the oak which was to form the permanent crop. This method seldom gives good results. If the conifers are cut out when they begin to top the oaks, the latter are left so far apart that they grow short and branchy. If, on the other hand, the conifers are left standing too long, the oaks are suppressed and the wood becomes practically a coniferous one, the so-called permanent crop being ruined. It is better to do without nurses. When oak is planted pure and dense, each tree nurses its neighbour, and if the wood is underplanted with beech, a far better crop is eventually obtained than under the system of planting with conifer nurses.

Although mixed woods with the species in groups are recommended wherever the area is extensive, yet pure woods are quite admissible under certain circumstances, more especially if the species is a soil improver; thus pure woods of beech, Sitka spruce, spruce, and Douglas fir may be grown if desired, though the conifers are more likely to suffer from insect and fungoid attacks. Coniferous woods are often found pure in nature, but in such places the soil and climate are usually thoroughly suited to them and they therefore do not suffer so much from insects and fungi as they do when artificially grown pure in less favourable spots, and if we plant them pure, we must understand that a risk is taken.

Scots, Austrian, and Corsican pines, and sweet chestnut are capable of preserving the fertility of the soil up to thirty or forty years and may therefore be grown pure, provided they are to be cut at this age to provide pit-wood or other small produce.

Other cases where pure woods are allowable are, when the soil is obviously suited for one species only, e.g. Scots pine on poor, dry, sandy soils; or when only one species is saleable at

PLATE IV

OAK AGED 50 YEARS

Height 43 feet, volume 1268 cubic feet per acre. Much over-
thinned but still worth underplanting. (The wood appears
more open in the photograph than is really the case)

present, and when it is unlikely that other species will be saleable in the future.

Ash, elm, maple, sycamore, and tree willows are never found in large masses in natural woods, and they do not flourish in artificially formed pure woods. They should, therefore, always be scattered here and there in small groups in woods consisting chiefly of other species.

CHAPTER IV
NURSERY MANAGEMENT

In existing woods one often finds young plants of oak, ash, sycamore, and other species springing up where they are not wanted, and these may be dug up and planted in other places. Usually, however, they do not give good results, for two reasons —firstly, because they have been growing in the shade of older trees and are often partially suppressed, and do not flourish when transferred out into the full light; secondly, because their roots have not been trained to withstand the operation of transplanting. As a rule the plants are so scattered that the cost of digging them up, and of carriage, is excessive.

Young plants may be obtained by purchase from public nurseries or they may be raised in home nurseries. The latter procedure is strongly recommended where the planting is on an extensive scale, as the plants can be raised very cheaply and usually prove more satisfactory than bought plants. As one can choose the day for taking the plants out of the nursery and can plant them without delay there are usually fewer failures in the plantation, whereas when sent by rail the plants may dry up or become heated if there is any delay in delivery.

When, however, planting is done at irregular intervals, so that a steady supply of plants is not required, or when it is only carried out on a small scale, it is best to purchase plants from one of the well-known nurserymen.

On many estates it is the practice to purchase one-year-old or two-year-old seedling plants and to grow these on for a few years in the home nursery. This is a good system, especially for the rarer exotics, though, if a nursery is kept at all, it would not add much to the work to grow the plants from seed. This is a perfectly simple business with all the common forest trees and presents no difficulty, as is explained later.

Purchase of plants from public nurseries. When purchasing

plants the woodman should, if practicable, visit the nursery, from which he proposes to get his plants, in the summer preceding the planting season; he will thus see the plants in full leaf and can be sure that they are well grown and healthy. He should have a few samples dug up and should see that the roots are well shaped, with plenty of fibrous roots, and that they are not all on one side. The plants should be well-proportioned, with well-formed buds, and they should not be drawn up and lanky.

If a visit cannot be made to the nursery, samples should be obtained before purchasing.

If the situation to be planted is at a high elevation or in an exposed spot it will be as well to obtain plants from a nurseryman whose nurseries are situated in a similar place, preferably from the north of Great Britain, taking care that the plants have been actually grown in the nursery from which they are ordered, and that they are not second-hand ones from elsewhere; a large 'exchange' trade is done in this way.

On arrival of the plants they should be unpacked, examined and counted, watered, and at once planted; if this cannot be done immediately, they must be 'heeled in'. A trench is dug, the roots are placed in this and are well covered with soil. Should the plants arrive during a hard frost they should be placed, just as they are, in a shed and should not be unpacked till the frost comes to an end. Bundles should be opened out before they are heeled in.

Home nurseries. These may be temporary or permanent. A temporary nursery is one laid out roughly about the middle of the area to be planted, strips being dug up about 1 foot wide and 2 feet apart in which young plants are planted 3 or 4 inches apart. When these are large enough they are planted out, leaving plants at about 4 feet apart throughout the temporary nursery to form a crop.

Such a nursery has certain advantages as follows:

1. The plants are trained on the soil and situation where they are to be permanently planted.

2. At the time of planting they have to be carried a short distance only.

3. The area of the nursery has not to be planted again, but is already stocked with a crop.

4. It is cheap, as fencing is unnecessary except against rabbits.

5. It saves the cost of a permanent nursery when but little planting is done.

This method was once tried in the Forest of Dean for some years, but it was then found that, unless a large expenditure is incurred in weeding, many plants are lost. Moreover, as the soil is not well worked after planting, it is hard to dig up the plants without doing great damage to the roots. In fact, the disadvantages have been found to outweigh the advantages and the system was long ago given up in favour of permanent nurseries.

Permanent nurseries cost more to prepare, but they yield much better plants and can be used for a great number of years; the saving on the cost of the plants as compared with bought ones soon repays the cost of forming the nursery.

Preparation of a permament nursery.

Choice of site. The following points require consideration:

1. The nursery should be near the centre of the forest, so that the plants can easily be carted to all parts. In extensive forests there should be several nurseries.

2. It should be near a woodman's lodge, so that it can easily be looked after.

3. It should be near water, which should, if possible, be above the nursery, so that it can flow down to any part of the area in pipes laid down for the purpose.

4. It should be near a road or ride to make cartage easy.

5. It should be on a gentle slope to ensure good drainage.

6. It should not be in a deep narrow valley where frost is likely to be bad. A fairly open position sheltered by surrounding woods, but open to the free circulation of air, is best. Regarding aspect, probably sheltered north or north-west aspects are the

best, as cold east winds do much harm on an east aspect, and the soil dries up too quickly on a south aspect. Moreover, south and east aspects receive sunlight early, and thaws after a night of frost will be too rapid. Too much shelter, however, is not good.

7. The soil should, if possible, be a light sandy loam, free from stones, as this is easily worked. It should not be too fertile or the plants will suffer when transplanted to less fertile soils. It should be of fair depth, because a shallow soil dries up quickly; from 18 inches to 2 feet is sufficient. If there is a choice only between a very light and very heavy soil, the light one is preferable.

The area of the nursery depends on the amount of planting to be done; as a general rule, where four-year-old plants are used, which are left two years in the seed-bed and two years in the nursery lines, an area of four or five acres of nursery is required for every hundred acres of land to be planted annually.

Formation of the nursery. The shape should be a square or rectangle, as this is cheapest to fence; and the beds are more easily laid out without waste of ground, and look neater. The nursery should be well fenced with a good wire fence, with rabbit netting attached, to keep out all cattle and ground game; if on an exposed situation, an evergreen hedge should be planted within the wire fence to give shelter against cold winds. Draining should not be necessary, as land wet enough to require draining should not be chosen; if, however, this must be done, it is advisable to lead the drains into a well at the lowest point of the nursery, whence the water can be raised by a pump for use in hot summers. As soon as the land is fenced the whole area should be carefully trenched to a depth of 18 inches to 2 feet, removing all stones and roots and levelling the surface at the same time. If the soil is of fair quality throughout, the top and bottom soil may be mixed while trenching is going on, but if the bottom soil is poor it will be best to leave it underneath, keeping the best soil on the top, as it is not desired to encourage young plants to grow deep roots. The trenching should be done during the summer, leaving the ground rough for the frost to pulverize the soil during winter. It should be dug over again and harrowed in spring and is then ready to be stocked.

With regard to the necessity for manure, as a general rule all strong manures should be avoided, as the young trees should not be forced. All that is necessary is to use a plentiful supply of well-decayed humus or leaf-mould. Well-rotted humus from ditches in the woods should be carted on to the ground and should be dug in at the time of trenching, and this may be repeated in future years whenever a piece of land is vacant. If this is done regularly no other form of manuring will be necessary, though it is as well to give a dressing of lime when putting on the humus, if the soil is deficient in this mineral. A crop of lucerne or other leguminous plant, grown on the area and ploughed or dug in, will enrich the soil considerably; this is often a good way of improving poor sandy soil before it is used as a nursery, if humus is difficult to obtain in large quantities.

To collect humus a ditch may be dug outside the nursery, and into this all dead leaves and rotting humus from the ditches in the forest may be thrown, together with all weeds from the nursery. These can then be allowed to rot and can easily be thrown over into the nursery when required. Fresh humus must not be mixed with old well-rotted stuff, but should be placed in a different part of the ditch to mature for two years. Care must be taken not to throw flowering weeds into the ditch; these should be burnt to destroy the seeds. An occasional dressing of lime to the dead leaves in the ditch will hasten their decomposition and will improve the manure.

Laying out the nursery. The area should be divided up by paths into squares or rectangles of about one-quarter of an acre each. In a small nursery of about one acre a cart road is seldom necessary, but if the area is large a good cart road 10 feet wide should be made down the centre with a turning space at the end, and paths 3 feet wide should then be made at right angles to the road, so that a wheelbarrow can be taken to all parts.

These paths may be lined with an edging of privet to prevent the soil falling on to them, or a line of stones may be used for this purpose. The paths should be made hard with small stones and gravel.

About one-tenth of the area of the nursery will be required for seed-beds, and this should be further divided into beds about 3 feet in width with a sufficiently wide footpath between them. A bed 4 feet wide is difficult to weed, and narrow beds are therefore preferable. The rest of the area will be used for nursery lines and the parts devoted to this work need not be further subdivided.

The nursery having been laid out, it should be stocked by purchasing one- and two-year-old seedlings of the species required, which should be lined out in nursery lines, and by sowing seed.

Sowing the seed-beds. The soil on the seed-beds must be brought to a fine state of division by raking. If the seed is to be sown broadcast a wooden rake without teeth is used to draw away the top soil to the sides, the amount drawn away depending on the depth to which the seed must be sown. The seed is then sown equally over the surface and the drawn-up earth is pushed over the bed with the wooden rake so as to cover the seeds. A light roller should then be passed over the bed.

If the seed is to be sown in drills these should be made to run across the bed to facilitate future weeding. A drill is made with a small hoe, or by pressing the edge of a board into the soil, other drills being then made parallel to the first at the proper distance apart.

When the seed is sown it is covered by drawing soil over the drills with a rake, or by sprinkling fine earth on the surface.

Sowing in drills is more satisfactory than broadcast sowing, as the plants have more light and root-space, but it takes up a lot of ground and broadcast sowing is therefore usually preferred. In both cases care must be taken not to sow too thickly, though, if seedlings are to be pricked out at the end of one year, the seed may be sown more thickly than if they are to remain two years in the seed-bed.

The following table is compiled from Schlich's *Manual of Forestry*, Nisbet's *The Forester*, and Simpson's *Estate Nursery*,

Species.	Number of clean seeds in 1 lb. about	Percentage of seed expected to germinate, about	Average number of plants per lb. fit to be planted out in the forest, about	Season when seed should be collected.
Ash	7,000	65	2,300	Oct., Nov.
Alder	300,000	25	37,000	Oct. to Dec.
Beech	2,000	50	750	Oct., Nov.
Birch	800,000	20	80,000	July to Sept.
Elm	60,000	30	9,000	May, June.
Hornbeam	15,000	65	7,000	Oct.
Oak	130	65	65	Oct., Nov.
Sycamore	5,000	50	2,000	Sept., Oct.
Sweet Chestnut	115	60	60	Oct., Nov.
Austrian pine	25,000	70	6,000	Nov. to Jan.
Corsican pine	32,000	70	7,500	Nov. to Jan.
Douglas fir	40,000	50	10,000	Oct.
Larch	70,000	35	8,000	Oct. to Dec.
Japanese larch	100,000	35	10,000	Oct. to Dec.
Scots pine	75,000	60	15,000	Dec., Jan.
Sitka spruce	200,000	50	30,000	Oct. to Dec.
Spruce	65,000	65	14,000	Oct. to Dec.

and the figures have been checked as far as possible by the author. The figures showing thickness of sowing have been amended in this edition to correspond with those given by the Forestry Commission in their Bulletin No. 14, 'Forestry Practice'.

This table must be used as a guide only as the figures vary very much under different conditions.

The number of seeds in one pound and the percentage which will germinate varies considerably according to the quality and age of the seed.

The number of plants, fit to plant in the forest, from one lb. of seed will vary a great deal according to the quality of the seed, weather conditions, losses during weeding operations, presence or absence of disease, care taken in protecting the seed-beds, and to other conditions. The figures given are average results under favourable conditions and assuming that no disaster occurs, such

Season to sow.	Thickness to sow in drills 1 inch wide and 4 inches apart.	Thickness to sow when broadcast.	Depth of soil covering, inches.
	Square yards per lb. of seed.		
April of 2nd year		12	$\frac{1}{2}$
April		Thick	Sprinkling
Dec. or March		4	$\frac{3}{4}$
As soon as gathered		25	$\frac{1}{4}$
,,		Thick	Sprinkling
April of 2nd year		12	$\frac{1}{2}$
Nov. or March		$\frac{1}{2}$	$1\frac{1}{2}$
Oct. or March		12	$\frac{1}{2}$
March		$\frac{1}{4}$	$1\frac{1}{2}$
April	27	20	$\frac{1}{2}$
,,	40	30	$\frac{1}{2}$
March	45	33	$\frac{1}{4}$
April	45	33	$\frac{1}{4}$
,,	95	65	$\frac{1}{4}$
,,	35	25	$\frac{1}{4}$
,,	95	65	$\frac{1}{4}$
,,	40	30	$\frac{1}{4}$

as a hard frost just when the seeds are germinating. From every sowing a certain number of bad plants, or culls, will be obtained and these should always be destroyed. The density of sowing is very important. The figures given in this edition are less dense than those in previous editions. During recent years the Forestry Commission have carried out extensive experiments in density of sowing and these figures are based on the results. It seems to be certain that the tendency is to sow too thickly, and this tendency must be resisted.

The depth of covering is also of very great importance and the depths given should be strictly adhered to.

Sowing should only be carried out when the soil is dry and in a fine state of division.

Germination is hastened if the seeds are kept wet for some time before sowing; twelve hours is enough for most species, but larch seed should be kept in a wet state for five or six days. It is also a good plan to roll the seeds in red lead while still wet, as this will, to a large extent, prevent their being eaten by mice and birds; and when thus coloured red it is easier to see that they are not sown too thickly. The seeds should not be sown till the red lead has become fairly dry, so that they do not stick together and fall in a lump.

Quality of seeds. It is very important to sow only good seed. As a general rule it is best to collect the seed of broad-leaved species from the home woods, and, if this is done, it should only be collected from well-grown, middle-aged trees. Seeds of common elm and of sweet chestnut are best obtained from abroad, as they seldom ripen in English woods. Elm, in fact, is usually propagated from suckers and not from seed.

The preparation of conifer seeds is a somewhat troublesome business, and it is generally best and cheapest to buy them from some firm of good reputation. If collected in the home woods the cones should be laid on shelves in a warm room to open.

A sample of the seeds to be sown may be tested in the following way. Place a piece of damp flannel across a dish with one end in another dish full of water. Put 100 of the seeds to be tested on this flannel and cover them with a second damp flannel. Keep them in a warm room at an even temperature. Examine daily and remove all seeds as they germinate, carefully counting the number. Seed may be considered good if a carefully carried out test shows that the percentage given in the table have germinated.

Time of sowing. Wych elm seed should be sown as soon as collected in June. Birch seed is usually collected and sown in August. The seeds of hornbeam, ash, hawthorn, lime, yew, and holly should be mixed with sand in a pit and should be sown along with the sand in the second spring after collection. The sand and seed in the pit should be turned every three months. This treatment is necessary to rot off the outer husk of the seed, and it is only a waste of space to sow direct on the seed-bed, as the majority of the seeds will not germinate till the second year. Large seeds like those of oak and chestnut may be sown in autumn, but they are then liable to be eaten by mice or birds. These seeds and those of all other species not mentioned above, are best kept till the following spring in an airy loft, being turned every now and then; they are then sown in spring. Seed can only be stored for a period longer than that mentioned above under very delicate conditions of temperature and in sealed vessels; even so it loses a lot of its germinative capacity and should generally be discarded.

Pricking out. In certain cases when the seedlings have been in the seed-beds two years they are transplanted direct into the woods. Such cases are few, and usually the plants are moved or pricked out into another part of the nursery and are placed in what are called nursery lines; the plants themselves being now called transplants.

Certain distinctive names are given to plants according to the number of years they have stood in the seed-beds and in the nursery lines. Thus 'two-year-two' plants are those which have been two years in the seed-bed and two years in the nursery lines; this sized plant is probably the most commonly used for planting into the woods. One-year-two plants generally have a well-developed root, but two years in the lines may give too strong a leading shoot and make them top-heavy. Quick growers may therefore be best as two-year-one plants. Corsican pine is best planted at one-year-one or two-year-one.

The reason for transplanting from the seed-bed to the nursery lines is to give each plant room to grow; the operation causes the plants to form bushy fibrous roots with which they are more successfully planted into the woods.

When a bed of seedlings is to be pricked out the soil should be well loosened by using two forks, one on each side of the bed, and the seedlings are then carefully drawn out by hand. The soil should not be shaken off the roots, as if this is done all the root hairs are torn away; there is no object in removing the little earth which clings on, as the plants have only to be carried a short distance to another part of the nursery. The seedlings, unless they are to be planted at once, should be promptly heeled in, in a shady place, their roots being well covered with soil.

The most important point is to see that the roots never get dry, therefore pricking out should be done in moist weather, or, if the day is dry and a wind is blowing, the roots should be dipped in water or liquid mud before being heeled in. Neglect of this precaution may cause the death of a large number of plants, whereas if carefully done there is no reason why any should die.

To plant into nursery lines, the ground having been well dug over, a garden line is put down across the area and a trench is dug out along it with a vertical side to a depth of at least 10 inches. Against this side the plants are placed at the proper distance apart and with their roots going straight downwards. A handful of earth is pressed against the plant to hold it in position, and when the whole line is completed the trench is filled up and the plants are gently firmed in with the foot. The garden line is then moved 9 or 12 inches and the process is repeated. A transplanting board may be used, and is very useful in soil which is not too full of stones.

In many cases the trench is made too shallow and the roots are therefore doubled up; this must be avoided at all costs.

While being pricked out the plants are often pruned, but pruning should be reduced to a minimum; a damaged or extra long root or a double leader may be pruned off with a sharp knife, but otherwise the less pruning is done the better, as disease often enters the wounds formed.

Pricking out may be done in any open weather during autumn and spring, the latter being the most favourable time. Care must be taken not to plant too deeply, as this is a common cause of failure; the plants should be placed in the ground to the same depth as they stood before.

The best general distance at which to place seedlings in the nursery lines is 9 inches by 4 inches, but very quick growers may be put in at 12 inches by 6 inches. As the plants will be taken out again in one or two years' time it is not necessary to give a larger space, and it is very important to get as many plants as possible into the nursery, as the cost of weeding per thousand plants is thus reduced; 9 inches between the rows just gives a man room to put his feet down and to work a hoe.

If very large plants, six or more years old, are required for planting out they must be transplanted more than once in order to keep the root system bushy and fibrous. Transplanting of such plants should be done every two years. If, owing to want of ground, or for any other reason, plants cannot be transplanted at the proper time, they should be undercut. This is done by pushing in a sharp spade in such a way as to cut off the lower roots. This retards growth and causes new fibrous roots to be formed, but the operation should only be substituted for transplantation in case of absolute necessity.

Tending the nursery. The young plants in the seed-beds and nursery lines must be protected against various dangers which threaten them. The chief are frost, drought, drying winds, weeds, destructive birds, mice, moles, squirrels, hares and rabbits, injurious insects—of which the cockchafer grub is the worst—and injurious fungi, which cause disease. Measures to be taken against these pests are dealt with in Chapters VIII, IX, and X.

CHAPTER V

SOWING AND PLANTING IN THE FOREST

SOWING

In some cases it is possible to sow the seeds directly in the woods; but this should not be attempted with seeds which are expensive to buy, or when there is a heavy growth of weeds, or where the species is a very slow grower, as in these cases the final cost is often more than the cost of planting large plants. Whereas in a nursery the seeds and seedlings can be protected from the numerous dangers to which they are exposed, in a forest nothing can be done except at great cost. Birds and mice may eat up a considerable amount of seed, and a strong growth of weeds will smother a large quantity of the seedlings, unless the ground is continually weeded, which is an expensive work. If, however, a piece of agricultural or other land clear of weeds is to be afforested it may be possible to sow direct ash, sycamore, birch, and pine, which grow rapidly, and in some cases oak, beech, and chestnut. Autumn is the season adopted by nature, as a rule, for the shedding of the seed, but in artificial sowings spring is a better period, because when sown in spring germination soon follows, while autumn-sown seed remains dormant all the winter, giving time for mice and birds to eat large quantities.

If sowing is adopted, the general method is the same as in the nursery, but the ground is only partially prepared, to reduce the cost. Strips 18 inches to 2 feet wide and from 3 to 4 feet apart should be ploughed or dug up; the soil should be well pulverized and the seed should then be sown in these strips, and covered with the proper amount of soil. When the seedlings have appeared the after management consists chiefly of keeping down the weeds. On hilly land the strips should follow the contour and should not run up and down the hill, as in this case a heavy rainfall may wash soil and seeds to the bottom of the strip.

Strip sowing of oak has been carried out in Dean Forest very successfully.

Instead of preparing strips the seeds may be sown in prepared patches about 15 inches square and from 4 to 5 feet apart.

The author has been responsible, under the Forestry Commission, for the sowing of extensive areas of various species, but, although these sowings have been successful in many places, yet he is not convinced that sowing should be done anywhere in preference to planting. There are so many difficulties to be overcome that there is often no eventual saving in cost over planting.

Although it is perfectly correct for the Forestry Commission to make extensive experiments with direct sowing, it is advisable for the woodman on private estates to form his plantations by the well understood methods of planting.

PLANTING

Both seedlings and transplants can be used for planting in the woods, and it depends on local circumstances which kind of plant should be preferred. Seedlings are much cheaper, and will sometimes stand the severe operation of transplanting better than larger plants, but on the other hand they are liable to be smothered by a rank growth of weeds unless a heavy expenditure is incurred in cutting this back annually for three or four years. In our moist climate, as a general rule, transplants are the best to use, preferring ordinarily two-year-two or one-year-two or two-year-one plants, which should be 10 to 20 inches high. Larger plants cost a good deal more, and very often a large proportion will fail, while three- or four-year-old plants, according to species, are generally large enough to outgrow rapidly any ordinary growth of bracken, bramble, and other weeds.

Two-year seedling pines may be used for planting up sandy soils, and seedlings of other species may also be used where there is not much danger of their being smothered. The woodman must decide for himself, after considering the local circumstances, which plants are best.

Plants either with balls of earth or with naked roots may be used, but the former are expensive to move, and in the vast majority of cases naked rooted plants are preferable.

Season for planting. Planting must be carried out in autumn or spring, as the plants are at rest in these seasons, and both temperature and moisture of air and soil are then favourable.

There are points in favour of both autumn and spring planting. If planted in autumn the trees get a good hold of the ground before growth commences, and may start growing rapidly early in spring; on the other hand the trees, especially conifers, may be blown about by high wind, and may be damaged by frost and snow. If planted in spring they escape this damage, and, if the weather is damp, the trees become established rapidly. Should, however, the weather be dry for a month after planting, the failures may be numerous. If there are a very large number of trees to be planted it would be difficult to get them all into the ground before the end of April if the work is only begun in spring. In practice, therefore, planting should be carried on in all open weather from November to April 15, avoiding dry frosty periods and commencing with the broad-leaved deciduous species and larch in autumn and ending with the evergreen conifers in spring. Corsican pine, which forms very few roots, is a difficult tree to transplant, and does best when planted as two-year-one plants in late October or in February.

Spruces planted on turfs are best left till quite late in the spring.

Lifting plants and transit to the woods. From the time the plants are lifted in the nursery till they are safely planted in the wood every care must be taken to prevent the roots becoming dry, as on this depends to a great extent the success of the operation; unfortunately sufficient care to see to this is not taken on all estates. Operations should take place as far as possible on damp cloudy days, but if it is absolutely necessary to lift or plant on sunny days, or when a dry wind is blowing, the roots of the plants should be dipped into water and this should be repeated whenever it is necessary. This simple precaution is easy, it costs nothing, and, if carefully carried out, it will prevent many failures.

Plants should be lifted by two men using forks one on each side, the plant being carefully drawn out when the soil is well loosened. It may be lightly shaken to remove the greater part of the earth, but this must not be done violently or the small fibrous roots will be lost. As soon as fifty or one hundred plants have been lifted, they should be tied into a bundle, taking care not to bruise the bark, and this should be heeled in. When sufficient bundles have been prepared they should be carted to the woods, if possible in the evening after the sun has set, but if moved in the daytime they should be well covered over with mats or branches. On arrival they should be at once heeled in, as near as possible to the ground to be planted and in a shady place. If they are not likely to be put out for some days it is best to open the bundles and to heel in the plants in thin layers in such a way that the roots are in close contact with the soil. If bundles of plants are left heeled in for some time, the plants in the middle of the bundle often fail, as, not being in contact with the soil, the roots dry up.

Only a few plants should be carried to each planter at a time, sufficient for him to plant during the next fifteen minutes or so; if he is given a large number he will probably lay them out in the holes, and those which are to be planted last may get dry before he comes to them.

Distribution of the plants. The trees should be planted, where possible, in regular lines as this facilitates weeding later on, but the lines need not be marked out perfectly straight with a garden line, though this is advisable if the plantation is near a much frequented road or ride, as it looks tidier. A fairly experienced man will be able to plant in sufficiently straight lines if he occasionally checks his distance with a stick cut to proper length. When planting up areas from which a previous crop has been cut it is often impossible to space the plants regularly owing to the stumps of the old trees, and the plants must be put in wherever there is room for them.

The most common forms of distribution are the *square*, where the distance between the lines is equal to the distance between the plants in a line, four plants thus standing in the four corners of a square; *equidistant lines*, in which case the plants stand closer together in the lines than the distance between the lines; and the *triangle*, when the plants stand at the three corners of an equilateral triangle, the distance between the lines being rather less than the distance between the plants in a line, and the plants in one row are opposite the spaces in the next row.

When once the young wood has formed thicket there is very little difference between these various forms of distribution, and for all practical purposes square planting is satisfactory and is the easiest to carry out.

If a mixed wood has been decided on, the planters should be instructed how to make the mixture; if it is to be by groups the woodman should mark out with stakes the areas where the different species are to be placed.

Density of planting. The number of trees which should be planted on an acre depends on the species to be planted, the size of plants used, the soil and climate, the object of the plantation, and the probable market for small poles.

The general object should be to obtain a complete cover over the ground within from five to ten years and therefore quick-growing light-demanding trees can be planted farther apart than slow-growing shade-bearers. Species which tend to branch heavily, such as oak and Scots pine, should be, however, planted rather densely in order to prevent the development of branches. In a fertile locality plants may be at greater distances than on poor soils or at high elevations, as the trees grow more quickly. Small plants must be planted more densely than large ones, as they take longer to form a thicket. Where the object is to produce small poles, or if small poles can be readily sold, it will usually pay to plant more densely than where only large timber is saleable.

Of course only a small proportion of the trees planted will come to maturity, but those trees which are crowded out will have done the work required of them, for they will have competed with the better trees, and will have helped to force them to grow tall, straight, and free from branches. Moreover, after the twentieth year such trees will be cut out gradually in the thinnings, and will often give a good revenue. Taking all things into consideration, the following distances are usually suitable on average sites where the intention is to grow clean timber of fair size. On very favourable sites the distance may be greater, while on poor soils or at very high elevations it should be rather smaller.

Larch, Japanese larch, Douglas fir, Sitka spruce, red cedar, ash, and chestnut may be planted at from 5 to 6 feet apart, $5\frac{1}{2}$ feet being a good distance under average conditions.

Scots pine, Corsican pine, spruce, silver fir, oak, and beech should be from $4\frac{1}{2}$ to 5 feet apart.

By planting at these distances the trees will clean themselves of branches sufficiently well, but it is essential that all failures should be filled up the year after planting. Six feet should ordinarily be the greatest distance apart at which trees should be planted, and this only exceptionally for rapid growers.

The number of plants required for a given area, by square or line planting, may be found as follows: Divide 43,560 (the number of square feet in an acre) by the product obtained by multiplying the distance between the lines by the distance between the plants in the lines, and multiply the result by the number of acres. Thus if 10 acres are to be planted at 4 feet by 4 feet the number of plants required is:

$$\frac{43,560}{4 \times 4} \times 10 = 27,220.$$

E

The number of plants required per acre for planting at different distances apart in square and triangle planting is as follows:

Planting distance.	Number of trees per acre.		Planting distance.	Number of trees per acre.	
Feet.	Square.	Triangle.	Feet.	Square.	Triangle.
1	43,560	50,312	4	2,722	3,144
1½	19,360	22,361	4¼	2,411	2,785
2	10,890	12,578	4½	2,151	2,484
2½	6,969	8,049	4¾	1,930	2,229
2¾	5,760	6,653	5	1,742	2,012
3	4,840	5,590	5½	1,440	1,663
3¼	4,124	4,763	6	1,210	1,398
3½	3,555	4,106	7	888	1,026
3¾	3,097	3,577	8	680	785

The distance between the lines in triangle planting is as follows:

Distance between the plants.	Distance between the lines.	Distance between the plants.	Distance between the lines.
Feet.	Feet. Inches.	Feet.	Feet. Inches.
2	1 8¾	4	3 5½
2½	2 2	4½	3 10¾
3	2 7¼	5	4 4
3¼	2 9¾	5½	4 9¼
3½	3 0¼	6	5 2½
3¾	3 3		

Methods of planting. There are three main methods of planting, pit-, notch-, and mattock-planting, while occasionally special tools are used which form long narrow holes, this method being called peg-planting. In *pit-planting*, holes, which vary in size according to the size of plants used, are dug out with a spade; they are usually about ten inches deep and of about the same width for three- or four-year-old plants. The soil taken out should be placed at the side of the hole in such a way that the poor soil is kept separate from the good. The bottom of the hole should be well loosened and the plant is then held in the middle of the hole by a boy, who arranges the roots in as natural a position as possible. The planter puts the finest and best earth round the roots, gently firming it down; then the rest of the hole is filled up to the level of the surrounding surface with the remaining earth, and finally the whole should be well trodden down. Where boys cannot be got a man working alone can do the work very efficiently after a little practice. In this case the man replaces about half the soil into the hole and then, holding the plant in his left hand, he makes a notch into the loose soil with the spade in his right hand and under his arm; he then puts in the plant, draws a little earth round it, and treads gently on it to steady the plant and fills in the hole as before. Holes are usually dug at the time of planting and are often made by a separate gang of men who do it piecework.

When the soil is very stiff, it is sometimes preferable to dig the holes in autumn to allow the earth to be pulverized by frost during winter, and the planting is then done in spring. Wherever possible, however, this should be avoided, as the holes often get filled up with water or dead leaves and have again to be cleared when planting.

Pit-planting is the best method of planting, but it is expensive, as a man can only plant from 120 to 150 plants a day. The method should therefore only be used for large plants which cannot be planted in any other way, or where only a few trees are to be planted.

Notch-planting. This is usually performed with an ordinary spade, an L or T shaped cut being made in the ground. The handle of the spade being pressed downwards, the slit in the ground is opened, and a young plant is inserted. The spade is then withdrawn and the soil is firmed with the foot. This method has been largely used for planting one- and two-year seedlings of larch and pine, but it cannot be recommended, as the roots are usually bent over into an unnatural position and do not get a firm hold on the ground. Trees planted thus are very apt to get blown down later on, more especially as the method can only be carried out on light sandy soils; if tried on stiff soils the plantation is almost bound to be a failure, as the roots get compressed out of shape, and also because the slits in the ground often open out in dry weather. On light soils, free from stones, the advantages of notch-planting, cheapness and rapidity, may be retained, while getting rid of the defects of the system, by using Schlich's vertical notching spade; this is a heavy V-shaped spade which makes a vertical cut into the ground some 10 inches deep. The plant is inserted by a boy with its roots going straight downwards, and the spade is then slantingly inserted two or three inches away, and being pushed backwards and forwards the hole is closed. Care must be taken to close the hole in such a way that the soil is well pressed against the roots and so as not to leave them in a pocket of air at the bottom of the hole. Planting with Schlich's spade can be done very rapidly in a sandy soil; a man and boy working together can plant about 1,000 plants a day. The method is quite successful if it is properly carried out, but it requires careful supervision. Before using the spade it is advisable to clear away the grass, heather, or other vegetation, from the planting spot. About a square foot should be cleared and this can be done with the side of the planting spade, though it is usually best to have a separate gang of men to do the work in advance of the planters and to do it with hoes or mattocks. The process, which is called *screefing*, enables the plants to get a start clear of weeds, and makes it easier to find the small plants later on when *beating-up* or filling up failures.

Mattock-planting. The mattock is a two-edged tool and resembles a short-bladed pickaxe. One side acts as a long strong hoe and the other is either a pick for use on stony ground, or has an axe-edge for cutting through roots.

The planter first screefs off the vegetation with the hoe end and then cuts into the soil with the pick to loosen it. With the hoe end he then digs up and further loosens the soil, and draws it towards him. He inserts a plant, withdraws the mattock and treads the soil firm. Mattock planting has many of the advantages of pit-planting combined with the convenience of notch-planting. An experienced planter can plant from 500 to 800 plants per day, so the method is not expensive. The Forestry Commission has planted thousands of acres with the mattock with excellent results and it is now perhaps the method mostly in use. It can be used on almost all kinds of soil. Mattocks vary in shape, size, and weight, and experiments should be made to find the particular tool which suits the soil and workmen.

Peg-planting. Where the soil is sandy, the surface free from weeds, and where small seedling plants are being used, it is sometimes possible to plant with a peg of iron or wood. The peg is driven into the soil and a plant is inserted into the hole with its roots straight downwards. The hole is closed in the same way as when using Schlich's vertical spade. The method is cheap and fairly satisfactory, but its use is limited.

Mound-planting. When the ground is very wet or stiff the young trees often get a better start when planted on small mounds. A few spadefuls of earth are dug up and a mound is formed about 15 inches square and 12 inches high; this will afterwards settle down to a lower height. The plant is notched into the centre and the soil is well pressed round it. The mound is covered with turf to protect the soil from sun or heavy rain. The method is not often used where there is much mineral soil, but in one form or another has been extensively used on peat, when it is known as turf-planting.

Turf-planting. The Forestry Commission has experimented on a large scale with the planting of wet peaty areas and by the adoption of methods described below it appears beyond doubt that successful crops of spruce and Sitka spruce can be established without a prolonged period of 'check' and at a cost not much greater than for normal planting when combined with heavy draining and expensive weeding. It has been proved that a thorough aeration of the root system is necessary for successful spruce growth. Turf-planting gives this aeration, and as the plant is raised above the ground level danger from frost and weeds is greatly reduced. This is an important advantage. Turf-planting is in no way a substitute for efficient drainage. The ordinary method of cutting out the turfs gives a grid-work of shallow drains, but unless the water is thoroughly trapped and led away success will not be attained. It is therefore necessary to commence by efficiently draining the area. When this has been done the lay-out of the turfs for planting is done by cutting a series of parallel ditches from each of which the turf obtained is laid' out at 5 or $5\frac{1}{2}$ feet apart over the ground between the ditches. Each turf is cut about 14 inches square and two rows of turf are laid to one side and three to the other side of each 'turf-drain'. If the turf-drains are $28\frac{1}{2}$ feet apart this allows for all the turf required at $5\frac{1}{2}$ feet spacing, an extra foot being allowed for the width of each drain in order that no turfs are placed too close to the sides of the drain. In practice of course variations occur, and there is no particular advantage in having a rigid grid-work of turf-drains between the main drains. The thickness of the turf should not exceed 5 inches, but it is sometimes impossible to cut it so thin. Where they have to be thicker, time must be allowed for them to settle and to become weathered, before inserting the plants. The turfs are placed upside down and are best left for at least a month, to cause the 'sandwiched' vegetation to become partially rotted, and thus to form a suitable rooting medium for the plants.

Turf-planting with spruces can be done at any time during the planting season, but as the plants are liable to suffer should there be severe frost shortly after planting it is best to postpone the work till spring. Provided the plants are heeled in close to the area they can be put in during any moist period even in April or May. The planting is done with a sharp spade or wide-bladed mattock, a single slit being made in the turf from the middle of one side into the centre of the turf. The turf is tilted and the plant inserted into the slit, the roots are spread out beneath, the turf is replaced and lightly stamped with the foot to close the slit. The roots should lie in the vegetation below the turf, hence the desirability of cutting the turf thin. With a thick turf the roots will be inside the turf, but to avoid this the plant may be planted deeply, covering the collar or even some of the foliage, and no great harm will follow.

General notes on planting. Whatever the method of planting, it may be necessary to prune the plants, but this should be reduced to the minimum. An extra long or damaged root may be cut off, and if there are two leading shoots one may be removed. Each plant should be looked at separately and the necessary pruning done. Sometimes a handful of plants is taken and the roots all cut off to a certain length; this practice is not to be recommended however.

After the plantation has been formed it should be carefully looked after until the plants are well established. The first care is to tread the young trees in firmly whenever they have been loosened by wind, as neglect of this precaution may cause great loss and the rubbing of the stem against the soil may cause a wound. This is specially necessary with autumn planting.

The year after planting, all failures should be filled up, and this should again be seen to in the second year. During the first three or four years weeds which are outgrowing the young plants must be cut back early in summer; when once the leading shoots of the plants are above the weeds these latter do no harm, and they will shortly be killed by the increasing shade of the young wood.

Very often plantations of broad-leaved trees, especially oak and ash, seem to stand still and the trees do not commence to grow for several years. In this case the plants should be cut back to the ground in early spring, three or four years after planting. The stools will then form new shoots which will grow rapidly. When these are two years old, all except the best one on each stool should be cut away. The shoot left will then grow into a healthy tree.

Planting grants and remission of taxes. At the time of writing (1933) the following grants are obtainable from the Forestry Commission, for planting areas of over 5 acres:

1. Up to £2 an acre for planting conifers.

2. Up to £3 an acre for beech, sycamore, and chestnut.

3. Up to £4 an acre for oak and ash.

4. Up to £1 an acre for clearance of scrub on large schemes. Sanction must be obtained before the planting is done, but the scheme is singularly free from awkward conditions as the aim is to encourage private planting as much as possible. Private enterprise in planting is also promoted by the following provisions:

5. No rates are now payable on woodlands.

6. If the owner elects to put his plantations under Schedule D the whole cost of planting may be deducted from his Income-tax and Super-tax returns. Any new owner is not bound by the decision of his predecessor and has the option of changing to Schedule B.

7. Upon the death of an owner the value of the standing timber is deducted from the total value of the estate, and death duty is paid only on the net amount. When the timber is afterwards sold, death duty is then paid on the amount of the proceeds, less the cost of fencing and replanting the area and less also the cost of other necessary outgoings consequent upon the sale of the timber.

The sum total of these grants and tax remissions may have the effect of very largely reducing the actual cost of producing and maintaining forest crops.

CHAPTER VI

TENDING OF WOODS

AFTER the young wood has been successfully formed it still requires careful attention, and this should continue to be given throughout its life. It will always be liable to damage by insects and fungi, and also by fire, while during the first few years care must be taken to protect it from frost, drought, cold winds, and weeds. Measures to be taken against these dangers have already been mentioned in some cases, while further details will be found in Chapters VIII, IX, and X.

During the first ten years or so the chief matter of importance is to cut down inferior species like aspen, birch, and willows, which so often spring up naturally, as soon as they threaten to injure the more valuable species. If coppice shoots from a previously existing crop are found these must also be kept down wherever they are outgrowing the young trees. The best procedure is to work over all young woods in succession, cutting out all such forest weeds at intervals of three or four years till the woods enter the thicket stage. As long as the material cut is of no value and the proceeds do not pay the expenses, the operation may be called a *cleaning*; the material cut can be left lying on the ground. When once the wood has formed a thicket, usually between the twelfth and fifteenth year, it should be left alone till the lower branches begin to fall off and the woods begin to enter the pole stage. As soon as this occurs regular thinnings commence; a *thinning* being a cutting made for the benefit of the remaining trees, while the produce cut is usually large enough to have some value.

In the thicket stage each tree is struggling against its neighbour for light and root space, and a regular *struggle for existence* is set up during which the weaker trees fall behind, become gradually suppressed, and finally die. The better trees, being pressed upon by their neighbours, are forced upwards and grow tall, straight, and clear of branches; but if the struggle is too long continued, they may be forced too much and may become weak and lanky. If left to nature the struggle for existence goes on all through life, the weaker trees gradually dropping out. The woodman steps in and regulates the struggle by making a thinning. While doing this he cuts and removes for sale the trees which are falling behind, and at the same time relieves the best trees of all excess of pressure, giving them just enough light and root space, thus reducing without stopping the struggle for existence. After a thinning has been made, the remaining trees soon close up and the struggle again commences, another thinning being necessary in a few years' time. This continues as long as the trees grow vigorously.

Thinnings are necessary for the following reasons:

1. They enable the woodman to guide the development of the wood, and to give the proper growing space to the best trees which will form the final crop.

2. In mixed woods the woodman can favour certain species, cutting others out gradually, so as to get the mixture he requires.

3. By the removal of dead, dying, and unhealthy trees, danger from insects, fungi, and fire is greatly reduced.

4. The trees which are to form the final crop are gradually strengthened against damage by wind.

5. They give, under favourable conditions, early and substantial money returns.

In any wood which is at all dense we can recognize four classes of trees. We find certain trees with their heads right out to the light and above all the surrounding trees; they are the tallest and best in the wood, and will probably form the final crop. Such trees are called *dominant* or *dominating* trees. Among these we find trees which are beginning to fall behind in the struggle for existence; their heads are still well up to the light, but they are partly shaded by the dominant trees, and they will obviously be gradually left behind. These are the *dominated* trees. Below the dominant and dominated trees we find others completely left behind. If left alone they will gradually die; these are the *suppressed* trees. Finally we find *dead* trees.

Now one of the chief objects of a properly conducted thinning is to give the proper growing space to the best trees which are to form the final crop, and therefore it follows that the trees to be cut must be those which are pressing too much on these dominating trees, and which are depriving them of the necessary light and root space. In all thinnings dead trees should be cut out, as these might prove breeding grounds for insects and fungi. In pure woods, suppressed trees should also usually be removed, if they are unhealthy, but they may be left if they are only partially suppressed, and are doing useful work by increasing the cover, or by shading the boles of well-shaped trees, and if they are of a species not specially liable to attack by insects and fungi.

With regard to the dominated trees it is usually best, in most cases, to leave them standing to cover the soil, but if they are so numerous that they interfere with each other's development, some of them may be cut out. The best rule to follow is to thin amongst these in such a way as to form no large break in the leaf-canopy, so that when the thinning is finished there is still a complete cover over the ground. Any dominated tree which is damaging or crowding out a dominant tree should be cut.

The dominant trees are left standing, except that a badly shaped, unhealthy, or very large-crowned one should be cut out if this will enable a well-shaped dominated tree to take its place; and also, when three or four dominant trees are struggling against each other, the best tree should be relieved by cutting one or more of the others.

In mixed woods matters are rather different, as it is often advisable to cut out a dominant tree of an inferior species for the sake of a dominated one of a more valuable species; thus a birch would be cut out if topping an oak. Moreover, in such woods care must be taken not to cut a shade-bearing species merely because it is under a light-demanding one. Such a tree is not necessarily suppressed, and is doing useful work in covering the soil. All light-demanders suppressed beyond recovery should be cut out, but shade-bearers should only be cut if they are suppressed by a taller shade-bearer. If a valuable light-demander is beneath an inferior one, the latter should be cut if the former is likely to recover.

In a mixed wood it is also necessary to consider the peculiar character of each species, and to carry out the thinning accordingly. Thus in a mixed beech and oak wood, while the beech should be kept close-grown the crowns of the oak must be more thoroughly freed.

In order to produce the highest quality of timber, thinnings should be *commenced early*, *repeated frequently*, and *moderately*. This is the golden rule for thinning.

The best procedure is to make the first thinning at about the fifteenth year for light-demanders, and at about the twentieth year for shade-bearers, when the struggle for existence has been properly set up, when a few dead trees are found here and there, and when the lower branches have been killed. The thinnings should then be repeated every five years for light-demanders, and every seven or eight years for shade-bearers, and be light in character till the woods are fifty or sixty years old. Conifer woods do not generally require thinning after this age except to remove dead or unhealthy trees, as they are usually felled at from seventy to eighty years of age; but with broad-leaved species, if these are to be left to grow into large timber, the thinnings are now made more heavily, so as gradually to isolate the crowns of a selected number of the best trees. At this time the thinning takes place chiefly among the dominating trees themselves, the dominated and partially suppressed trees being left to cover the soil; in addition the woods may be underplanted if the crop consists of light-demanding species.

The trees to be cut out in a thinning should be carefully marked while the leaf is still on them, as the effect of the removal of a tree can then be more easily estimated; they are cut in winter. A good rule for the marker is not to mark any tree unless he can put into words a reason why the tree should be cut. If it is doubtful whether a particular tree should be cut or not, it is better to leave it, as it can always be cut out later on, while if it is once cut it cannot be put back again! It is also best to mark lightly at first, as some of the trees to be left may be damaged in carrying out the thinning, and it is well to have others to take their place. After the cutting has been made, the area can be gone over again to remove any tree which it is then seen should come out. Care must be taken not to mark a tree simply because it is of bad shape, as such a tree may be doing useful work in clearing the branches off a better tree, and is helping to form cover over the ground. Badly shaped trees, which are otherwise doing good at present, will be removed in the later thinnings.

By keeping woods fairly dense while they are rapidly growing in height we cause the trees to become tall, straight, and free from branches, while by making the thinnings heavier towards the end of the principal height-growth we let in light to the crowns, which then enlarge, and, owing to the increased foliage, more food material is formed and the stems increase rapidly in girth. If we keep the woods too open to start with we get a small number per acre of short, thick trees, while if they are kept too dense we get a large number of tall, lanky trees. The proper state is to keep between the two extremes, inclining to density in youth and openness towards maturity.

No regard should be paid to the distance apart of the stems. It is at the crown that the woodman looks when making a thinning, and so long as the crowns are kept so close that there is a complete cover over the ground at all ages, it matters not whether the stems are regularly or irregularly spaced. The following figures given in the Forestry Commission's bulletin No. 10 may be taken as a guide as to what number of stems should stand on an acre at various ages on average soils if the production of high-class timber is aimed at, and if the woods have been well managed from the start. These figures are based on the measurement of 1,100 carefully selected sample plots throughout the United Kingdom. On first-class soils the number of trees will be smaller, and on poorer soils larger.

Number of trees per acre, after thinning.

Age of Wood.	Spruce.	Larch.	Scots Pine.	
			England.	Scotland.
30	1,310	800	1,040	1,230
35	930	620	835	990
40	665	510	680	795
45	500	430	570	655
50	410	370	480	550
55	350	325	405	470
60	300	285	350	410
65	260	250	305	360
70	230	220	270	325

As a general rule conifers can stand closer than broad-leaved trees, and shade-bearers than light-demanders. Species like oak, spruce, Douglas fir, and Scots pine, which tend to the formation of side branches, should be kept closer when young than species without this tendency.

A thinning is called *light* when only dead and suppressed trees are cut out; *moderate* when some dominated trees are also cut; *heavy* when some of the dominating trees are removed.

Sometimes, especially in woods from thirty to fifty years old, where oak has been grown with larch nurses, it is necessary, for the sake of the oak, to cut out all the larch, which are often of large size. In such an operation a very large proportion of the volume of the standing crop is removed. After the cutting has been made the woods are usually very open and have to be underplanted. Such a cutting is no longer a thinning in the correct sense of the word, but is a *partial clearance* of the crop.

Unfortunately the method of thinning practised in most British woods up to a recent date has been incorrect, and the result is that many of the older existing woods have been largely over-thinned. This has resulted in the standing crop being of

PLATE V

OAK AGED 95 YEARS. Height 40 feet. Very much over-thinned. Edgehills, Dean Forest
Photograph by R. C. MILWARD

far less value than it should have been; the trees, being far apart, have large branching crowns and short stems. There has been too much rule-of-thumb about the method. An ordinary rule was to thin the trees till they stood at one-third of their height apart. This means that a larch wood 60 feet high would contain only 109 trees per acre, instead of about 400, while the shade-bearing Douglas fir would be given the same, or possibly more, space than the light-demanding larch, which is not only unnecessary, but causes the formation of very knotty timber. Again, very often when timber was required for estate purposes, or to fetch an increased revenue, the tallest and best trees were cut, leaving the dominated and suppressed trees to form the crop. This is a ruinous procedure, as trees once suppressed seldom recover, and the final crop consists of poor badly grown trees.

It is largely owing to this over-thinning and early removal of the best trees that many of our woods are in such a poor state, and that foreign timber is preferred to British. If the owner requires an extra revenue, it is far better to clear cut an area large enough to bring in the required amount, than to over-thin the whole wood.

Thinning is the most important operation carried out in pole woods, as upon the way it is performed depends the future development of the woods; the marking of the trees should not therefore be left to a woodcutter, but should be done by the head forester or woodman himself. In felling, every precaution must be taken not to injure the standing crop; tall trees should be lopped and topped if they are likely to do damage in falling.

Short, small-girthed trees can often be saved from damage from falling timber by pulling their crowns partly to one side with a rope or with a long hooked pole. When the logs are being dragged out of the area, a stake should be held between the log and the butt of any tree which is likely to get rubbed.

Woodcutters engaged in thinning dense crops should be paid by the day, and not by piece-work, as otherwise they may not take sufficient care.

PRUNING

Pruning is apt to be a somewhat expensive operation, and it should seldom be necessary if woods are grown sufficiently dense from the beginning. When this is done, the side branches get killed off by the heavy shade before they are of any size, they drop off, and the timber formed is clean. If, however, woods have been grown in a too open manner, the trees will probably bear a considerable number of branches below the proper crown, which will reduce the value of the timber, and it may be desirable to prune them if the species is of sufficient value to warrant the expense.

A dead branch can be of no benefit to the tree, while, if it is allowed to remain, it will gradually rot, and this rot will travel down the branch into the stem, and will probably spoil a considerable length of timber below the branch. Moreover, even if it does not rot, the branch will be gradually enclosed in the stem, as it grows in girth, and will cause a hard knot lying loose in the timber. A dead branch may therefore always be cut off at any time of the year, and its removal will decidedly benefit the future value of the tree. Pruning of dead branches should be carried out while the trees are young, not later than about twenty to twenty-five years of age. A saw is usually the best instrument to use, and the branch should be cut off as close to the stem as possible; the cambium then gradually forms a layer of wood and bark over the cut surface, and if the wound is a small one the process, which is called *occlusion*, is completed in three or four years' time. Dead branches of larch should always be knocked off with a stick. If they are too green to snap off it is clear that the wood is not ready for pruning or that it is too thinly stocked.

The removal of a green branch is a more serious operation, as this reduces the area of foliage; the wound made is, moreover, a fresh one, and exposes living tissues upon which the spores of fungi may settle, thus introducing rot. As a general rule, there-

fore, it is not advisable to prune green branches unless they are
so small that the wound made will be occluded rapidly; generally
no green branch should be pruned if larger than two inches in
diameter. The knot made by a green branch is not so bad as
one from a dead branch, as the fibres are in connexion with those
of the stem, and thus the knot is never a loose one liable to drop
out of a board as does that of a dead branch. Oak will stand
pruning well, while conifers can also be fairly safely pruned, as
turpentine exudes and protects the cut surface. It is, however,
very seldom worth while to prune green branches off conifers
on any large scale, as if the woods are so open that pruning is
necessary the value of the timber will, in any case, be small, and
the amount spent on pruning will probably not be repaid by
increased value.

Large green branches should never be pruned except for a
special reason. There is always a flaw at the place operated
upon, and the removal of a large branch very seldom improves
the value, as timber merchants rightly look with suspicion upon
marks which show that pruning has taken place. Such a branch
should only be removed when it is necessary to give light to an
under crop of young trees, and when the removal of the whole
tree is impossible or undesirable.

Branches should be cut off as close to the stem as possible,
and in such a way as to leave a smooth surface, as this resists
rot better than a rough one. The work can be done with knife,
hatchet, bill-hook, or saw, and it is usually best to allow the
workman to use the tool he prefers. Heavy branches should
first be cut off 2 feet from the stem to reduce the weight, and to
prevent any possibility of tearing or splitting the stem, and the
work should begin with a cut on the lower side, for the same
reason.

When large branches are removed on ride sides or in parks,
the wound should be painted over with coal-tar, made sufficiently fluid by the addition of oil of turpentine, to prevent rot
or disease.

As a general rule in forestry, pruning on a large scale should be restricted to the removal of dead branches in young woods of oak, larch, pine, and Douglas fir, and even then only the best trees which are likely to form the final crop should be pruned, and not those which will come out in the thinnings.

In the case of Douglas fir, however close they are grown, the branches do not fall off when they are dead, but hang on for many years. It appears, therefore, to be best to plant Douglas fir rather far apart, at 6 feet, and then to prune off the dead branches carefully with a saw at the time when the first thinning is made. The cost of pruning will be more than covered by the saving effected on cost of plants and planting, and it may be possible to sell the pruned branches for peasticks, for which purpose they are quite suitable.

CHAPTER VII

METHODS OF TREATMENT

WHERE the woods are extensive it should be one of the chief objects of the woodman to manage them in such a way as to get a sustained and regular annual yield. All haphazard working must be put an end to, and an endeavour should be made to cut only that amount of timber which the forest is capable of producing annually. The owner then knows that his woods are not being overcut, and has the satisfaction of being able to depend upon a more or less steady income from them instead of receiving perhaps a large income one year and very little in the next.

Before putting into force a regular treatment the woodman must decide as nearly as possible the age at which the woods will give the most paying size of timber, or, in other words, he must fix the *rotation* or the period in which the whole of the woods shall be cut over once. He must also decide which of the main sylvicultural systems, or methods of treatment, will suit his purpose best. There are three main systems, called *high forest*, *coppice*, and *coppice-with-standards*.

A wood is called *high forest* when it consists solely of seedling trees, that is, of trees which have grown up from seed sown artificially or naturally on the spot, or of plants raised from seeds sown in a nursery; the term is, however, sometimes applied to a wood in which the trees are coppice shoots, though only one shoot has been allowed to remain on the stool to grow into a tree.

All species can be grown in high forest, and produce of any desired size can be obtained from such woods by fixing the rotation according to the size required.

Coppice is a wood consisting of shoots which have sprung up from the stools of felled trees. From such a wood only small produce is usually obtained, and broad-leaved trees alone can be treated under this system. *Coppice-with-standards* is a wood which consists partly of trees which form an overwood, and partly of coppice shoots which form an underwood. From such a wood both large and small produce is obtained, but the trees are not usually so tall, straight, or clean as those obtained from high forest.

With regard to the rotation it is impossible to say, when planting woods, at what age they will be exactly fit for the axe, but we may assume that this will be approximately the age at which we now find existing crops to be mature.

At present the following rotations are about the most profitable:

High Forest.

Oak . . .	100 to 130 years.
Beech . . .	90 to 100 years.
Ash, maple, sycamore, elm, and chestnut, 60 to 80 years.	
Conifers . .	60 to 80 years.

Coppice.

Alder and chestnut .	20 to 25 years.
Oak . . .	20 to 30 years.
Hazel . . .	8 to 15 years.

The length of the rotation depends greatly on the local demand; when, for instance, conifers can be sold as pit-wood, a rotation of forty years can be adopted, while where small stuff cannot be sold the rotation must be sixty or seventy years at least.

In coppices where fuel cannot be sold it is usually best to have as long a rotation as possible up to the age beyond which the stools will not give healthy shoots.

As a general rule, under all systems with long rotations the fertility of the soil is well maintained and the timber produced is of first-class quality, but, on the other hand, the owner's capital is locked up for a long time and his only returns are from thinnings. With short rotations the soil is exposed frequently and may deteriorate, the timber obtained is soft, as it mostly consists of sap-wood, and it is usually short in length. If the produce is readily saleable, however, more profitable results are obtained.

High forest system.

Where high forest has been decided upon, the cutting of the existing crop and formation of the new crop may be carried out under one of the following methods of treatment:

1. Clear cutting.
2. Successive regeneration fellings, or Compartment method.
3. Group method.
4. Selection method.

The Clear cutting method.

Cuttings should be so carried out that at the end of the first rotation there will be upon the ground a series of approximately equal areas of even aged woods, varying in age from one year up to the number of years in the rotation. The total area of the woods is divided by the rotation, and this gives the area to be cut annually. Thus if there are 600 acres of wood, and the rotation is fixed at sixty years, an area of 10 acres is cut over each year and is at once planted up. At the end of the first rotation there will be upon the ground:

10 acres covered with wood 60 years old.

| 10 | ,, | ,, | ,, | 59 | ,, |
| 10 | ,, | ,, | ,, | 58 | ,, |

and so on to

10 acres covered with wood 2 years old.

| 10 | ,, | ,, | ,, | 1 year | ,, |

the age here meaning the number of years since the plantation was formed. After the first rotation the owner, in theory, will be able to cut 10 acres of mature wood for ever, assuming that the fertility of the soil is maintained. If the present crop is even aged, the crop cut at the end of the first rotation will of course be older than that cut at the beginning. The value of all the crops (with the exception of the mature wood on 10 acres), together with the value of the land, represents the capital invested, while the value of the 10 acres of mature trees, plus the value of thinnings in the younger woods, minus the annual expenses, represents the interest the owner receives.

In practice there is no reason why the falls should follow each other regularly over the area, in fact for reasons given in Chapter VIII it is better that this should not be the case. The oldest crops should generally be dealt with first, together with those which are growing badly, but the protective measures against insects, fungi, and storms mentioned in Chapters VIII, IX, and X must also be taken into consideration in determining the order of cutting. The theoretically correct area need not be invariably cut every year and under all conditions; where, for instance, the soil and growing crop is poor, a larger area may be cut than where it is good, to equalize the yield.

The area decided upon for the year's working is clean cut, leaving nothing whatever standing upon the ground; a new crop is then formed as soon as possible by sowing or planting, and this is tended on to maturity with the necessary thinnings, and is then again clean cut. The crop in any block is even aged, and as, after the thicket stage, the sunlight only reaches the tops of the crowns the trees grow tall, have clean boles, and produce fine timber. At any felling the produce obtained is all of about the same size, and as it is all lying together it is usually readily saleable. The method is a simple one, and easy to carry out. No damage is done to young growth in the fellings; on the other hand, as the young crop is formed on cleared ground there is considerable danger of damage by frost and drought, while weeds are also troublesome, and the ground being exposed for some years the soil may deteriorate. As compared with methods where natural regeneration is possible, the formation of the new crop may be dearer.

All species can be treated under this method, but it is chiefly suitable for hardy soil-improving species, such as spruce and Douglas fir, and for pines. Where light-demanders like oak, ash, and larch are grown under this method they should be mixed with soil-improving trees, or a modification of the method called *two-storied high forest* employed. This consists of first planting the light-demanders, and when these are thirty to forty years old under-planting them with shade-bearers. The two crops grow on together and the whole is then clear cut when the light-demanders have reached the desired age.

On the whole, when the soil is of good quality, and where the conditions are unfavourable for natural regeneration, this is a suitable system for many woods. Where, however, the existing woods act beneficially in a mechanical way such as by holding up the soil on steep slopes, or when they are situated in exposed positions where it would be difficult to form a new crop, or where they are required for shelter, clear cutting should not be employed.

The method of successive regeneration fellings, or the Compartment method.

In order to decrease the damage done to young crops by insects, weeds, frost, and drought, the new crop can be formed under the shelter of the old crop, or of part of it, instead of on a large blank area. The shelter given by the old trees then protects the young plants and also prevents to a considerable extent the deterioration of the soil by exposure. The new crop can be formed by sowing or planting or by natural regeneration from seed falling from the shelter trees, which in this case are called the *mother* trees. When conditions are favourable, as much as possible should be done by natural regeneration; planting should be undertaken only when the former fails.

Where the new crop is formed by sowing or planting, the size of the annual cut is found, as in clear cutting, by dividing the total area by the number of years in the rotation. This area is then cut over each year, but, instead of making a clean cut, a certain number of trees are left standing. These should be evenly scattered over the area and should be trees of which the crowns are small and without branches low down on the stem. The number left depends on the species to be planted. If this is a tender shade-bearing species such as beech the cover left should be fairly heavy, while if it is a light-demanding and hardy species such as oak the cover should be light. The young trees are planted under this shelter wood, and when they are well established the shelter trees are removed. After this has been done, the future management is like that under the clear cutting method. With a little care the shelter wood can be removed without doing any great harm to the young crop, and the increased value of the shelter trees, which put on girth rapidly, will usually make up for the damage done.

Where the existing crop contains coppice, a very efficient shelter can be got by leaving tall coppice shoots evenly scattered over the area. These can be removed three to five years after the young crop has been planted, and can be easily carried away by men, or can be left on the ground if they are not saleable.

The method is, however, chiefly used when the new crop is to be formed by natural regeneration. In this case a number of annual cutting areas should be dealt with together, as it is impossible to work with the same regularity as when the crop is planted, owing to the irregularity of seed years. If, for instance, it is found that ten years is the usual period for completing the regeneration from start to finish, ten times the average cutting area should be dealt with at one and the same time; when this has been successfully regenerated, another block is taken in hand.

With natural regeneration an equal annual outturn can seldom be obtained, but this inconvenience is, to a certain extent, counterbalanced by the low cost of the new crop.

By *natural regeneration* we mean the production of a new crop by seed thrown from trees already on the ground. As the new crop becomes established the existing trees are gradually removed, so that the old wood, in the course of a few years, is cut down and replaced by a new one. It is by natural regeneration that a wood untouched by man gets reproduced; when a tree dies, from old age or other cause, an opening is formed in the cover and seed falling from surrounding trees germinates and springs up. In nature this process is a slow one, but in sylviculture it is hastened by the removal of mature trees and by aiding the young crop.

British foresters mainly rely on planting, but there is no reason why under favourable conditions, where rabbits are kept down and where weeds are not luxuriant, natural regeneration should not often be carried out for the reproduction of beech, oak, ash, birch, sycamore, and Scots pine.

Natural regeneration is usually cheaper than planting, and under very favourable conditions the cost may be practically nothing. Where, however, weeds are very luxuriant the cost of cutting them away may amount to more than the cost of planting.

The young crop is greatly protected from frost and drought by the shelter trees, and weed growth is also reduced, while another advantage is that a very large number of plants are obtained on an acre, and consequently, with good after management, cleaner and straighter stems are produced. On the other hand the operation is more complicated than planting and requires more highly skilled woodmen; other disadvantages are that the removal of felled timber is more difficult and expensive, and that it is not easy, owing to the irregularity of good seed years, to arrange for an equal annual yield of timber, cuttings being heavier in some years than in others.

To describe how natural regeneration is carried out, the general theory will first be explained, and then such modifications as are usually necessary in British woods will be alluded to.

The theory of natural regeneration.

Let it be assumed that a very dense beech wood about eighty years old is to be cut and regenerated. In such a wood it will be found that there is overhead a very dark cover, and that the individual trees are tall stemmed and have small crowns; it will also be found that they do not bear much fertile seed. Below, the surface of the ground will be covered with a thick layer of dead leaves and partly decomposed humus, which is not a favourable germinating bed, as the mineral soil is too far from the surface. Under such a wood very few seedlings will, in fact, be found. The first object of the woodman is therefore to get the wood into a fit state for regeneration by inducing the mature trees to produce fertile seed, and, by causing the dead leaves to decompose quickly, to get the soil into a proper condition to receive it. He does this by making one, two, or more *preparatory cuttings* or heavy thinnings. By doing this, air, light, and rain are let into the wood; the crowns of the trees left standing soon grow larger and bear better seed; and the humus decomposes more rapidly. This preparatory stage may take ten or fifteen years. Before starting these cuttings the future shelter trees should be marked evenly over the area and the thinnings should then be made so as to open these out gradually, starting operations by cutting out any undesirable species which may be standing in the wood, and all very badly shaped or diseased and overmature trees. Those with well-developed crowns should be left as future mother trees. In the course of time the conditions will be nearly ready for regeneration, and mineral soil will be seen here and there on kicking up the humus with the foot. Operations now cease till a good mast year arrives. Pigs may be admitted to the woods till the seed begins to fall, as they grub up the soil and improve the germinating bed. When the mother trees are seen to be covered with a good crop of seed another cutting is made called a *seeding cutting*. This has for its object the removal of all trees not wanted as future shelter to the young crop. It may be made when the seed is quite ripe, and probably the best period is just as the seed begins to fall naturally from the trees. The seed on the felled trees is thus well scattered over the area during felling operations. Care must be taken to leave the proper number of trees to form an efficient shelter. Rather a dark shelter is required for beech, as the seedlings are frost-tender and shade-bearing. On soils where weeds grow rapidly or where the woods are exposed to strong winds or on poor loose stony soils, the shelter wood should be kept darker than under opposite conditions.

All trees not required for future shelter are cut down, usually about one-third to one-half of the crop on the ground being now removed. The felled trees must be at once taken out of the area, and this work must be completed before the seedlings germinate in spring. The dragging out of the timber will bury a considerable quantity of the seed, but if thought desirable a harrow may be dragged over the ground to make matters more sure; the admission of cattle at this stage is advantageous, as they tread in the seed. If the operations have been well carried out, a thick crop of seedlings will shortly appear, and the final work is to remove the shelter wood. This is done by one or more *final* cuttings, during which the shelter wood is gradually cut down at such intervals as appear necessary for the benefit of the young crop. As long as this looks healthy and is growing well, the shelter trees may be allowed to stand as they rapidly increase in girth and value owing to their isolated position.

Usually with beech a cutting is made when the seedlings are two years old, and this is repeated at intervals of three or four years till the young crop is completely uncovered; matters may be hastened when there is little or no danger from frost or weeds. Under favourable circumstances the final stage is completed in six to eight years, while occasionally it may take as long as fifteen.

When the last of the shelter trees have been removed, any blanks in the young crop are filled up by transplanting trees from patches where the regeneration has been successful, or by introducing another species. In fact this is a good opportunity to plant larch, oak, ash, and other species into the beech wood to form a mixture.

It would appear at first sight that the removal of the shelter wood must do considerable damage to the young crop. This, however, is not the case if the fellings are carried out with reasonable care. There are usually a very large number of seedlings on the ground, and a considerable proportion of these may be destroyed in the final operations without endangering the success of the regeneration. What appears to be great damage while the plants are two or three years old will not be noticeable after a few years when the surrounding plants have grown taller. Nevertheless care must of course be taken; the larger trees should be removed in the earlier cuttings, as they can then be got out with the least damage; trees must be lopped if they are large crowned, and they must be felled in the direction where least damage will be done. They should be removed on timber-carts and should not be dragged out of the area.

Modifications in practice.

In British woods it is very seldom necessary to carry out any preparatory cuttings whatever, as they are usually already open enough, and there is seldom an excess of humus. It is unfortunately more often the case that the soil is covered with a mass of weeds or with a hard turf. In these cases the preparatory stage consists of cutting the weeds and working up the soil just before making the seeding felling. A light forest plough may be run over the ground, or the soil may be hoed up in strips about 2 feet wide and 4 feet apart. The seeding felling being completed, the seed may be raked into these strips and be lightly covered.

In British *beech* woods no preparatory cuttings are usually required. When a good mast year comes all except about 50 trees per acre are cut in the seeding felling. When the seedlings are two years old a final cut, removing about half the crop, should be made, and the rest should be removed in a few years' time.

With *oak* about 40 trees per acre should be left as a shelter wood, all others being cut away in the seeding felling. As soon

PLATE VI

NATURAL REGENERATION OF OAK AGED ABOUT 8 YEARS
Blakeney Hill, Dean Forest

as the seedlings are three years old, the whole of the shelter wood should be removed, as the young plants are light-demanders and do not suffer from frost. An area of about 370 acres of oak wood in the Forest of Dean was, during the years 1900–4, most successfully regenerated, and there was at 10 years old a dense crop on the ground of all heights up to 12 feet, the average being about 5 feet; 40 plants were counted on an area of 5 feet by 5 feet. The area was by no means an exceptionally favourable one, as the ground became covered with a thick growth of bracken as soon as the wood was enclosed; this was cut annually till the young oak was safe: rabbits, however, did not exist.

With *ash*, *sycamore*, and *birch*, 15 to 20 mother trees per acre are all that is usually necessary, as the seeds are winged and travel to a distance. If, however, the area is exposed to frost a heavier cover is necessary with ash, and, as the seedlings are distinctly shade-enduring during the first few years, this can easily be given. Provided sufficient mother trees are present, and that rabbits are absent, regeneration is very easy with these species and it is usually only necessary to keep down weeds. No soil preparation is necessary. The shelter wood should be removed in three or four years. As with the oak, a considerable area of ash has been very successfully regenerated in the High-meadow woods near Dean Forest.

With *Scots pine*, the young crop being hardy and very light-demanding, no shelter is required; the mother trees should therefore stand far apart, about 15 to 20 trees being sufficient on an acre. These should be removed as soon as seedlings in sufficient quantity have appeared over the greater part of the ground, blanks being filled up by planting. Where there is danger of the mother trees being blown down they may be left in clumps or in strips instead of leaving a single tree here and there. Some soil preparation is necessary if there is a thick layer of needles on the ground. Pine seedlings will come up well through heather, if not very thick, so this need not be cut away; in fact dry heath land is just the place where regeneration will prove most successful.

In British woods, where weeds usually abound, it is seldom desirable to await a second seed year if the regeneration fails at the first. It is usually better to plant up the area as soon as it is certain that the regeneration has failed. When there is a very good mast of oak or other light-demanders, it is often possible to cut all the trees at the seeding cut, leaving no shelter.

When considering the desirability of naturally regenerating woods it is important to take into consideration the age of the existing trees.

The different species begin to produce good seed at the following ages:

Birch, acacia, aspen at 25 to 30 years.

Pines, larch, Douglas fir, alder at 30 to 40 years.

Hornbeam, wych elm, ash, sycamore at 40 to 50 years.

Spruce at 50 to 60 years.

Beech at 60 to 70 years.

Oak, silver fir at 70 to 80 years.

Group method.

Wherever it is not desirable to have large clearings this method is a good one. Throughout the forest, groups of moderate size and of any shape are cut and are regenerated. In succeeding years other groups are taken in hand, and those first formed are enlarged periodically till in the course of time all merge into one another. The forest is thus continually changing in character, and is uneven aged, patches of all ages and sizes being found. The groups first attacked should be those where the trees are mature or are growing badly; and wherever patches of natural regeneration are found on the ground the old trees are removed from over them. The new crop can often be obtained by natural regeneration, more especially with shade-bearing species like beech, silver fir, and spruce, but regeneration of oak, ash, and other light-demanders can also be got by making the groups fairly large, so that sufficient light is given to the young crops; in fact the method is essentially one for natural regeneration.

In order to obtain a fairly equal annual yield, about the same area should be cut over each year; thus if the total area divided by the rotation comes to ten, about ten acres should be cut annually, in scattered groups. It is usual, however, to fix the volume of timber which may be cut, and not the area, but this must be done by an expert. The groups may be clear cut if there is natural regeneration already on the ground, or if the new crop is to be formed by planting, or if the cleared patches are not larger than 20 to 25 yards in diameter and there are seed-bearing trees on the edges, of species whose seeds travel some distance. Where the patches cleared are larger than this, some mother trees must be left to seed up the area. Trees should always be felled outwards into the untouched area, and with care the timber can be taken out without having to pass through young crops. Where there are plenty of rides through the forest each group may be so formed that it touches a ride, and it may take the form of a strip. This method is very suitable for the natural regeneration of mixed woods. Thus where a few ash are found it is easy to cut away all other species, ensuring the regeneration of ash only in that group. In another place oak may be left, in a third beech, and so on. It is also an excellent method for the regeneration of beech woods. The soil is very well preserved and the new crop is well protected against frost, drought, and weeds, and there is never any large area uncovered. Insects and fungi do less damage in woods managed under this method than under those already described. The woods remain very wild looking, and are beautiful, as there is no formal arrangement of the crop, and trees of all sizes are found mixed together in groups as they are in natural woods. Such woods are also good pheasant preserves.

The whole area should be worked over once in the rotation. At the end of that time there will be found groups of trees of all ages from one up to the number of years in the rotation, irregularly scattered over the area.

An objection to the group method is that the woods get little rest, as work is going on more or less over the whole area. On the other hand it is easier to obtain an equal annual yield than under the last method, because it is not difficult to find groups where some cutting is necessary. To avoid disturbance of the whole area every year, the woods may be divided into four or five blocks. One block may then be worked in, year after year, till it is regenerated and then another block may be taken in hand.

The Selection method.

Under this method the forest is theoretically worked over throughout its full extent every year, taking out single trees or small groups of three or four trees here and there, always cutting all trees which are dying, diseased, or mature wherever they are found, and making necessary thinnings wherever the crop is too thick. It is like the group method, where the group is reduced to the space left by removing only one or two trees. In practice, in order to localize the fellings, it is usual to divide the forest into from seven to twelve equal blocks and to work in a different block each year. The forest is entirely uneven aged, trees of all ages and sizes being found mixed up together. As no blanks are made, the method is only really suitable for shade-bearing species such as beech, and the new crop is usually formed by natural regeneration. The method approaches what is found in natural woods untouched by man. Wherever a little light is let in seedlings appear; these usually grow slowly under the heavy shade, but they may be assisted, by removing trees which overshadow them, in the future cuttings. Unfortunately brambles also appear in the openings, and this adds to the difficulties. The beech woods in Buckinghamshire are mostly managed under this method, but it would probably prove more advantageous to work them under the group method, as the young trees would grow more rapidly.

There is great danger of overcutting where woods are worked under this method, as it is very difficult to calculate the number of cubic feet which should be cut, and there is no area check. Hence, unless the woodman is very skilful, a time may come when no trees of mature size will be found standing in the wood. Where, however, there is a working plan prepared by an expert the volume of timber which may be cut annually is laid down.

The soil is excellently preserved, while damage by frost or drought is reduced to a minimum; on the other hand, the trees grow slowly, and the carrying out of the fellings is expensive and difficult, as more damage is done in felling in woods where the trees are of varying heights than where all trees are of more or less the same height. The trees are often crooked when grown under this method, as each tree, as it were, feels round and grows towards a hole in the canopy. The method is only suitable in those places where it is essential to keep a continuous shelter over the ground, e.g. on steep slopes and exposed hill-tops. It can also be used in very small woods which are not large enough for an equal area to be cut each year. Woods which are left out of the general scheme, such as those round the owner's mansion, or those worked solely with a view to beauty and not for revenue, may sometimes be managed under this method with advantage.

Coppice system.

All broad-leaved trees can be coppiced, the reproductive power of oak, sweet chestnut, sycamore, alder, hazel, and ash being, however, greater than that of birch, beech, sallow, and aspen. When a young wood of the above species is cut down a number of shoots arise from the stools, and, growing rapidly, soon form a dense thicket; this is allowed to grow to the size desired, and is then cut down to reproduce itself. To obtain strong shoots the cut should be made as near the ground as possible, as the new shoot then often forms roots of its own, and becomes independent of the old stool. The only exception to this is where floods are likely, as in alder coppices; here the stools may be cut a foot from the ground. The cut should be smooth, and slanting, so that water cannot lodge on it, and the bark must not be separated from the wood. The best season for cutting coppice is February and March, as if it is done in autumn frost may separate the bark. As few species have the power of sending out good shoots from stools over forty years of age, only small produce can be obtained from coppice woods. Formerly oak was largely grown on a rotation of from eight to sixteen years for bark; alder and other species were coppiced for charcoal for the manufacture of gunpowder, chestnut for hop-poles, and ash for various purposes, but, with the exception of alder, owing to the fall in prices, it will now seldom pay to grow any of these as coppice.

There is, however, a considerable area of osier holts, or coppices of various species of willow, used for basket-making, in Great Britain, and this industry might be extended on deep, rich, alluvial land liable to be flooded occasionally. *Salix viminalis*, *triandra*, and *purpurea* are the chief willows employed. To form an osier holt the land is thoroughly cleaned the summer before planting, and is ploughed or dug to a depth of 14 to 16 inches. The willows are planted in February or March, using sets or cuttings from wood of two years' growth, 16 inches long, of which 10 inches are put in the ground. The shoots are cut back annually, and the holt usually lasts about fifteen years before the stock must be replaced. For further details regarding this work the woodman should obtain the Board of Agriculture leaflet No. 36.

For coppices of other species the age of the produce most easily sold should be ascertained, and this should be taken as the rotation. The amount to be cut annually will then be the total area divided by this rotation. It is, however, seldom that the woodman will now be called on to manage a simple coppice; he is more likely to have to convert existing coppices into high forest. Oak coppice is still grown in parts of Wales for pitwood.

Coppice-with-standards system.

This system is the one most commonly found in the Midlands and South of England. The overwood consists of oak, ash, larch, birch, or any other species which only throw a light shade; and the underwood of hazel, ash, sycamore, sweet chestnut, oak, and beech, or any other broad-leaved species which will bear the shade thrown by the overwood. The rotation of the coppice is fixed at the age at which the produce is most easily saleable, and the total area divided by the rotation gives the area to be cut annually.

Each year the coppice on this area is clean cut. Then the standards are thinned, taking out all mature trees and those which are diseased or very badly shaped. The number of standards to be left depends upon the size and age of the existing trees. For instance, in an oak wood, where the rotation of the coppice is 35 years, the normal number of standards to be left per acre after each cut is as follows:

$$
\begin{array}{r}
\text{Aged} \quad 35 \text{ years} = 40 \\
\text{,,} \quad 70 \quad \text{,,} \quad = 20 \\
\text{,,} \quad 105 \quad \text{,,} \quad = 10 \\
\text{,,} \quad 140 \quad \text{,,} \quad = 5 \\
\hline
75
\end{array}
$$

Where trees of the larger sizes are not to be found, a greater number of the younger classes are left standing. In most woods the standards are left equally distributed over the area, but better timber is obtained if they are left in groups, each group consisting of standards of the same age.

The age of the standards will always be some multiple of the rotation of the coppice; thus, if the coppice rotation is twenty years, the standards on the area cut in any year will be twenty, forty, sixty, eighty, and one hundred years, and so on up to the desired age. While cutting the coppice care is taken not to cut any saplings which will do for standards; if these are absent good coppice shoots may even be left for this purpose. If no saplings worth leaving can be found, young trees are planted in the spaces to form future standards. When the coppice has formed thicket again, periodical cleanings should be made to clear the saplings from any shoots which are threatening to damage them.

In a well-managed coppice-with-standards there should be found on any area standards of several ages, though this is seldom the case in English woods owing to the neglect to plant new saplings, or to allowing them, if planted, to be killed out by the coppice.

Existing woods have often two faults: first the standards, usually oak, are grown singly and far apart, with the result that they are much branched and produce short timber only; secondly, the coppice consists chiefly of hazel, which is now of no value. Such woods may be improved as follows. After a cut has been made, assuming that the rotation is twenty years, about 400 strong plants should be planted per acre *in groups*. About 100 of these may be oak, 250 ash, and 50 larch, sycamore, and other desired species. These grow on and should be visited every four years to cut back all coppice shoots injuring them. At the next cutting about 50 of the best of these trees, now twenty years old, will be reserved, about 25 being oak, and 25 ash, larch, &c., another 400 plants being planted as before. At the third cut the 50 standards, now forty years old, will be thinned where necessary, leaving about 30, of which half are oak. At the fourth cut they are reduced to 15 per acre, and at the fifth cut, when the trees are eighty years old, they are reduced to 5, and these must all be oak, the ash and larch being now finally removed. These 5 oaks will be left till they are 100 years old and will then be cleared, or, if desired, one or two of them can be left to 120 or 140 years. Another 400 plants are put in after every cut, and each lot is treated as above. Thus, after one complete rotation of one hundred years of the overwood, there will be on an acre immediately before cutting:

    5 oaks 100 years old.
    5 oak and 10 ash, &c., 80 years old.
    15 oak and 15 ash, &c., 60 ,,   ,,
    25 oak and 25 ash, &c., 40 ,,   ,,
    300 to 400 tellers or young standards of the age of the coppice, 20 years.

When the felling is made the following are removed:

5 oaks	100 years old.
10 ash, &c.	80 ,, ,,
10 oak and 5 ash, &c.	60 ,, ,,
10 oak and 10 ash, &c.	40 ,, ,,
All except 50 trees	20 ,, ,,
All the coppice	20 ,, ,,

and the correct number of each age is left to grow another rotation.

The oak, ash, and other broad-leaved trees cut at the age of twenty years, of which there will be about 300 per acre, will coppice and form an improved underwood in the future, and in the course of time the hazel will be got rid of.

As the standards will all be in small even-aged groups they will form better timber than has been usually obtained from such woods. Larch does very well over a dense coppice and often escapes disease when grown in this way, as may be seen in the State woods at Tintern. Groups of any other species can be introduced as desired.

Coppice-with-standard woods suffer very little from frost, drought, storms, insects, and fungi, and if the cover is kept dense the fertility of the soil is well preserved. The only real danger is from rabbits, which often completely destroy the coppice. These must, therefore, be kept within reasonable limits.

Woods for timber and game coverts combined.

A modified form of coppice-with-standards will often be found the best on estates where pheasant preserving is important, and when the management of the woods must be such that the sport is not interfered with. With a little arrangement there is no reason why a good revenue should not be obtained without friction between the gamekeeper and woodman, provided always that the owner insists on rabbits being kept down. In pheasant preserves it is essential that the underwood should be full and dense, and therefore the rotation should be such that this effect is obtained. With long rotations the underwood gets thin below, and therefore about twenty years should be fixed upon.

In order to provide food for the pheasants, groups of such trees and shrubs as crab-apple, hawthorn, mountain-ash, elder, holly, cherry, sloe, privet, snowberry, and barberry can easily be formed on ride sides, on the margins of woods, and here and there in blank spaces without unduly reducing the area for the growth of more valuable species. A few spruce should be grown in an open manner, three or four together to provide roosting-places. These trees should be allowed to branch right down, and clean timber is not expected from them. With this modification, the crop should be formed as described under coppice-with-standards.

Another essential matter is that the woods shall be disturbed as little as possible and only at intervals of a few years. This can be ensured by carrying out the cuttings as indicated in the following example:

Let us assume that there are 200 acres of woods in four blocks of 50 acres each, and that the rotation chosen is twenty years, the work being carried out as already described. The average annual cut will be 10 acres, so that the whole area will be worked over once in twenty years.

Then the first cut is made in block 1

,,	second	,,	,,	2
,,	third	,,	,,	3
,,	fourth	,,	,,	4
,,	fifth	,,	,,	1

and so on.

Thus in any year three blocks are left entirely alone and work goes on in one only. Arrangements should be made to have this block shot over early in the season before the forest operations commence.

At the end of twenty years, block 1 will contain 10 acres each of woods 20, 16, 12, 8, and 4 years old.

Block 2 will contain woods 19, 15, 11, 7, 3 years old.
Block 3   ,,   ,,   18, 14, 10, 6, 2   ,,   ,,
Block 4   ,,   ,,   17, 13, 9, 5, 1   ,,   ,,

Thus each block will have old, middle-aged, and young coppice and will give excellent cover. Shelter belts should be left on the north and east sides to keep off cold winds, and the cuttings should proceed against the prevailing wind direction, usually therefore from north-east towards the south-west. By doing this young shoots and standards will be protected from wind by the uncut wood to the windward side.

This method can easily be made to suit all woods, whatever their size or arrangement. It matters not whether all the woods are in one large block, in which case they can be divided into four or more moderate-sized parts, each worked as above as if it were a separate block; or whether they consist of a large number of small blocks, in which case two or more can be grouped together for the arrangement of the cuttings.

Conversion of coppice-with-standards into high forest.

In many localities where coppice is now unsaleable the owner may wish to convert his existing coppice-with-standard woods into high forest. Where the underwood is hazel the simplest method of doing this is to convert the wood gradually, taking so long about it that by the time the wood has been worked over once, the first formed plantations of the new crop will come in for felling. If conifers are planted this period should be at least forty years, and the area cut annually will be the total area divided by 40. This area of the oldest coppice is cut, and the standards are also cleared with the exception of any groups young enough to take their place in the new crop. It is, however, useless to leave single trees, or very small groups, as these will never form good timber. The area is then planted up with larch, ash, Douglas fir, Sitka spruce, Corsican or Scots pines, or other quick-growing trees according to the soil. The future treatment consists of keeping back the coppice shoots which should be cut in the third year after planting, and it may be necessary to repeat the operation up to the sixth year. After this the seedling plants will be able to keep above the coppice shoots, which will then gradually die out. In each year of the rotation another area is dealt with, till in the fortieth year the whole of the coppice-with-standards is replaced by high forest.

Where the existing underwood contains a large proportion of oak, ash, sycamore, chestnut, or beech, it can be converted into a false high forest which will grow to a paying size before it is finally removed and replaced by seedling trees. In this case the area of ripe coppice should not be clear cut, but a heavy thinning should be made among the shoots, reducing the number to one or two on each stool, the straightest and stoutest being left. All the large-sized standards are also removed, leaving the younger and well-grown ones. The standing crop may then be allowed to grow on, with necessary thinnings periodically, till it is fifty to sixty years of age, by which time a considerable amount of saleable timber will be obtained. It can then be clear cut and the new crop formed by planting, or in some cases it will be possible to obtain natural regeneration. This method delays the formation of true high forest, and the timber will not be first class, as the trees are stool shoots and are often rotten at the butt; on the other hand the cost of planting is saved, and small stuff which may be hardly saleable is allowed to grow on to a fair size. This method has been carried out with success on a fairly large scale in oak and beech woods at Tintern. The conversion was begun in about 1906, and thinnings have been made at intervals of about eight years until in 1933 the conversion is practically completed. The woods which were originally coppice are now vigorous high forest from forty-five to fifty-five years old, and there is little sign of rot from the stumps.

When carrying out this method there is some danger of converting too large an area at one time. Thus if the total area is 600 acres and the old coppice rotation was twenty years, it may seem desirable to cut 30 acres annually, but if this is done, at the end of twenty years the oldest wood will only be forty years of age, while the crop will probably not mature till sixty years is reached. There will thus be nothing to cut from the fortieth to the sixtieth year. To prevent this, one must convert a smaller area annually.

In this example, if the future wood is considered likely to be mature at sixty years, it will be necessary to take forty years to convert it, because the oldest coppice is already twenty years old to start with. Thus 15 acres must be converted annually.

The best procedure is to select 150 acres of the oldest coppice and to convert this in the first period of ten years. Another 150 acres of the next oldest coppice is left alone, to be converted in the second period of ten years. The remaining 300 acres is managed for the first twenty years as ordinary coppice-with-standards, and is taken in hand for conversion in the third and fourth periods.

In the fortieth year the wood will consist of forty 15-acre blocks, covered with woods from twenty to sixty years old, looking like high forest though really consisting of coppice shoots.

Henceforward only 10 acres would be regenerated annually unless the rotation is to be altered.

CHAPTER VIII

PROTECTION OF WOODS AGAINST DESTRUC-TIVE ANIMALS, BIRDS, AND INSECTS

ANIMALS

HARES and rabbits, squirrels, mice, and voles are the most destructive animals in the British woods.

Hares and rabbits do damage by gnawing the bark of young plants and by biting off the buds and young shoots; they also eat the bark of large-sized trees of beech and other smooth-barked species. Nearly all species are attacked with the exception of lime, which has a stringy bast; Corsican pine also is sometimes avoided. When rabbits are at all numerous it is useless attempting to raise plantations, as there is little or no chance of obtaining a full crop. Wherever serious forestry is to be attempted it is absolutely necessary to get rid of them, as otherwise extensive fencing with netting must be done, the cost of which will run away with a large proportion of the profits. Where the owner desires rabbits, it is far preferable to enclose them in a warren and to get rid of them elsewhere, than to have to fence every young plantation. If the owner does not wish to do this, he must understand that his woods are never likely to pay. When woods are netted against rabbits it is only fair that the cost of the work should be debited to the sporting account, and not against the woods. The easiest way to get rid of rabbits is to shoot them persistently; but it will also be necessary to dig out those that escape the gun, as even one rabbit can do immense destruction in a young plantation. They must also be trapped. Where they are few in number any rare or specially valuable trees may be painted with one of the preparations on the market, or can be enclosed with a small ring of wire netting.

Wherever netting has been erected plantations should be periodically visited, preferably when there is snow on the ground, and if any trace of rabbits is found the animals must be hunted down and killed. Foxes may be encouraged.

Squirrels. These do more damage than is generally imagined; they eat fruit and seeds, cotyledons and buds; they bite off young shoots, girdle trees by eating the bark, and destroy eggs and young birds. Squirrels especially attack Scots pine, but larch suffers considerably by being barked some 12 to 15 feet below the top, which then dies or is broken off in the next gale. Squirrels should therefore be kept down to a reasonable number by shooting them, though they do a certain amount of good by carrying and dropping seeds, thus aiding natural regeneration.

Mice and voles. Voles are distinguished from mice by their thicker, shorter head, by having their ears buried in their fur, and by their short legs and tails. These animals do damage by burrowing in nurseries and young plantations, just under the ground, thus uprooting young plants. They eat fruit and seeds and cut through the roots of plants of some size, while they sometimes aid the spread of fungi by carrying the spores from one root to another. During winter they may gnaw the bark for some inches above the ground. They are especially harmful in nurseries, often eating considerable quantities of acorns and other large seeds. Ordinarily the damage done is small, but occasionally they increase rapidly and they then do great harm. To protect woods and nurseries against these pests, the following measures may be taken.

1. When mice are abundant, do not sow acorns or other large seeds in autumn, but keep them till spring, when they germinate quickly.

2. In nurseries sow broadcast instead of in drills and scatter small pieces of gorse in the seed-beds, among the seeds.

3. Give the seed a coating of red-lead before sowing.

4. Protect mice-eating birds, such as kestrels, buzzards, and owls, which destroy large numbers.

5. In nurseries lay spring traps about on the seed-beds and

visit daily to remove the mice which are caught. The traps should be attached with strong cords to pegs.

Another good plan is to bury glass jam-pots in the ground with their tops level with the surface. Into these place a few grains of wheat as a bait; the mice fall in and cannot get out.

6. If great care is taken poison may be used, but there is always danger of this being taken by other animals. When used it should be placed in short narrow drain-pipes, so small that only mice can enter them. Liverpool virus is harmless to all animals excepting mice and rats.

BIRDS

The great majority of birds are useful, as they eat a great number of grubs and injurious insects, and care should therefore be taken not to destroy them without careful thought. At certain times of the year, more especially in nurseries, birds may be a nuisance, but it is usually better to protect the seed-beds with netting rather than to shoot the birds, which are probably the woodman's best friend at other times of the year.

Pigeons, doves, jays, and chaffinches are decidedly destructive; they eat great quantities of seeds and also destroy buds and seedlings in nurseries, and should be kept down by shooting. Most of the other birds do more good than harm.

Nurseries may be protected from damage by birds as follows:

1. Mix the seed well with red-lead before sowing.
2. Cover the seed-beds with wire netting.
3. Use scarecrows.
4. Fire off blank cartridges, or if necessary shoot the birds.

Woodpeckers do damage by making holes in standing trees, but on investigation it is nearly always found that trees so attacked are already rotten within, or have been attacked by bark beetles. The woodpecker eats these beetles and thus does good. On the whole we may say that woodpeckers do more good than harm, and should be preserved.

From a forester's point of view birds may be classified as follows:

1. *Decidedly harmful.*

Capercailzie (eats pine buds).
Black game   „
Wood pigeon (eats seeds and buds).
Jay (destroys eggs).
Hawfinch (strips buds).
Chaffinch (eats seedlings).
Crossbill (strips cones).

2. *Sometimes useful and sometimes harmful.*

Most hawks (kill birds, but also mice, voles, rabbits, and chafers).
Rooks (destroy eggs, but eat grubs).
Larks (insect feeders, but sometimes do harm in conifer seed-beds).
Bullfinch (eats insects, but strips buds).
Starling (mostly useful, but harmful at roosting places).

3. *Decidedly useful.*

Cuckoo	Tree-creeper	Robin	Tits
Woodpeckers	Swallows	Redstart	Wagtails
Wryneck	Thrush	Wheatear	Pipits
Nightjar	Blackbird	Stonechat	Owls
Swift	Wren	Hedge-sparrow	

INSECTS

An insect generally passes through a series of changes before reaching maturity. Typically it commences as an *egg*, this hatches out into a *larva*, grub or caterpillar, which is a stage in which growth and active feeding takes place; the larva often changes its skin or moults several times, and then turns into a *pupa* or chrysalis. In this stage it remains inactive, does not feed, and is often enclosed in a cocoon. Finally, out of the pupa emerges the *imago*, or perfect insect. The female lays eggs, and a new generation then commences. Thoroughly to understand the above, the woodman should collect a few common caterpillars from his garden and should place them in a box covered with muslin. If they are kept well supplied with fresh food, for example, the leaves of the plant they were found eating, they will go through all the above stages and can be easily observed.

Insects do no harm in the egg or pupa stage; with the majority of species the damage is done in the larva or grub stage, whilst in some cases the perfect insect also does damage. The time which elapses between the egg stage and the fresh production of eggs is termed a generation; this may be annual, or there may be several generations in the year, while in some cases there is only one generation in several years.

There are a great many species of injurious insects which do damage to forest crops in Britain. The damage done depends on the species, and may be very slight or so bad that large areas of woods are destroyed. Injurious insects may do damage by eating leaves, flowers, or fruits of trees, by gnawing the roots or by boring in bark or timber. Some attack dead trees only and are therefore not so injurious as those which attack and kill healthy trees.

As a general rule conifers suffer from insect attack more than broad-leaved trees.

Fortunately we have not so far had in Britain such severe plagues of insects as have sometimes ravaged huge forest tracts on the Continent. This is no doubt due partly to the scattered and mixed nature of our woodlands. In years to come, however, the risk will increase, as there are coming into existence large tracts of forest of more or less pure woods.

Prevention is always better than cure, and danger can be largely reduced by careful attention to the following general rules, the great thing being to keep the woods in a clean, healthy condition.

1. Careful choice of species to suit soil and climate.

2. Formation of mixed woods, more especially mixing broad-leaved trees with conifers. Pure woods on a large scale are especially susceptible to insect attacks.

3. Early and frequent thinnings should be made to remove all dead and dying trees.

4. Careful preservation of the fertility of the soil, by mixing soil-improving trees with light-demanders.

5. Removal of all trees broken by wind or injured by fire.

6. Avoidance of large felling areas in one place. It is, for instance, better to cut 10 acres in one part, and 10 acres in another part of the forest, than to clear 20 acres in one spot. Moreover, a cutting should not be made adjoining a previous one till the young trees on the latter are well established; this is specially important in conifer woods.

7. All material felled should be rapidly removed from the wood, and should not be left lying about.

8. All insectivorous birds should be protected and encouraged. These are included in the list already given, under the headings 2 and 3.

To encourage birds a few hollow trees and clumps of under-wood should be left standing in the woods, here and there, to provide nesting-places.

Toads and frogs are useful in nurseries, and spiders are great destroyers of insects.

With regard to remedial measures, it is unfortunately very difficult to take steps against most species, owing to the heavy expense of doing things on a large scale. In orchards and in small plantations remedial measures will often be successful, but in a large forest it is seldom possible to fight effectively against these pests. The following measures may be tried in certain cases:

1. Collection and destruction of larva, pupa, and perfect insect. With a knowledge of the life-history of the insect, the woodman will choose that stage in which it is easiest to destroy it.

2. Preparation of traps. A few dead or sickly trees are left standing in the woods, or felled logs are left here and there. These are visited periodically, and when found to be full of the insects they are burnt.

3. Grease-bands may be put round the trunks of trees to

catch insects, such as the winter moth, which climb up from the ground and cannot fly.

4. In nurseries spraying with an insecticide is often practicable. Paraffin emulsion is particularly useful; to make it, dissolve one pound of soft soap in half a gallon of boiling water, add one gallon of paraffin oil, and churn this well by using a garden syringe till the oil is well mixed into the soapy water. For use, dilute by gradually stirring in twelve to fifteen gallons of water.

Other measures are indicated in the following pages when dealing with each insect.

Although very little can be done by the woodman, it is comforting to know that parasitic insects, diseases, birds, damp and cold weather kill off myriads of injurious insects which would otherwise multiply enormously. It is not possible in this book to enter into great detail regarding the various insects, but the following short notes deal with a few of the most harmful to be found in the British woods. Further details about some of these pests can be obtained in the leaflets issued by the Forestry Commission, which are given away free. A list of these should be obtained by the woodman, who can then ask for those leaflets he requires. The number of the appropriate leaflet is given in the following pages and these leaflets should certainly be obtained.

Coleoptera (Beetles).

The Cockchafer (Melolontha vulgaris). (Leaflet No. 17.)

This beetle is common in our woods, and does damage in forest nurseries. It is a large reddish-brown beetle, about one inch in length; it appears in April and May, and lays eggs in the ground, preferring bare loose soils, such as ground recently dug. The grubs hatch out from four to six weeks afterwards, and live in the ground three or four years, eating the roots of plants. The grub is large, white, and curved, and is often found while digging nursery ground, or when taking up turf. The beetle flies off to the surrounding woods and does some damage by eating the leaves of broad-leaved trees. It is, however, in the grub stage that the worst damage is done, as a few grubs in a seed-bed will bite off the roots of many plants, which droop and die. The roots of all species are eaten. The only effective protective measure against this pest is persistently to collect and

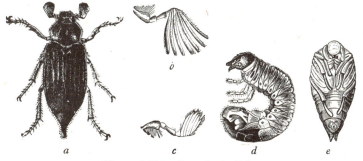

Fig. 1. *Melolontha vulgaris*, Fabr.

a Imago (male).   *b* Antenna of male with 7 lamellae.   *c* Antenna of female with 6 lamellae.   *d* Grub.   *e* Pupa (ventral surface).

destroy all grubs found in the nursery whenever any part is being dug over. If they get into a seed-bed this will be suspected, as seedlings here and there will droop, and if pulled up will be found to have had their roots bitten off. If this happens, the best procedure is to go systematically through the seed-beds, running the plants up between the fingers. Loose plants will be pulled up without damaging the sound ones. When a loose plant is found, dig down at and round that spot with a narrow trowel. Very often the grub will be found at work and can be destroyed. All beetles found should also be destroyed. To aid collection of grubs a trench should be dug round the nursery and filled with humus; this should be turned over every now and then, and probably many grubs will be found. Birds, especially rooks and starlings, eat the grubs and beetles, while moles also eat quantities of the grubs, but are, unfortunately, undesirable in a nursery.

H

Pine weevil (*Hylobius abietis*). (Leaflet No. 1.)

This beetle is from three-eighths to half an inch long, dark brown to black, with two or three golden stripes across the back. Its head has a long snout. The beetle is found from May to September, and it lays its eggs on stumps and roots of conifers

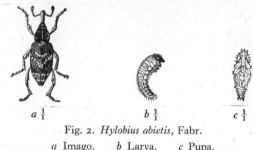

Fig. 2. *Hylobius abietis*, Fabr.

a Imago.   *b* Larva.   *c* Pupa.

which have been felled one or two years. The grubs eat galleries in the bast and sapwood of the stumps, and finally turn into pupae in them. As the grubs pass their life in stumps they do not do any harm, but the beetles, which come out in the second year, attack young plants of Douglas fir, pines, spruce, and other conifers, preferring those from three to six years old. They gnaw the bark off the young stem, exposing the wood in patches. Very often the plants are girdled, and in some cases are completely peeled. On older plants only bark from one to five years old is eaten, as six-year-old bark is too hard for them. The beetle is very destructive and often causes the failure of large plantations. The following protective measures may be tried:

1. The areas cut should be small and isolated, a belt of old wood being left between successive cuts. If then the beetles get into one area, they are more easily prevented from spreading into other young plantations.

2. Stumps of conifers should be extracted, but as this is usually too expensive, all rubbish should be piled and burnt on

them, when clearing an area for planting, to kill the stumps. Unburnt stumps may be barked.

3. Any area containing conifer stumps may be left for four years unplanted after felling, as the stumps and roots will then dry up, and the beetles will hatch out and leave the area. While the ground is bare, sheep and cattle may be admitted for grazing. This measure is very effective, but four years are lost, weed growth springs up and it should only be carried out in extreme cases.

When beetles have actually appeared, the best remedial measures are:

1. To employ children to collect them off the plants. If persistently done, this will keep them down.

2. To put down traps in June, consisting of smooth-barked pine sticks 3 feet long and 2 to 4 inches thick. These should be buried in the ground, here and there over the area, obliquely so that one end is 10 inches deep and the other 2 inches out of the ground. The beetles lay their eggs in these, and in September the sticks are pulled out and burnt. A stake put at every trap will enable it to be easily found.

3. Pieces of bark about 12 inches square may be placed on the ground bast downwards, with stones to keep them in place; about fifty per acre are required. Children can visit these bark traps daily and collect the beetles found under them; the bark should be renewed when it loses its resinous smell. The beetle can be quite effectively dealt with if these measures are adopted.

Pine-beetle (*Myelophilus piniperda*). (Leaflet No. 3.)

This is one of the commonest of our destructive beetles. It is about $\frac{1}{6}$ inch long, and dark brown or black in colour. Eggs are laid in spring in felled stems and dead or dying trees of Scots and other pines, large trees being preferred. The grubs hatch in April or May, and the beetles appear in June or July. The grubs eat out galleries in the bast but it is the beetle itself which does the damage by boring into the pith of young pine shoots a few inches from their end, eating out a gallery an inch long. These shoots fall off when the next heavy wind comes, and thus the tree loses a great deal of its foliage. The broken twigs may often be found in thousands lying on the ground. Wherever

$a\frac{7}{1}$ $b\frac{4}{1}$ $c\frac{4}{1}$

Fig. 3. *Myelophilus piniperda*, L.

a Imago.   *b* Larva.   *c* Pupa.

large fellings of conifers are made this beetle is apt to become a serious pest.

The following protective measures are often effective:

1. Carry out frequent thinnings to remove dead and sickly trees, and burn the branches.

2. Clear all felled timber from the forest by April.

3. Periodically, from January to September, fell a tree or two here and there to act as traps. Strip the bark off them as soon as grubs are found at work, and burn the bark.

4. Standing trees found to contain the grubs should be felled and the bark stripped and burned.

Lepidoptera (*Moths*).

Oak-leaf roller moth (*Tortrix viridana*). (Leaflet No. 10.)

This is a small moth, with its fore wings light green, and hind wings light grey, which may be found in thousands in almost any oak wood in June. The caterpillar is about half an inch long, greenish-grey to dull green, with its head and anal flap black, and with warts on its back. The caterpillars appear in April and May, often in enormous numbers, and spin threads, by which they let themselves up and down from the branches; they very often completely defoliate extensive areas, chiefly attacking

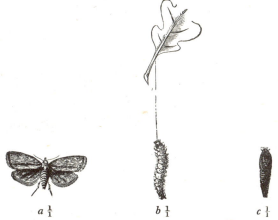

a $\frac{1}{1}$ *b* $\frac{1}{1}$ *c* $\frac{1}{1}$

Fig. 4. *Tortrix viridana*, L.

a Moth. *b* Caterpillar suspended by a thread. *c* Pupa.

the mature trees. At the beginning of June they roll up a leaf and pupate inside the cover thus formed. Owing to the destruction of the foliage the tree may form very little timber in the year of attack, and the formation of acorns may be prevented. Fortunately, the second flush of leaves which appear in July are never attacked, and the trees are not killed. Pedunculate oak suffers more than sessile oak.

Unfortunately, no remedial measure is possible on a large scale. The destruction of the pest must be left to birds, especially starlings, and to unfavourable weather.

Larch-miner moth (Coleophora laricella).

A very small moth, with a wing expansion of about $\frac{3}{8}$ inch. The wings are very narrow, shining ashy grey with very long fringes. The caterpillar is dark reddish-brown, about ⅛ inch long. The moth flies in May and June, and lays its eggs singly on larch needles. The caterpillars hatch in June and grow till September, boring into young larch needles to about half their length, so that the upper ends turn yellow and shrivel up, looking as if they had been touched by frost. In September the cater-

a ³⁄₁   *b* ³⁄₁   *c* ³⁄₁   *d* ³⁄₁

Fig. 5. *Coleophora laricella*, Hbn.

a Moth.   *b* Caterpillar.   *c* Larval case.   *d* Pupa.

pillar prepares a case out of the dry part of a needle and hibernates in this, near the tips of the twigs, or in cracks in the bark. It pupates in spring after enlarging the case by attaching a second hollowed-out needle to the first. Owing to its appearing in very large numbers year after year in the same place, the foliage of the larch is often so reduced that the health of the tree is affected, and it then becomes liable to attack by the larch canker. It must therefore be considered as a very serious pest. No remedial measures can be taken on a large scale, but the chief object of the woodman should be to keep the larch in healthy condition by the accepted sylvicultural methods. Late frosts, and wet or cold weather, kill off millions of this insect.

Hymenoptera (Sawflies).

Pine sawfly (Lophyrus pini). (Leaflet No. 103.)

The larva of this insect has twenty-two legs (whereas that of a moth has sixteen), and is of a dull green colour. It is social, and feeds in colonies. The sawfly appears in April and May, and again in July and August. The female does not appear to fly, but crawls along on the twigs and needles of pines. She cuts slits into pine needles and lays an egg in each slit. The larvae hatch out in May and June, and the second brood in August and September. They pupate in long leathery dark brown cocoons.

They attack chiefly Scots pine, preferring sickly trees, and eat the needles in companies of eighty to one hundred, leaving the midrib untouched. When disturbed they bend the front part of their bodies into the shape of the letter S.

Fig. 6. Pine needles, with larvae and cocoon of *L. pini*, L.

The insect is very destructive, but unfortunately it is difficult to deal with on a large scale. In young plantations the larvae may be easily destroyed by crushing them with a gloved hand. This should be attempted in the early stage of an attack, as at that time the larvae are in fairly compact groups and are more easily dealt with than when they are scattered at a later stage. When the attack is on a small scale this method is quite successful, but on an extensive area a large gang of men must be employed to cover the ground, and it becomes expensive.

The fox-coloured sawfly (*Lophyrus rufus*) does similar damage and its attacks should be combated in the same way.

The large larch sawfly (*Nematus Erichsoni*).

The sawfly measures $\frac{3}{8}$ inch and is, on the whole, black in colour. The caterpillar measures $\frac{3}{4}$ inch, and has a black hairy head, a greenish body, with twenty legs. The caterpillars eat the needles of larch in July and August, and may completely defoliate the trees. They prefer trees from twenty to seventy years of age. This makes it difficult to carry out any remedial measure, as the caterpillars are out of reach. When they appear on small trees they should be squeezed in a gloved hand, or infested shoots may be cut off and burnt. On dull days the trees might be jarred to bring down the caterpillars. Full details about this pest will be found in leaflet 186.

Hemiptera (*Plant lice and scale insects*).

Spruce-gall aphis (*Chermes viridis*). (Leaflet No. 7.)

The spruce-gall aphids have a life-cycle which, when complete, consists of a series of five generations and is passed on two different host trees, of which one is always a spruce and the other may be a larch, pine, silver fir, or Douglas fir. In Britain, however, the life-cycle is often shortened.

Chermes viridis alternates on the spruce and larch. On the spruce it forms a gall (Fig. 7) which is due to the swelling of the bases of the needles in the bud stage where the insects feed. The gall, which is generally on one side of the shoot, causes distortion of the twig, but the damage done is not serious except when the leading shoot is attacked. On the larch the aphis feeds on the needles and bark. An attacked needle is bent over (Fig. 8). The insect looks like a black spot at first, but gets covered with a woolly down. When numerous the health of the tree suffers. Nothing can be done on a large scale against this chermes, but in the nursery attacks by this and other chermes can be checked by spraying infested trees with an emulsion of paraffin.

Chermes strobilobius forms a gall at the tip of the shoot on spruce. The gall is smaller and more circular than that of *viridis* and it completely encircles the twig. On larch, the alternate host, the woolly patches are not prominent. They occur at the base of young shoots and on the main stems of young trees. They are more harmful to the larch than to the spruce.

Chermes nüsslini forms a gall on spruce, but this gall is rarely found in Britain. The alternate host is silver fir, on which tree white woolly patches appear at the base of the needles and on branches of old and young trees. It is very destructive to trees

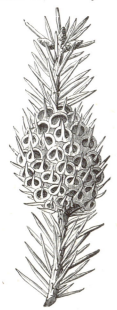

Fig. 8. Larch-shoot attacked by *Chermes viridis*. (*Natural size.*) *a* Insects feeding on the needles, which show a characteristic angular bend.

Fig. 7. Gall of *Chermes viridis* on a spruce-twig. (*Natural size*).

under twenty-five years old, and is perhaps the chief cause of the failure of silver fir.

Chermes Cooleyi. (Leaflet No. 2.)

This insect is common on Douglas fir. In America it has an alternate generation which makes large galls on Sitka spruce, but this has not been found in Britain. The small black insects, with their copious exudation of woolly-looking wax, are commonly seen on young Douglas fir plantations and, for a few years, growth is considerably retarded and the plants weakened. When growing under favourable conditions, however, the infestation usually becomes less and less severe, and by the time the thicket stage is reached the wood is more or less free from attack. During this period, however, the growth of the trees is checked. The foliage of infected nursery plants should be dipped in soapy water and be well rinsed before being planted out, but this can hardly be done on a large scale.

Spruce green-fly (*Aphis abietina*).

This green blight often appears in vast numbers in plantations of Sitka spruce and causes serious defoliation. This and many other aphids are largely kept in check by ladybirds and their larvae.

Beech woolly aphis (*Cryptococcus fagi*). (Leaflet No. 15.)

This scale insect attacks beech and is a common pest, often seriously injuring fine old trees. It is covered with a white felt, which is very conspicuous on the bark where the insect sucks the sap. Valuable trees in parks may be saved by scrubbing them with paraffin emulsion.

CHAPTER IX

PROTECTION OF WOODS AGAINST WEEDS AND FUNGI

WEEDS

ALL plants which are not required in the forest may be termed 'weeds', whether they are trees, shrubs, or annuals.

The most common weeds in our woods are bramble, heather, wild briar, bilberry, ivy, traveller's-joy, honeysuckle, bracken, gorse, foxgloves, broom, and grasses. Sometimes such plants as birch, willows, aspens, blackthorn, whitethorn, and holly may also be considered as weeds where they interfere with the growth of valuable species.

Most of these weeds damage forest plants by closely surrounding and covering them, thus depriving them of light, air, and rain. Climbing plants smother or wind round trees, and, in addition to depriving them of light, they spoil the shape of the stem, which often grows into a corkscrew-like shape. Moss on stems is a sign of dampness, but does no harm.

Bracken and similar weeds are often laid flat over the plants in winter by the weight of snow, and thus bend and smother them. Weeds also take up valuable mineral matter from the soil and thus impoverish it; although these substances are returned to the soil when the weeds die, yet too often a new crop of weeds again comes up and the mineral matter is therefore not available for the forest trees. A dense growth of grass or annuals prevents dew and light rain from reaching the ground, and may thus be harmful in dry years. Weeds, in addition, harbour mice, voles, and rabbits, and are a great source of danger with regard to fire.

It is therefore of importance to keep weed growth under proper control. Before planting a blank area weeds may often be cheaply got rid of by burning them as they stand, and this is the best mode of dealing with a thick growth of heather or gorse.

A short growth of heather, however, is not detrimental and such ground can generally be planted without burning as the trees soon grow beyond the heather, which provides a little shelter during the first year or two. A strong growth of bracken can often be weakened by mowing in June for one or two years prior to planting; this is not always an advantage, however, as coarse grasses may spring up in place of the bracken. Brambles should be beaten down, and not cut, as cutting increases the number of suckers; nevertheless, if these new suckers are also cut regularly, the brambles will die out in two or three years' time. Foxgloves should be cut when in flower.

In a young plantation this cutting of weeds may be necessary annually for two or three years after planting. After that period the trees will usually form cover over the weeds, and low-growing weeds need not then be taken notice of, as they will die in course of time.

When the trees are forming a thicket, only climbing weeds such as honeysuckle and traveller's-joy need be cut back.

Once the thicket stage is formed, a densely planted wood becomes clear of weeds, and the ground remains clean till the woods open out naturally at about the twentieth to fortieth year. Under light-demanders there usually then springs up a new crop of weeds of some sort, and this is an indication that the time has come for underplanting with beech or some other shade-bearer, as if there is light enough for weeds there is also enough for beech.

Under certain conditions a moderate growth of certain kinds of weeds may do more good than harm. Where, for instance, there is a growth of birch, sallow, aspen, coppice shoots of any species, or even broom and gorse, in a young plantation, these should not be cut without taking into consideration the fact that they may be of use in affording shelter from wind or frost to the young forest trees. Where this appears to be the case they should not be cut wholesale, but only those which are actually doing damage need be destroyed. The rest may be left standing ill their shelter is no longer required, and may then be cut out.

A very good instance of this sheltering effect of what would ordinarily be called weeds occurred some time ago in the woods at Tintern. Here an excellent crop of larch, Douglas fir, and Scots pine, in groups, over about 10 acres in all, had been raised on a somewhat exposed position at an elevation of 850 feet, by leaving coppice shoots of oak and other woody weeds on the ground, the young trees being planted between them. The area was gone through occasionally and, at very small expense, just those shoots which were actually injuring a tree were cut back. When the trees had been planted eight years, they were forming thicket, and the coppice shoots were left alone to die out. This example shows how advantage may be taken of coppice shoots or other weeds to give valuable shelter; another advantage is that the great expense of wholesale cutting of weeds is saved. The tendency is to overdo weeding and thus to waste money.

Herbaceous weeds may also be left alone unless actually interfering with growth.

It is worth noting that where no regeneration is required, and where no planting is being carried out, brambles are useful because they keep the soil moist and prevent leaves being blown away. They are a sign of moisture in the soil, and are absent in open woods where dry conditions obtain, though they are found in fairly thick woods if the soil is rich and moist. Under such circumstances they are not killed out by the cover unless this is very dense, low, and continued for five or six years, as the seeds lie dormant for about four years.

FUNGI

Fungi belong to the lowest form of plant-life, and possess no chlorophyll; they are therefore unable to form food material for themselves and obtain it from dead or living plants.

Fungi which obtain their food from dead plants are called

saprophytes; these are not of great importance to the woodman. Those which live upon living plants are called *parasites*, and are of the greatest importance in forestry as they cause many bad, and sometimes fatal, diseases among forest trees.

Fungi are usually formed of many long filaments called *hyphae*, which together form a mass called the *mycelium*. This sometimes grows and spreads through living wood or bark, and is often only distinguishable with a microscope. Instead of flowers the reproductive organs are a special collection of cells, the whole being called a *fructification*, which produces large numbers of minute reproductive bodies called *spores*, which are, as it were, the seeds of the fungus. In the ordinary mushroom the part above ground, which we eat, is the fructification, the spores being borne on the gills. The mycelium of the fungus is below ground, and is often called the *spawn* by mushroom growers. The fructifications of most species usually appear for a few weeks only, chiefly about October, but in some species they are permanent, and are then often hard or woody. Warm damp weather is favourable to the spread of the fungi, while strong sunlight is unfavourable to them.

Some fungi attack sickly trees only, while others damage perfectly healthy ones. It is difficult sometimes to say whether a fungus is the cause of disease, or whether it is the result of previous debility in the tree.

Fungi are the cause of a great many diseases, especially in coniferous species, and with the larger planting of conifers which is taking place in Great Britain nowadays, disease is likely to spread, and woodmen must be on the look-out so as to take measures early.

The best general rules for prevention of disease are to grow species only on soils and situations really suitable to them, as they are then stronger and can withstand attack better;—to plant good strong plants; to form mixed woods so that trees liable to attack are isolated, especially mixing broad-leaved trees with conifers; to keep woods in a clean state by having timely thinnings; and to prevent wounds being formed in standing trees. Special measures which may be taken in certain cases are: isolation of attacked plants by trenches; the cutting down and removal of diseased trees; pruning and burning of attacked

Fig. 9. Eight-year-old Scots pine killed by *A. mellea*, Vahl. *a* Sterile rhizomorphic strands. *b* and *c* Fertile ditto; some of the fructifications are abortive. *d* Fructifications springing from mycelia under the bark. (*Reduced*.)

branches; and the spraying of diseased young plants with fungicides.

The Honey fungus (*Armillarea mellea*). (Leaflet No. 6.)

This fungus is one of the most destructive to young conifer plantations. When the tree is attacked the needles become yellow and gradually dry up and fall, the base of the stem swells up, the bark peels off and turpentine exudes in quantities, often clogging together the soil round the tree. In the soil will be found black or brown root-like growths, termed *rhizomorphs*, which almost look like the leaf-stalks of a maidenhair fern; the thin, firm, white ribbon-like mycelium will be found between the wood and bark at the base of the tree.

The trees usually die very shortly after being attacked.

The fructifications or toadstools appear in numbers closely collected together round the base of the stem or on the surrounding ground in October, and are either of a bright yellow colour, or of a dirty brownish yellow, and vary in diameter from 2 to 6 inches.

When one plant has been attacked infection spreads to surrounding ones, as the rhizomorphs bore into the roots of neighbouring trees.

The fungus attacks nearly all conifers, of all ages, but especially trees from four to fifteen years old. It also attacks broad-leaved trees, living and dead, and is found on the stumps of felled oak and beech. Here it does no harm, but it spreads to conifers planted among these stumps, and is then destructive. It also attacks gate-posts and other dead timber placed in the ground. When the disease has appeared steps should be at once taken to prevent it spreading. All conifers attacked should be dug up with their roots, and these latter should be burnt.

The ground around the plant may be trenched and all rhizomorphs collected and burnt. Where the surrounding trees appear healthy a small trench, a foot deep, should be dug round the attacked plant, or group of plants, at some little distance away, so as to prevent the rhizomorphs spreading. This is best done in autumn when the toadstools are visible, so that the whole area can be included. No really effective measure is, however, known.

Any spot attacked and treated as above should be visited periodically to see whether surrounding plants have been infected, and if so, the measures should be repeated. The blanks caused by the removal of the infected plants should be filled up with some broad-leaved species.

Conifer heart rot (*Fomes annosus*). (Leaflet No. 5.)

This fungus is very destructive to conifers, especially spruce, larch, Scots pine, and Douglas fir. It attacks both young and old trees, spreading upwards from the roots. Infected young trees appear very like those attacked by honey fungus, but the mycelium, which is found between the wood and bark, is more delicate and silky. The fructifications are below ground, on the

Fig. 10. Fructification of *Fomes annosus*, Fries., on a Scots pine root. (*Reduced.*)

roots, in masses like yellow or white grapes, though sometimes the mass is bracket-shaped. In the rotting wood black spots surrounded by soft white patches appear. There are no rhizomorphs. Nothing can be done except to dig up and burn infected young plants.

On older trees, over ten years old, the disease is very serious. Trees are seldom killed, but they become heart-rotted or 'pumped', and this is seldom discovered till the trees are felled. The heart-wood rots away and becomes fibrous or slimy and eventually the tree becomes hollow. The value of the timber is seriously reduced, and all the trees in a wood may be attacked. It is specially liable to appear on areas which have been planted with conifers a second time, also on old agricultural land planted for the first time. There is no cure for the disease; if it is discovered while thinnings are being carried out, the crop should be felled as early as possible and the area should be replanted with broad-leaved species.

Pine blister (Peridermium pini).

This disease is very common in pine woods in Great Britain, and trees attacked by it are often called 'foxy' trees. On infected

pines orange-yellow tufts or fructifications are seen breaking through the bark in June. These liberate their spores and then become white. The mycelium develops chiefly in bark and bast, but also in the timber, forming a canker which is covered with resin. The canker increases in size annually, working round the stem, and if it gets completely round, the portion of the stem above it dies. Pines of all ages are attacked, but the damage done is greatest in woods from fifteen to twenty years of age.

The only measure which can be taken against it is to cut out all infected trees in the thinnings. These can be more easily distinguished in June when the fructifications are visible, and they should therefore be marked for felling then.

Fig. 11. *Peridermium pini,* Wallr. (corticola), on a 5-year-old shoot of a mountain pine. The fructifications are closed (*a*), or have already burst (*b*). (*Natural size.*)

Silver fir canker (Melampsorella Caryophyllacearum).

This fungus is fairly common wherever silver fir is grown. It causes the silver fir canker and 'witches'-broom'. The shoots attacked become brush-like and erect, and are of an entirely different appearance from the ordinary shoots. Such abnormal growths are called the witches'-broom. The mycelium grows in the bast, causing a swollen canker on which the bark is deeply cracked. Should the fungus attack a part where there is no living bud, a canker is formed but not the witches'-broom. The fructifications are orange-coloured, and appear on the under side of the leaves of the witches'-broom. They give out their spores in June, and the needles then die. The witches'-broom lives about sixteen years, and branches freely, somewhat resembling a bunch of mistletoe. It then dies, and only the canker remains.

Badly cankered trees may die outright, but more often they live on, the timber however being spoilt.

The best preventive measures are to prune off branches affected in June and July before the spores ripen, close to the stem, tarring the wounds. Cankered stems should be cut out in the thinnings.

The larch canker (*Dasyscypha calycina*). (Leaflet No. 16.)

This fungus is without doubt the most destructive one found in British woods and has done an enormous amount of damage. It is found in almost every young larch wood in England, Scotland, and Wales, but fortunately it is less common in Ireland, especially in mixed woods.

The disease is recognized by the appearance of swellings on the stem and branches; the bark splits, the resin flows out, and the wood is often exposed. In the cracks round the swelling, cup-shaped fructifications, about the size of a large pin's head, appear; these are white outside and orange yellow within the cup. When the weather is damp these produce spores which infect other trees. As time goes on the canker increases in size, and becomes black and spoon-shaped. It gradually spreads round the stem, and may finally kill the tree. A great number of cankers may appear on the same tree. When the canker is high up, or when the tree is vigorous and is growing under favourable conditions, it will probably overcome the disease, or at any rate the tree will live on for years, although of course the timber is spoilt at the canker. When young trees are attacked low down, and when the soil and climate are not suitable for larch, the tree will probably die before many years have passed. From a few infected trees the disease will spread throughout a young plantation, the spores germinating if they settle on a wound however

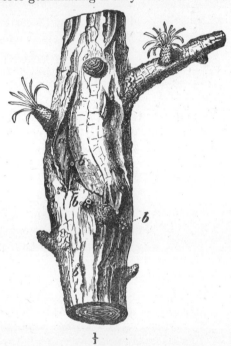

Fig. 12. Portion of Larch-stem attacked by *Dasyscypha calycina*, Fuckel.
        a Cracks with outflow of resin.   *b* Fructifications.

small. Such wounds are always present on the younger parts of the stem, being caused in a variety of ways. The fungus, however, according to Hiley, chiefly enters the stem by growing down from the dying branches. Trees from ten to twenty years old suffer most. It has been found on Japanese larch, but fortunately very rarely and this tree appears to be practically immune from the canker. The disease is worse in low-lying damp situations and in frosty places than on high-lying land. It is usually worse in pure, densely grown larch woods than when the larch is scattered amongst other species. Bark which is over fifteen years old is usually not pierced by the fungus, so that, in a larch thirty years old and 45 feet high, the bottom 20 feet or so are safe, if not already cankered, and if clear of branches.

The chief protective measures to be taken against this disease are: to grow it in localities as nearly as possible resembling its native Alps, in elevated well-ventilated places and preferably on a northern aspect and on a good, fresh, well-drained, but not arid, soil; to allow ample light and air beneath the canopy by planting it in mixture with slower-growing shade bearers; and, most important of all, to thin the woods rather heavily after the fifteenth to twentieth year, and to repeat the thinnings every few years thereafter. It seems in fact that the canker was so much dreaded some years ago because larch had been planted on many unsuitable sites, and early and fairly heavy thinnings were not then known to be necessary for the well-being of this tree.

The great object should be to induce vigorous growth of the larch. If this is obtained the disease will not get the upper hand, and the timber, even if cankered here and there, will still be of considerable value. If the larch gets into a bad state of health it soon gets covered with canker and its value is then much reduced. Lower branches should be snapped off with a stout stick, as soon as this can *easily* be done, to a height of about 6 feet. Thinnings should begin shortly after this operation has been found possible.

Polyporus sulphureus.

This fungus causes red-rot in the timber of oak, sweet chestnut, poplars, willows, alder, birch, fruit trees, larch, and silver fir. Infection occurs through wounds on the branches and on the stems; the timber attacked becomes reddish brown, cracked

and dry. The mycelium spreads through the cracks and forms large felted white sheets. The fructifications appear annually, and are very conspicuous, being large, bright yellow, smooth, and cheese-like.

The only remedial measure is to cut down infected trees, care being taken not to damage other trees in removing them. Other forms of *Polyporus*, which often have bracket-like fructifications, cause various forms of rot in different species.

Nectria ditissima. The canker of broad-leaved trees.

This fungus is a very common one on beech, oak, ash, hornbeam, hazel, alder, lime, cherry, and apple, but is chiefly found on beech and ash. The part infected becomes cankered, and on careful examination in spring, dark red globular fructifications will be found on it. Trees of all ages are attacked, and the parts infected often become greatly malformed. Beech timber turns brown, and ash timber black, and, if badly attacked, the wood is only fit for fuel. Cankered trees should be cut out in the thinnings, and great care should be taken not to wound standing trees while felling.

Fig. 13. *Nectria ditissima*, Tul., on a beech. *a* Commencement of the disease, which has proceeded deeper into the wood at *b*.

Beech seedling mildew. Phytophthora omnivora.

This very destructive fungus attacks chiefly seedlings of beech, but also those of maple, ash, acacia, spruce, and Scots pine. It may do considerable damage in natural regenerations, and may kill off whole beds of seedlings in nurseries. Damp warm years are favourable to the spread of the fungus, which may be carried about by wind and mice, or on the feet of men and horses. Infected seedlings turn black, and die from below upwards, during germination or immediately afterwards. The stem shrivels up and turns brown, and dark spots appear on the cotyledons, or young leaves. The fungus spreads very rapidly.

The most effective measure against it is to spray the seedlings, immediately the disease appears, with Bordeaux mixture—two pounds of sulphate of copper dissolved in ten gallons of water, with one pound of freshly burned lime added. All infected plants and dead leaves lying near by should be burnt. Those parts of the nursery where the disease has appeared should be used for transplants for a few years, and seed-beds should be formed in a new place.

Other diseases.

Space does not permit of a description of the following fungi which have become of importance since the second edition of this book was published. The leaflets mentioned give details and should be obtained.

The *Phomopsis* disease of conifers, *Phomopsis pseudotsugae* . . . . (Leaflet 14).

Douglas fir leaf-cast disease, *Rhabdocline pseudotsugae* . . . . (Leaflet 18).

The Dutch elm disease, *Graphium ulmi* . (Leaflet 19).

CHAPTER X

PROTECTION OF WOODS AGAINST FROST, DROUGHT, STORMS, AND FIRES

THE measures to be taken against ordinary damage by frost have already been mentioned in Chapter II, and it remains only to deal with two peculiar effects of frost—frost-crack and frost-lifting.

FROST-CRACK

Oak, beech, walnut, elm, ash, and sweet chestnut are most liable to frost-crack; it is, however, found in other species, though it is rare on conifers. Frost-cracks usually occur on the lower part of the stem and take the form of a long crack running up and down it. They usually are formed in late winter, when the sap is rising, if very cold weather prevails. The sapwood then contracts with the cold while the heart-wood, being warm, does not; the result is a crack in the sapwood, which is often accompanied by a loud report like a pistol-shot. The crack is healed over by the growth of timber during the summer, but is usually opened out again the following winter. Pressure of the bark being thus relieved, the timber formed at the spot is laid on in thick layers, and a projecting rib of wood is formed called a *frost-rib*.

Frost-cracks are mostly found in open woods or in those which have been over-thinned after growing in a dense state. They do not affect the health of the tree, but spoil the most valuable part of the timber. The best protective measure is to keep woods in a properly dense state. Nothing can be done when once a crack has been formed, and affected trees should therefore be cut out in the thinnings.

FROST-LIFTING

In February and March when there are frosts at night with a thaw in the day-time we find that young seedlings are often lifted out of the ground. This is due to the fact that the soil rises with the frost, and the plants are raised also; then when the thaw comes the soil sinks again, but the plants do not. When this has been repeated three or four times the plants fall over and lie on the surface, and die if long exposed. Nearly all species may be lifted, though this happens but rarely with seedlings, such as oak and sweet chestnut, which have long tap-roots. Sitka spruce is specially liable, and frost-lifting is often serious amongst newly planted spruce and Sitka spruce on turfs or mounds. This can be largely avoided by planting deeply in the turf and by planting rather late in spring. Frost-lifting is not so bad on sandy soils as on stiffer ones.

To prevent damage in nurseries the spaces between the rows of seedlings should be covered with dead leaves. Seed-beds and nursery lines consisting of small plants should be inspected daily in frosty weather, and all plants lifted should be at once replaced in the ground. Seed-beds should be covered over at night with mats.

DROUGHT

Drought is seldom to be feared in Great Britain, at any rate not to such an extent as to damage established woods. A long spell of dry weather in summer will, however, cause a large proportion of failures in recently formed plantations and, unless care is taken, in the nursery. It is seldom worth while to take measures against drought in the forest; failures in plantations must be filled up the following planting season. Drought is often serious on newly planted areas when turf or mound planting has been carried out, as the mounds get very dry.

In the nursery drought may be guarded against by covering spaces between the plants with a good layer of humus or dead leaves, as this will keep the soil moist; by sticking branches of evergreen trees into the soil on the south side of beds of seedlings in such a way that these will shade the bed in the hottest part of the day; by covering beds with mats, lifted up on short supports, during the hottest hours; by hoeing the surface periodically to prevent it caking; or, if absolutely necessary, by watering the plants in the evening; if this is done the watering must be thorough, as it is useless to give a mere sprinkling.

WINDS AND STORMS

There are three types of wind—dry east and north-east winds, sea-breezes carrying salt, and westerly or south-westerly gales— which do serious harm to woods in the British Isles; the wood-man should take every possible precaution to reduce such damage to a minimum.

The chief measures to be taken against *dry east winds* and against *sea-breezes* have been indicated in Chapter II, the main object being to form an efficient wind-break some twelve to fif⁺een years in advance of the regeneration of the woods behind them. In existing young woods, where it is too late to form a shelter belt of evergreen trees, every endeavour should be made to keep the east and north-east sides in as thick a condition as possible by reducing thinnings to a minimum along a belt 40 to 50 feet wide, and by carefully preserving all undergrowth which springs up.

East winds prevail in spring and dry up the soil, blow dead leaves away from ridges and slopes, and thus prevent the forma-tion of humus, hinder the formation of dew, injure the foliage and flowers, and if planting is going on they dry up the roots unless precautions are taken. Together with other winds they spread the spores of fungi. Broad-leaved trees suffer more than conifers from such winds, while seedlings, young transplants, and young coppice shoots suffer more than older trees.

Storms are more serious and are more difficult to deal with, as the power of the woodman is limited, and he cannot hope to overcome successfully the force of nature. Nevertheless a good deal can be done to reduce damage. Storms either break trees or uproot them, and if a large quantity of timber is thrown in a gale the market is glutted, and the price obtainable for the timber is small; this adds considerably to the loss sustained. In addition, large blanks may be made in the woods; and large trees may fall on young growth and injure it. In coniferous woods, owing to the large amount of dead timber lying about, insects may increase rapidly, and thus cause damage to other standing woods. The chief damage is, however, done by the stunting effect of wind, as trees grown in exposed places will be short and misshapen and of small volume.

Conifers and evergreen trees suffer from storms more than broad-leaved and deciduous trees, while shallow-rooted trees are more easily uprooted than those with deep roots. Ash, sycamore, Norway maple, alder, lime, and oaks are fairly storm firm. Trees grown always in the open resist storms better than those which have grown up in a dense wood, and which have then been opened out.

The following protective measures should be carefully carried out, as the fight against storms must be begun when the woods are planted, and must be continued throughout their life.

Measures to be taken while forming woods.

1. In places where storms are bad, plant broad-leaved species, especially beech and sycamore, in preference to conifers.

2. Plant the trees on the exposed edge at distances rather far apart, at least 6 feet, so as to encourage them to grow sturdy.

3. Mix deep-rooted species with shallow-rooted ones; thus, mix beech, sycamore, or Scots pine, with spruce. In spruce woods five or six rows of a deep-rooted species may be planted across the storm direction every 150 yards.

4. Form protective belts, if none already exist, along all exposed sides and along roads.

5. Form wide rides through the woods. The trees along them will grow up storm firm, and will afterwards protect woods behind them. The main rides should be formed parallel to the storm direction so that the wind blows harmlessly down them.

Cross rides can be formed between the main rides. These rides should be formed when the woods are planted; if they are afterwards cut through existing woods there is a chance of wind doing damage.

Measures to be taken during tending of woods.

1. Make early, frequent, and moderate thinnings. Heavy thinnings in densely growing woods must be avoided.

2. Keep the woods dense along a 50 feet wide belt on exposed sides, but allow the outside row of trees to branch low down, by never allowing them to become crowded.

Measures to be taken during the felling of woods.

1. All places badly exposed, such as hill-tops, should be regenerated under the selection method, so that the area is never blank.

2. Fellings in any wood should be commenced on the side farthest away from the storm direction; in Great Britain they should therefore usually commence on the north-east side of the woods, and gradually proceed towards the south-west. By doing this a cutting will never expose a middle-aged or mature wood to storms, while the young plantation, which is not apt to suffer much in any case, grows up behind the shelter of woods still uncut. This measure is one of the most effective, and should never be neglected. To ensure its being done it is even worth while to cut a middle-aged crop before a mature one, if this happens to be necessary.

If two parts of a wood are separated by a broad ride or road, along which the trees are storm firm, each part may be treated as a separate wood, and cuttings may be made in both parts.

3. Felling areas should take the form of long narrow strips instead of large square blocks.

4. No standards of shallow-rooted species should be left standing, as they are almost sure to be blown down.

5. When felling woods, the strip of weather-beaten trees along

the exposed edge, to a width of 50 or 60 feet, should not be felled, but should be left standing to protect the new crop. These trees are usually misshapen and stunted, and it is a mistake to cut them and replant, as the new crop will be no better than the existing one.

Should windfall occur on any large scale, especially in coniferous woods, every endeavour should be made to sell the fallen timber as soon as possible, as if left in the forest the logs act as breeding-grounds for numerous species of insects. If a sale cannot be effected at once all conifers should be stripped of bark.

FIRES (Leaflet No. 9)

Fires are caused chiefly by carelessness, but occasionally on purpose by persons having a grudge against the owner or woodman. The chief causes of forest fires are: carelessness in throwing away cigarette ends or lighted matches, carelessness on the part of picnic parties in leaving fires alight, and sparks from railway engines and steam lorries.

Fires do harm by burning young trees, and by scorching the bark of older trees. They also burn dead leaves and dry humus lying on the ground, thus rendering the soil poor. On an area through which fire has passed there is an additional risk of insects, especially in coniferous woods.

Danger from fire is greatest in young pine woods, owing to the early drying up of the lower branches; spruce also burns easily owing to the resinous needles. Amongst broad-leaved trees, rough-barked ones such as oak and elm will stand fires better than smooth-barked trees, such as beech and ash.

Young plantations are most exposed to damage, as weeds are plentiful, and when these have been killed out in the thicket stage, the danger is still great as the lower branches are dry. After the woods have passed the age of thirty years the danger of damage rapidly decreases.

Taking all things into consideration the danger of fire is

greatest in young conifer woods with a vegetation of heather, bracken, or molinia grass. The most dangerous season is March, when dry winds prevail, and bracken or heather is still dry. August is also a dangerous month if rainfall is deficient.

Under the Railway Fires Act 1905, the Railway Companies are liable for damage done by fire to the extent of £100, but this will often not cover the injury done.

The following measures may be taken to reduce the danger of fire and to limit the area likely to be burnt.

1. Strips, 25 to 35 feet broad, of broad-leaved trees may be planted through coniferous woods. Where the risk of fire is very great these strips may be kept clear of weeds.

2. In young pine woods all inflammable material such as heather, fern, &c., may be burnt early in the season, on either side of railways and much-frequented roads or rides. Such burnt fire-lines limit the area burnt, and form lines of defence should a fire occur. In preparing them a guide line 6 feet broad is first cut on the side farthest from the road or ride, and then the weeds on the line are burnt *in situ*, care being taken to have sufficient men on the spot to prevent the fire getting out of hand, and to stop burning should a heavy wind get up. Each man should have a large flat long-handled shovel with which he can beat out any fire which crosses the guide line. One or two men should follow the firing gang, and should see that all smouldering embers are extinguished.

Fire-lines should be 50 feet broad along railway lines, but 20 to 30 feet is usually sufficient along roads or rides.

3. Belts of alder or false acacia should be planted along railways, on the forest side of the burnt fire-line. The non-inflammable foliage of these species intercepts sparks which are blown over the fire-line.

Conifers planted close to a railway will kill out all grass and weeds, but may, when in the thicket stage, catch fire themselves.

4. A good system of roads and rides through the forest will greatly help in limiting a fire to one block.

5. Workmen should be cautioned at the commencement of every fire season against carelessness in leaving fires, and regarding smoking.

6. As it is of great importance to commence extinguishing a fire as soon as possible after it starts, a sharp look-out should be kept over the woods in dry weather by all woodmen. If the lodges are on high land overlooking the woods, the woodman can easily take a look round, periodically, and especially just before going to bed. If the lodge is surrounded closely by woods, a long ladder standing against a tall tree will enable the woodman to climb the tree easily, and he can then see to a distance.

7. On public holidays in dry weather, in woods liable to be overrun with holiday makers, it is advisable to have all the staff patrolling the woods to warn people against making fires, and to be ready to concentrate on any fire which arises. This measure is carried out in the Forestry Commission's woods with satisfactory results. The men can be given a holiday on some other day to make up for their own lost day.

8. If all lodges in large woods are linked together by telephone, rapid concentration on a fire is greatly facilitated.

Should a fire break out, as many men as are available should be at once sent off to the place, and should take with them billhooks, axes, rakes, large flat shovels, and besoms, or green branches. Previous arrangements should be made with local police and neighbours for help.

If the work is likely to take a long time, the head woodman should arrange for a supply of tea or lime-juice for the men; cold water must not be taken. The fire should be attacked on both sides by beating it out, or by sweeping the burning material into the already burnt area. It is seldom possible to attack it from the front owing to the smoke and heat, but attack from the sides will gradually narrow the fire. If there is no wind this work will usually be successful, the time taken depending on the number of men available.

If the fire is in the crowns of trees in the thicket stage, beating is usually useless. In this case, and wherever beating proves of no avail, *counter-firing* must be carried out, sacrificing a portion of the woods in order to save the rest. A cleared ride, road, fire-line, or stream some little way in advance of the fire is chosen as a point of attack, and all the men available are concentrated on this line. When the fire is some two chains away, each man lights another fire 3 or 4 yards from the side of the line. This he watches, and takes care to prevent it or any sparks crossing the line. When the main fire approaches, a draught will be caused towards it, the small fires will be drawn inwards, and will meet the main fire, when the whole will go out for want of fuel. While this is in progress, every care must be taken to extinguish at once any fire which may manage to cross the line. In many cases where the nearest cleared ride is some distance away from the fire, it is possible to clear a line a short distance ahead, by cutting the weeds, and·by brushing away dead leaves, and to counter-fire from the swept line. If this can be done it may be possible to save much woodland which would otherwise have to be sacrificed.

Counter-firing is difficult to carry out, and is risky, and must only be undertaken in extreme cases, where it is obviously impossible to put out the fire by beating. Indiscriminate lighting of counter-fires will do more harm than good if these fires are not kept properly under control.

When the fire is out the area should be gone over carefully, and all smouldering wood should be extinguished by heaping earth upon it. Care must be taken that it does not start afresh if a wind springs up.

Young coniferous woods much injured by fire should usually be felled and replanted, while young broad-leaved trees may be left a year or two to see whether they recover; if not they will often throw up coppice shoots if cut back.

Where the soil is peaty a fire may burn in the ground for days. It should be ringed round by ditches specially dug and carefully watched till rain falls.

There are now very large areas of young plantations in the country, mainly in the State forests under the control of the Forestry Commission. In every dry spring or summer there are numerous fires largely caused by carelessness on the part of holiday-makers. Every endeavour should be made to educate people to be more careful in lighting and extinguishing picnic fires and in throwing away cigarette ends. A small fire soon becomes a large one unless immediately put out, and very serious financial loss may be caused. The beauty of the countryside is also destroyed for some years.

CHAPTER XI

SYLVICULTURAL NOTES ON THE BROAD-LEAVED TREES

Acacia, False Acacia or Locust-tree (*Robinia pseudacacia*).

A NATIVE of North America, introduced into Great Britain in 1638. It requires a good deal of warmth, and should be grown only in situations with a mild climate, and is more suitable for the south of England than for the north. South aspects are best. It is frost-tender, and requires shelter when young. It is highly light-demanding. Deep, dry, light, and moderately rich soil suits it best, but it grows fairly well on poor sandy soils.

It produces good seed, which should be kept in the pod until it is sown; it coppices well and throws up numerous suckers. It can be grown in high forest mixed with pines in groups, and is useful as a belt along railway lines running through pine woods where there is danger of fire. It does well as standards-over-coppice, and also as coppice, if not shaded by standards. It is a very ornamental tree, and can be grown in parks and along the edges of plantations.

It does not suffer much from attacks of insects or fungi, but is often damaged by rabbits. It is ripe for the axe at about forty to sixty years in high forest, and at from ten to twenty-five years in coppice, small sizes being useful for hoops for casks, and for hop-poles.

Alder (*Alnus glutinosa*).

A native of Great Britain and of Europe, it is found up to an elevation of 1,600 feet in Scotland. It is hardy against frost, but cannot stand drought. Any aspect will suit it. It is light-demanding, but will bear a fairly heavy shade when young or as coppice. It requires a wet soil, but does not do in stagnant water. It does well on fairly deep sandy loams; cold clays and dry sands are unsuitable. It is a good tree for planting on low-lying wet places and along streams, and it can often be grown with profit as coppice under ash or poplar standards in wet places. It is a quick grower. It produces plenty of seed and coppices well; it also sends up many suckers. It is not often grown in high forest, but when so grown reaches maturity at about sixty years. In coppice it can be cut at any age up to forty years. It does not suffer to any great extent from insects or fungi. The chief dangers to which it is exposed are frost-lifting shortly after being planted, and drought.

The White or Grey Alder (*Alnus incana*).

Can bear a considerable amount of shade, and does well on shallow, poor soils, and even on dry ground. It may be substituted for the common alder under these conditions. It is a useful tree on an exposed spot as a shelter tree for a more valuable species, which can be planted between the lines of alder when the latter is large enough to give the required shelter. It is also useful for covering spoil heaps from stone quarries and other unsightly banks of poor soil.

Ash (*Fraxinus excelsior*).

A native of Great Britain and of Europe, it is found up to an elevation of 1,350 feet in Yorkshire. It does not require much heat, but is tender against late frosts, and a light shelter is useful when young. It does best in moist situations on north and east aspects. It is storm firm. It is very light-demanding in later life, but seedlings will stand a heavy shade for a few years, and as coppice it stands light shade. It prefers a fresh, deep, light, loamy soil, with some lime, and plenty of humus, and grows well on the sides of ravines.

It produces good crops of seed about every second year after forty years of age, and is easily reproduced naturally. It forms good shoots when coppiced.

Ash is best grown in high forest scattered here and there singly, or in small groups, in woods of other broad-leaved species, especially beech. It can be grown as standards-over-coppice, or as coppice under a light shade. Existing young pure woods should be underplanted.

It is a fast grower, and forms a straight stem which forks at about half its height. The roots are extensive and deep-growing. In the thinnings ash should be given plenty of space, and other species should never be allowed to top it. It is ripe for cutting at from sixty to seventy years, and is a very profitable tree, being saleable at all sizes. It does not suffer much from disease, though it turns black-hearted on unsuitable soils and is injured by a fungus (*Nectria ditissima*). The shoots may be badly stunted by a moth (*Prays curtisella*). The ash bark-beetle kills weakly trees.

White Ash (*Fraxinus americana*) has much the same characteristics as the ash, but it stands frost better and grows well on dry, sandy soils which are not good enough for common ash. Its seed germinates in the first year after ripening.

Beech (*Fagus sylvatica*).

A native of England and of Europe, it is found up to an elevation of 1,200 feet in Derbyshire. It is tender against late frosts, but otherwise it is hardy. It grows best on north or east aspects, and does well near the sea; it withstands an exposed situation fairly well. It does best on a fairly deep, porous, fresh, and fertile soil, especially where there is a good deal of lime. It is essentially the tree for marls and chalky soils, but does well on moist sandy soils or on moderately stiff clayey soils with lime. It is a great shade-bearer, and for the first few years, when it is very subject to damage by frost or by hot sun, it may be considered as shade-demanding. It produces good seed from sixty years of age, but usually only at intervals of from five to nine years. It coppices badly, and the stools only last three or four rotations.

Beech is best grown as high forest in pure woods on rotations from 80 to 120 years, but first-class timber of ash, oak, larch, &c., can be produced by introducing these trees into the beech

PLATE VII

BEECH PLANTED AT 4 FEET BY 4 FEET

Aged 18 years. Height 35 feet, girth up to 16 inches. The ground is covered with dead leaves. Coopers Hill

woods, either singly or in small groups, and it is chiefly as a nurse to the valuable light-demanders that beech will be grown in Great Britain. It is the best tree for underplanting open woods of light-demanding species. It is unsuitable for standards-over-coppice, and is not very good as coppice except as a soil improver. It must be grown densely, or the stems will not get naturally pruned; thinnings may be moderately heavy. It is a slow grower at first, but after twenty to thirty years the rate of growth increases. Beech woods are very suited to natural regeneration, especially when the soil contains lime. An aphis (*Cryptococcus fagi*) does much damage, otherwise beech does not suffer much from insects or fungi, though it is attacked by a good many species. The bark of trees suddenly exposed to the sun is very often blistered.

Birch (*Betula pubescens*).

A native of Great Britain and Europe, and is found up to an elevation of 2,500 feet in Scotland. It is very hardy, does not suffer from frost, and does well on any aspect. It is highly light-demanding. It is very accommodating as to soil, and can be grown on almost any kind of soil and situation. It produces large quantities of seed, is easily regenerated naturally, and is apt to come up wherever there is clear ground, and is often a troublesome weed in plantations. Coppice shoots are usually weak, and the stools die after two or three rotations. It is not a good tree for pure woods as the soil deteriorates under it, but it is found growing alone where the soil is too poor for other species. Being of little value birch is seldom grown except as a nurse crop, but as such it is usefully introduced with conifers on exposed places and on certain types of heath land. It is important, however, to see that it does not spoil the conifers by the whipping action of its slender branches, and is best used in small groups or belts. It is a quick grower, and is usually cut at from forty to sixty years of age. It does not suffer much from insects or fungi.

Cherry or Gean (Prunus Avium).

A native of Europe. It is found here and there in most English woods. It is fairly hardy against frost and will grow on any aspect. It is a light-demander. It will grow on almost any soil, but does best where it is not too wet and where there is some lime. It is propagated by sowing the stones shortly after collection in July. It coppices well, and also sends out suckers. It usually is grown singly here and there in high forest, and often forms part of the coppice in coppice-with-standards where there is not too much shade. It will grow to a height of 60 or 70 feet in close canopy with other trees, and reaches maturity at fifty or sixty years. The timber takes a fine polish and is valuable for furniture.

It is only of small importance in British woods, but is a very ornamental tree along the edges of plantations.

The English Elm (Ulmus campestris).

A native of Central and South Europe, it was introduced into Great Britain by the Romans. It is found up to an elevation of 1,500 feet in Derbyshire. It requires a mild climate, but is fairly hardy against frost. It does best on flat land, and south aspects are preferable in hilly places. It is a light-demander, but will bear a light shade better than oak or ash. It requires a deep, porous, moist, and fertile soil, and does best in low lands and valleys. It seldom produces fertile seed in England, and is best propagated from suckers. Where there are a few elms in a hedge, suckers will be found coming up plentifully in the neighbouring field, and a strip of land can be fenced off and used as a nursery. Elm is chiefly found in hedgerows and in parks, but it could be grown as a forest tree in small groups mixed with other broad-leaved trees. It should not be grown in pure woods. It must be given plenty of space for its crown from middle age upwards. It is a rapid grower, and attains a good height. It ordinarily reaches maturity at about eighty years. Elm suffers badly from insects and fungi. The bark-beetle (*Scolytus Geoffroyi*) does much damage to weakly trees. The Dutch elm-disease (*Graphium ulmi*) may kill trees very rapidly. The branches of large elms are very apt to fall off and are often dangerous in avenues and parks and along roads.

Wych Elm (Ulmus glabra).

A native of Great Britain and Europe, and is found up to an elevation of 1,300 feet in Yorkshire. It does better in Scotland than the common elm, and is more a tree for hilly land than the latter. It does well in ravines and near the sides of streams. It is hardier than the common elm and is more accommodating as to soil and situation. It does fairly well on stiff loams, but does not thrive on sand. It produces large quantities of seed and also good stool shoots. It should be grown, like common elm, in groups here and there in woods of other broad-leaved trees. In other respects its characteristics are much the same as those of the common elm.

Hazel (Corylus avellana).

A native of Great Britain, Europe, and Asia Minor. It is found up to an elevation of 1,900 feet in Scotland. It is frost-hardy and will succeed on any aspect. It is a moderate shade-bearer. It prefers a fresh, porous soil of moderate depth, but will grow on almost any soil provided it is not marshy. It seeds well, and also coppices easily. It can be layered or 'plashed', and this method of reproducing it is useful for filling up blanks in existing coppices. It is chiefly grown as coppice under oak standards, and is cut on rotations of from seven to twenty-five years. Its value has greatly declined recently, and new coppices of hazel are hardly required, except possibly in woods kept mainly for sport.

Holly (Ilex aquifolium).

A native of Central Europe. It is hardy, but does best when sheltered. It is not particular as to aspect. It is a great shade-bearer. It does best on a light, dry soil with plenty of humus, and prefers soil containing lime. It seeds well and produces good coppice shoots. It can hardly be regarded as a useful forest tree and is usually grown for ornament. It is, however, a very good plant for evergreen hedges. Seeds should be treated like those of ash, as they do not germinate till the second spring after ripening.

Hornbeam (*Carpinus Betulus*).

A native of Great Britain and Central Europe, it is generally a tree of low lands and low hills. It is hardy, and will do better than other species in cold, damp situations; it prefers north and east aspects. It is a good shade-bearer, but not so good as beech. It does best on a loose, fresh, rich, and fairly deep soil, but it will succeed on soils of most descriptions and is useful on a heavy clay. It seeds and coppices well. It can be grown as a pure wood either as high forest or as coppice, but is hardly valuable enough to be grown on a large scale. Its chief use in Great Britain is as a substitute for beech for mixing with or under-planting woods of light-demanding species on heavy clays or in very frosty places. It also makes an excellent hedge. It can be cut at any age up to 100 years in high forest, and at from fifteen to thirty-five years as coppice. It reaches a height of 50 to 60 feet. It suffers but little from insects and fungi.

Horse-chestnut (*Aesculus hippocastanum*).

A native of Greece and parts of Asia. It is a hardy tree, and grows on any aspect, but its branches are often broken by wind in exposed situations. It will bear a light shade. It does best on a good, rich, loamy, fairly dry soil. It is used as an ornamental tree, and is not valuable enough to be grown in woods, its timber being soft and not durable; it might, however, become valuable for the manufacture of wood-pulp. It is a rapid grower. Its chief enemy is a fungus (*Nectria cinnabarina*), which may be recognized by the bright red fructifications which break out on the branches.

PLATE VIII

HORNBEAM PLANTED AT 4 FEET BY 4 FEET
Aged 18 years. Height 35 feet, girth up to 16 inches
In the background is pure birch. Coopers Hill

Laburnum (Laburnum vulgare).

A native of Central and South Europe, and has long been cultivated in Great Britain. It is chiefly of use as an ornament in parks and gardens and on the edges of plantations. It will grow on most soils, but to reach a large size it requires a deep, loamy, and fairly dry soil and a sheltered situation. The timber is valuable for cabinet-making, and fetches a good price if large.

Lime-tree or Linden (Tilia europaea).

There are three varieties of the lime-tree: the large-leaved lime (*Tilia grandifolia*), the small-leaved lime (*Tilia parvifolia*), and the intermediate form (*Tilia intermedia*). The lime-tree is a native of Central and South Europe and has long been grown in England. It is a tree of the plains, and does not do well at high elevations. It is frost-hardy; it stands half-way between the light-demanders and the shade-bearers; that is to say, it will bear a light shade in favourable situations. It does best on a fresh, fertile soil, the large-leaved variety being more exacting than the small-leaved tree in this respect. The latter should therefore be preferred on poorer soils. It can be grown from seed, or from layers; it coppices well, and produces good straight shoots. The timber is not good enough to warrant the growth of this tree in woods, and it is chiefly used as an ornamental tree in parks, and for avenues. It is, however, useful in coppice woods when there are many rabbits, as it is not touched by them owing to its stringy bark.

Mountain Ash (Pyrus Aucuparia).

A native of Great Britain, and the hardiest of all our trees; it will grow at high elevations on all aspects and on most soils. It bears some shade. Its timber is good for cart-making and for agricultural implements owing to its toughness, but it can hardly be regarded as a forest tree. It is useful as an ornamental tree along roads and rides, and sylviculturally it may be useful as a nurse to conifers, especially on some types of mountain moorland ground where exposed and peaty, also for fire-belts in such places.

The English or Pedunculate Oak (Quercus Robur).

A native of Great Britain and Europe, it is found up to an elevation of 1,500 feet in England. It requires warmth, and does better on southern than northern aspects. It suffers from late frost, but it comes into leaf so late that it usually escapes damage. It is highly light-demanding and should have its head free throughout life. It is very storm-firm. It requires a deep, fresh, fertile soil to do really well, but it will grow on stiff clays and also on moist, sandy soils and limestones. It produces seed heavily every three or four years, and also throws up good coppice shoots, the stools living for many rotations. Oak is not suitable for pure woods, but it may be grown pure up to the fortieth year, when it should be underplanted with beech. It can also be planted in groups surrounded by other species, of which beech is the best; in fact first-class oak timber can hardly be produced without an admixture of beech. Oak of a very fair quality can be grown as standards-over-coppice, though in this case the timber is short, unless the standards are left in groups. It used to be largely grown as coppice when bark was of more value than it is now. It is a moderately fast grower and has a deep root-system. It has a decided tendency to throw out large branches, so the thinnings should be light in character till the fiftieth or sixtieth year, and then they should gradually be made more heavy so as to isolate the crowns. Oak matures at about 120 years. A large number of insects live on this tree, but on the whole damage is not serious. The oak-leaf-roller moth defoliates whole woods, but the trees recover with the second flush of leaves. Canker is caused by the fungus *Nectria ditissima*.

The Sessile or Durmast Oak (Quercus sessiliflora) has much the same characteristics as the English oak; it is the more common species in Wales. It is on the whole a hardier tree, and is content

PLATE IX

OAK AND LARCH WITH COPPICED BEECH. Oak aged about 120 years, height 70 feet
Highmeadow Woods. *Photograph by* R. C. MILWARD

with poorer soil than is the English oak; it should be preferred at high elevations and on the poorer and drier soils. It does not tend to produce horizontal branches, and it is therefore easier to obtain straight clean timber from woods of sessile oak. It suffers less from mildew and from the leaf-roller moth.

Occasionally when an oak has been felled the timber is found to be brown in colour. This is 'brown oak', which is worth a high price if well figured.

The Turkey Oak (Quercus Cerris).

A native of South Europe, it was introduced into Great Britain in 1735. It does best on southern aspects and sheltered positions, and prefers dry, loamy soils; limy loams or clayey limes suit it well. It grows quicker than the English oak, but it will never be a valuable forest tree as its timber is not so durable as that of the English or sessile oak, and is very heavy. It is used for furniture and cabinet-making. It forms a fine ornamental tree in a park, but it gets injured if much exposed to wind.

Plane.

There are two species often planted in avenues and parks in large towns: the Western plane (Platanus occidentalis); and the London plane (Platanus acerifolia). Neither can be regarded as a forest tree, but they are very ornamental and flourish in towns where other trees are killed by the smoke and dirt, and they are chiefly used for town planting. They do best on deep, light, moist soil and in sheltered positions. They can be grown from seed, but they are best propagated from layers or cuttings. The timber is of good quality, and is used for the framework for veneering.

Poplar.

The following species are often grown or are found in British woods:

The Black poplar (Populus nigra).
The Black Italian poplar (Populus serotina).

The Lombardy poplar (*Populus pyramidalis*).
The White poplar (*Populus alba*).
The Grey poplar (*Populus canescens*).
The Aspen (*Populus tremula*).

Of these the black Italian poplar is the most profitable timber tree. It grows rapidly, and will give large-sized timber at from forty to fifty years of age. It should be planted on a good, deep, moist soil in sheltered positions, but large trees will also be obtained on poor soils if situated on a sloping bank where there is plenty of moisture. The black Italian is the most accommodating of the poplars as to soil.

The Lombardy poplar is not a forest tree, and is chiefly used for providing shelter, as when planted closely in a line it soon forms a tall hedge.

The white and grey poplars provide timber suitable for industries requiring a light and soft wood. They thrive best in moist sandy loams and in sheltered situations, but the grey poplar is very accommodating and will grow to a large size on many different soils, while the white poplar does well on clays. Both these trees are best raised from suckers.

The aspen is very hardy, and will grow in most soils and situations; it comes up naturally in many woods, and often becomes a troublesome weed in plantations of more valuable species owing to the great number of suckers it produces.

As a whole the poplars are hardy trees and light-demanders; they prefer moist soils and situations sheltered from wind, and are useful for planting up damp hollows and along the sides of streams. They are usually propagated from cuttings or from suckers, and are rapid growers. The leaves of poplars are much eaten by the larvae of many species of moths, but no great amount of damage is done. The timber is bored by the goat-moth caterpillar. The small poplar longicorn beetle (*Saperda populnea*) does a considerable amount of damage to young plants. Fungi do no serious damage.

Sweet or Spanish Chestnut (Castanea sativa).

A native of Southern Europe, it was probably introduced into Great Britain by the Romans. It is a tree which should be restricted to warm situations and low elevations, southern or western aspects being best, though it does well on northern aspects in the south of England. It is tender against frost, and cannot withstand severe winter cold. It is a light-demanding tree after early youth, but not so much so as the oak. It stands a fair amount of shade till about twenty years of age, and also when grown as coppice. It is storm-firm. It does best on a deep, porous, fresh, and fertile soil, but can grow on rather dry soils if deep; it does not like wet or limy soils, but will produce fair timber of small size on clays.

It seldom produces good seed except in the south of England, but it sends up very good stool shoots even from old stools, and it is therefore a very good tree for coppices and underwoods. It also produces suckers. It can be grown as high forest, standards-over-coppice, and especially as coppice. It should not be grown as a pure wood as high forest except on short rotations and on good soil, but pure coppices are allowable as, with a short rotation, it keeps up the fertility of the soil. As high forest it is best grown in groups mixed with beech and oak, while a mixture of larch and chestnut is also good on a fertile soil. It is a rapid grower and attains a large size, but large timber is usually much shaken, and it is therefore best to cut it at an age of forty to fifty years. As coppice it pays well on a rotation of fifteen to twenty years where there is a demand for hop-poles, or for split chestnut fencing material. It deserves more attention as an underwood tree than it has yet received in England. With regard to thinnings, these should be made in the same manner as for oak. Insects and fungi do but little damage.

Sycamore or Great Maple (Acer Pseudo-platanus).

A native of Central Europe and Western Asia, it was introduced into Great Britain during the fifteenth century. It is a tree of the hills and withstands strong winds well. It is rather tender to late frosts. It stands half-way between light-demanders and shade-bearers, and to do well as high forest requires a full amount of light. As coppice it will stand a fair amount of shade, and it can be used for underplanting the more open spaces in oak, ash, and larch woods. It requires a deep, fertile, fresh soil to do well, but it will grow on most kinds of soil provided there is a good depth. Some lime in the soil is advantageous. It grows well from seed, and its natural regeneration is easy. It coppices well when cut for the first time, but the stools do not last long. It can be grown as high forest, standards-over-coppice, or as coppice, and is best grown in high forest in groups mixed with other species, especially beech. It should be given plenty of space when its height growth begins to fall off. It is a rapid grower, and produces a tall clean stem if grown in crowded woods. It reaches maturity at from eighty to one hundred years. Large timber usually sells well, but small trees are of little value. Insects and fungi do but little damage. The fungus *Rhytisma acerina* causes the black spots found on the leaves.

The Norway Maple (Acer platanoides).

Has much the same sylvicultural characteristics as the sycamore, but thrives farther north. It is more a tree of the plains than of the hills, and is specially suitable for planting near the sea. It suffers less from late frosts, and is not so exacting as to soil. Its timber is not quite so valuable as that of the sycamore.

Tulip tree (Liriodendron tulipifera).

A native of the United States, it was introduced into Europe in 1663. It is an ornamental tree for park planting, and has not been planted in woods. It suffers from late frosts and should therefore be grown in sheltered situations; it does best in the south of England, and thrives in London parks. It is a light-demander. It does best on a deep loamy soil. It is a difficult tree to transplant, and therefore is not likely to be grown on a large scale as a forest tree in England, though its timber is used for furniture and other purposes under the names of 'White Wood', 'Canary Wood', and 'Yellow Poplar'.

Walnut (Juglans regia).

A native of Greece, but has been cultivated in Great Britain for many centuries. Although here grown chiefly as a fruit tree, its timber is of considerable value for gun-stocks and for furniture, and it would pay well if grown as a timber tree. It could be introduced in groups here and there in woods of other species on deep, dry, rather light loamy soils. It is a light-demander, and requires plenty of space. It should be grown in sheltered positions as it is extremely frost-tender. It is grown from nuts which should be sown in rows two inches deep, and the seedlings should be transplanted at one year old.

The *Black walnut (Juglans nigra)* and the *Grey walnut (Juglans cinerea)* would also perhaps prove to be good forest trees in the warmer parts of England. Walnuts should be grown on a rotation of over 100 years, as the valuable heartwood is not produced till the tree is fifty to sixty years old.

WILLOWS

The Sallow, Saugh, or Goat Willow (Salix caprea).

A native of Great Britain and Europe. It is found up to an elevation of 2,000 feet in Scotland. It will succeed on any aspect and on almost any soil, and is very hardy. It is light-demanding and a rapid grower. It is not of much value and is usually considered as a weed, and is cut out in the cleanings and thinnings. It seeds well, but is ordinarily propagated from cuttings. It could be used to provide temporary shelter to more valuable trees in unfavourable situations.

The White Willow (Salix alba).

A native of Europe and Asia, and probably of Great Britain. It is very accommodating as to soil and situation in the southern counties so long as there is enough moisture, and is very useful along the banks of rivers and streams. It is light-demanding and hardy. It coppices and pollards well, and is the best willow for providing small material for cask-hoops and basket-work. It is propagated from cuttings about 5 feet long. It may be kept free from side branches by careful pruning but should not be grown in close woods.

A variety of this willow (*Salix alba caerulea*) is the best for cricket-bats, and *Salix alba* is the next best willow for this purpose. The female trees are said to be better than the male, and therefore cuttings of female trees should be obtained from districts such as Essex, Suffolk, and Herts., where the best willow for cricket-bats is now grown. Well-grown timber fit for bats fetches a very good price. Trees are usually ready for cutting at about twenty years of age. Timber with large rings and no heartwood is the most valuable. It is badly attacked by water-mark disease (leaflet No. 20).

Crack Willow (*Salix fragilis*).

This willow will grow in most soils and situations provided there is sufficient moisture. It is a very hardy and quick-growing tree. It is treated and propagated like the white willow. It is not so good for basket-making, and only makes inferior cricket-bats.

The Osier (*Salix viminalis*).

The osier is not a tree-willow, and is solely planted for coppicing in osier beds to provide material for basket-making. It requires a fertile soil, and succeeds best along river beds in low-lying land which is occasionally flooded. It is light-demanding and a rapid grower. It is fairly hardy, but sometimes suffers from frost.

For full details regarding the cultivation of osiers for basket-making the Board of Agriculture leaflet No. 36 should be consulted. The name 'osier' is in practice used for all willows cultivated for basket- and wicker-work.

Osiers are grown in plantations known as 'holts' and the

produce of the osier holt is known commercially as 'rods'. The land must be thoroughly cleaned, and in autumn should be ploughed or dug over to a depth of 14 inches. Planting at about 15 inches apart in rows 30 inches apart is done in February or March. The sets are cut from two-year-old wood, and should be about 18 inches long of which 10 inches is put into the ground. The spaces between the rows must be kept well cleaned during the first two years, after which the growth is dense enough to kill out all vegetation. The holt reaches its full production in about four or five years, and will last from twelve to fifteen years. The rods are cut annually before the sap rises, with a sharp hook, and are tied up into bundles or 'bunches', an average crop giving about 150 bunches per acre, each bunch having a girth of 45 inches one foot from the butt. The rods are peeled and graded into sizes.

Various local names are given to varieties of the osiers used. Glibskins, Black Mauls, Green sucklings, and Black Hollanders are varieties of *Salix triandra*. The Welsh osier is *Salix purpurea*, Mottled Spaniard is *Salix decipiens*, and the Cane osier is *Salix viminalis*.

CHAPTER XII

SYLVICULTURAL NOTES ON THE CONIFERS

THE CYPRESSES

The large-coned Cypress (Cupressus macrocarpa).

A NATIVE of California, it was introduced into Great Britain in 1838 as an ornamental tree, but it will probably prove of use to foresters for planting as a windbreak, and also for underplanting as it is a good shade-bearer. It is fairly hardy and does well in open situations, but is apt to be injured by frost in low-lying damp places. It is storm-firm and withstands sea-breezes and gales. It does best on deep, fresh, sandy loams. It is a quick grower. When grown in an open manner it branches down to the ground, and a belt of this species, planted on exposed sides of woods, would form an excellent shelter-belt for young plantations against cold winds. It is a difficult tree to transplant without heavy losses and, for small-scale planting, it should be grown or bought in pots to avoid loss. It makes an excellent hedge and bears clipping well.

Lawson's Cypress (Cupressus Lawsoniana).

A native of California, it was introduced into Great Britain in 1854. It is an ornamental tree, and as its timber is of good quality, it may prove valuable for planting in woods, as it is a quick grower and hardy. It is a moderate shade-bearer, and does well on most soils provided they are not too wet, and on most situations except exposed places. It may be treated sylviculturally like spruce. It is good for underplanting.

The Red Cedar (Thuya plicata).

A native of California, it was introduced into Great Britain in 1854. It is very hardy against frost and will succeed on exposed situations, being storm-firm, though it does best in sheltered places, especially on northern aspects. It will stand a good deal of shade. It is accommodating as to soil, but prefers a deep fresh one, and likes some lime. It is a rapid grower, but not so fast as Douglas fir or larch. This tree may prove useful for underplanting on moist soils in the place of spruce as it bears more shade than the latter. It could also be grown as a mixture in lines with Douglas fir, but as its timber has not yet been proved to be valuable when grown in Great Britain, it should only be planted on an experimental scale at present. Its timber will probably prove to be excellent for gate-posts and for fencing purposes.

A fungus, *Keithia thujina*, does great damage in the nursery, and being very common makes it difficult to raise plants.

THE FIRS

Douglas Fir (Pseudotsuga taxifolia).

There are three distinct varieties of this important species: the Pacific or Green Douglas fir, the Colorado or Blue Douglas fir, and the Fraser River Douglas fir.

The Colorado variety has shorter and bluer needles, which are stiffer than those of the Pacific Douglas fir. If the needles of the two species are rubbed they have a distinctive scent, and it will be found that the Colorado has a much coarser smell than the Pacific. The Fraser River variety resembles the Colorado rather than the Pacific, but the needles are green and not blue. The Pacific variety should always be chosen for planting.

The *Pacific* Douglas fir is a native of the Rocky Mountains and Vancouver Island; it was introduced into Great Britain in 1828. It is a fairly hardy tree, but requires sheltered situations as its long leading shoot gets easily broken off, or bent, by wind. It also requires a damp atmosphere. It suffers from autumn frost in low-lying situations, but does not get much injured by spring frosts. Northern aspects are best. It bears only moderate shade. It is a very rapid grower, and in favourable situations will outgrow larch. It is fairly accommodating as to soil, but does best on a deep, fresh, sandy loam; it also does fairly well on stiff soils on the slopes of hills where there is a good natural drainage. It does not thrive on chalks or limy soils, or on dry soils. It can be grown in high forest as a pure wood, as it is soil-improving; or it can be mixed with larch, preferably in groups; when mixed with other species it will probably outgrow and suppress them. It may be used for underplanting larch or other light-foliaged trees. When grown pure it should be planted at not more than 6 feet apart as, unless grown closely, the branches will not die off early. It should be carefully planted as its root growth is slow at first and the trees become top heavy. On felled woodlands its protection by coppice shoots should be preserved until the thicket stage. It will not stand smoke or fumes.

The timber is of much the same character as that of larch, but ranks between it and Scots pine in value. It is largely imported under the name of 'Oregon pine'. Although of less value than larch per cubic foot, it will possibly pay better, as a very much larger quantity can be grown on an acre.

Until recently it had not suffered in Britain to any great extent from insects and fungi, but *Chermes cooleyi* (leaflet No. 2) considerably retards its growth. *Phomopsis pseudotsugae* (leaflet No. 14) causes the die-back of young shoots and also causes canker of the stem. *Rhabdocline pseudotsugae* (leaflet No. 18) causes leaf-cast. These pests may increase and do serious damage. The pine weevil (*Hylobius abietis*) and the cockchafer seriously injure young Douglas fir, and other insects attacking conifers may spread to this species. *Megastigmus spermotrophus* (leaflet No. 8) destroys the seed.

The *Colorado* and *Fraser River* varieties are much slower-growing trees and are not worth planting on a large scale, at any rate in the south of England. Care should be taken when purchasing Douglas fir to see that these varieties are not supplied in place of the green one.

PLATE X

DOUGLAS FIR PLANTED AT 4 FEET BY 4 FEET
Aged 16 years. Height 35 feet, girth up to 17 inches
Coopers Hill

The Silver Fir (Abies alba).

A native of Central Europe, it was introduced into Great Britain in 1603. It requires warmth and is more suitable for the south of England than for Scotland. It does best on northern and eastern aspects in situations sheltered from wind, but does not thrive in low-lying frosty valleys. It is extremely sensitive to late spring frosts. This fact and the danger of the tree being killed by chermes result in common silver fir being little planted nowadays. It is a great shade-bearer. It does best on a deep, fresh, stiffish loam, and prefers soils inclined to be stiff rather than sandy ones. The roots are deep going, and shallow soils are unsuitable. It can be grown in pure woods, but is better mixed with spruce. One of its chief uses would be for underplanting larch or pine woods which are to be grown to long rotations, as when growing under shelter it escapes damage by frost and greatly improves the fertility of the soil. If grown on blank areas it must be protected by larch or birch nurses planted beforehand. It grows extremely slowly for the first ten or fifteen years, but it then pushes ahead rapidly, and finally reaches a greater height than any other British tree with the exception of spruce and Douglas fir. To get clean timber it must be kept very dense, as the branches bear much shade and do not easily get killed off. It reaches maturity in Great Britain at about seventy years, its timber being used for the same purposes as that of spruce. On the whole it is not a profitable tree to plant, as it requires a good soil where more valuable species could be grown. In addition to insect-damage the fungus *Melampsorella Caryophyllacearum* causes witches'-broom and canker, and does serious harm.

Silver fir is a difficult tree to transplant and succeeds best where five-year-old plants are used, the planting being done in the late spring.

Nordmann's Silver Fir (Abies Nordmanniana).

This tree is a native of the Crimea, and was introduced into Great Britain in 1845. It is a far hardier tree than the common

Silver fir, and it does not get injured by frost. It will therefore probably prove useful as a substitute for the common species. When once established it grows rapidly. It is accommodating as to soil, and resembles the spruce in this respect, doing fairly well on all soils which are neither very wet nor very dry. In other respects it resembles the Silver fir. It may be used for underplanting larch or pines.

THE LARCHES

Common Larch (Larix decidua).

A native of the hilly parts of Central Europe, especially of the Alps, it was introduced into England in 1629 and into the Lowlands of Scotland in 1725. It does best in a situation resembling as far as possible that of its natural home; that is, on high elevations and on cool north and east aspects. It is found in the Highlands up to an elevation of 2,000 feet, though it hardly pays to plant it at this height. Larch suffers from drought, but is fairly hardy against frost, though its foliage gets cut back by late frosts in low-lying damp situations, as it sprouts early in spring. It is storm-firm and a quick grower. It is a great light-demander and must not be grown where it gets in the least shaded by other trees.

A deep, porous, and fresh soil suits the larch best, and it does well on stony, well-drained soils along ravines. It will not thrive to a large size on land which is not well drained, but it will produce small timber on clayey soils. It does well on limy soils, but on gravels it is very liable to heart-rot. Dry sands are also unsuitable. It will not stand fumes in the air.

Larch should not be grown in large pure woods as it gets much diseased, and after the thicket stage is passed the soil deteriorates under it. It should be grown as standards-over-coppice, or in small groups here and there in woods of other species, especially where there is plenty of beech or chestnut. It is essential to give it plenty of space, and thinnings in pure woods should be fairly

PLATE XI

LARCH PLANTED AT 4 FEET BY 4 FEET

Aged 18 years. Thinned when 12 years old and underplanted with silver fir. Height 45 feet, girth up to 26 inches.
Coopers Hill

heavy throughout, underplanting being resorted to, to keep up the fertility of the soil. The timber is usually ripe for the axe at from sixty to eighty years of age, though in favourable situations it can be grown on to much larger size. It is, perhaps, the most valuable timber grown in Great Britain, being used for a great variety of purposes. It suffers considerably from insects and fungi. Of the insects, the worst are the larch aphis (*Chermes viridis*), the larch miner moth (*Coleophora laricella*), and the larch shoot moth (*Argyresthia atmoriella*), while the sawfly (*Nematus Erichsoni*) has locally done very serious damage. Of fungi, the worst is the well-known larch canker, *Dasyscypha calycina*; in the nursery *Meria laricis* (leaflet No. 21) is often very injurious, and the heart-rots, chiefly *Fomes annosus*, do much damage to both young and old trees.

The Japanese Larch (Larix Kaempferi).

A native of Japan, this tree was introduced into Great Britain in 1861. It is of more rapid growth during youth, but when about twenty years old it is overtaken by the common larch. It is a more hardy tree and suffers less from insects and fungi. It is far more accommodating in its soil requirements, and does quite well on some peaty soils where carefully drained. It may be treated sylviculturally like the larch. Japanese larch is very useful for planting in colliery districts, such as South Wales, where there are many fumes. It withstands these far better than the common larch and makes excellent pit-wood.

Of other larches, the western larch (*Larix occidentalis*) may prove to be a useful tree, but neither the Kurile larch (*Larix kurilensis*) nor the Siberian larch (*Larix sibirica*) is likely to be of much value for forest growth.

THE PINES

The Scots Pine (Pinus sylvestris).

A native of Scotland and of the countries round the Baltic. It is found up to an elevation of 2,200 feet in Scotland, but does best on low lands. At high elevations southern aspects are best for it, as it succeeds best in a warm climate, but at low elevations it will do well on all aspects. It is hardy against frost and drought. It is very light-demanding and should not be grown in the shade of other trees. It is storm-firm, being deep rooted, but heavy snow breaks off many branches. It is a rapid grower. It is very accommodating as to soil, and can be grown on almost any class of land except very shallow soils. It succeeds best, however, on gravelly loams and sandy soils, and is useful on dry, shallow peats. Depth and moderate moisture are necessary for its finest development, but useful timber can also be obtained on dry and moderately shallow soils. It is one of the best trees for a first crop on land not previously wooded, at a moderate elevation.

Scots pine may be grown in pure woods up to an age of forty or fifty years, as it preserves the fertility of the soil till then. After this age the woods open out, and if they are to be grown on to a long rotation they should be underplanted. It is, however, better to mix Scots pine in fair-sized groups with beech, spruce, or Douglas fir, while groups of larch may be planted here and there in pine woods to improve the revenue. High forest with clear cutting is the most suitable sylvicultural system with a rotation of about sixty to eighty years. On sandy lands covered with a short growth of heather natural regeneration will usually be successful. The timber of Scots pine is largely imported under the names of 'red deal', 'red fir', 'red pine', and 'yellow pine'. British-grown timber only fetches a small price as it is almost invariably knotty and soft, having been grown in too open a manner, but if grown properly in crowded woods there is no reason why home-grown timber should not be quite as good as the foreign. Insects do serious damage, the chief pests being the pine weevil (*Hylobius abietis*), the pine beetle (*Myelophilus piniperda*), the pine saw-fly (*Lophyrus pini*), and the pine-shoot moth (*Retinia buoliana*). Fungi, especially the honey fungus (*Armillarea mellea*), the red-rot root fungus (*Fomes annosus*), and the pine blister (*Peridermium pini*), do much harm. With so many insects and fungi attacking Scots (and other) pines, it is especially necessary to keep the woods clean by having light thinnings made every five years to remove dead wood and unhealthy trees. In pure woods the thinnings should be light in character throughout the rotation so as to keep a complete cover over the ground, but if the woods are to be underplanted, with the intention of growing them to a long rotation, they should be made heavier about the fortieth year so as to admit sufficient light for the undercrop, and to encourage the pines to increase rapidly in girth.

The Austrian Pine (*Pinus nigra* var. *austriaca*).

A native of Austria, it was introduced into Great Britain in 1835. It is a very hardy tree and can be grown at high elevations, and also near the sea, as it withstands wind. It will do well on any aspect. It is a light-demander, but will stand side-shade rather better than the Scots pine. It is very accommodating as to soil, but does not do well on stiff wet ground; it thrives on limy soil. It is not as valuable as the Scots or Corsican pines and should not be grown on a large scale. Its chief use will be as a shelter-belt; for this purpose it is excellent, as it forms a thick hedge when allowed to branch low down, and grows rapidly when young. It is also useful for planting on poor limy soil and on dry chalks which have deteriorated; it would soon improve such a soil and could be cut at an early age, when a more valuable species could be substituted for it. The timber is coarser than that of Scots pine. Austrian pine is attacked by the same insects and fungi which damage the Scots pine.

The Corsican Pine (*Pinus nigra* var. *calabrica*).

This tree is a very close relative of the Austrian pine, but it is a native of Corsica and southern Europe. It was introduced into Great Britain in 1759. It is a hardy tree, but does not do so well as the Austrian pine on high elevations or in windy places. It does well near the sea. It is a light-demander. It is of much more rapid growth than the Austrian pine and is a more valuable tree altogether, as it grows with a taller, cleaner, and straighter stem. It is deep rooted and does best on deep, light, dry, sandy loams, and thrives on limy soils. It does not grow well on wet clays. It can be treated sylviculturally like the Scots pine, with the exception that greater care must be taken in transplanting it, as it forms very weak roots in the nursery and is therefore a bad transplanter. After two years in seed-beds it must be transplanted each year, and is best planted out as a two-year-one transplant in late October or February. Where larger plants are used, often fifty per cent. die if there happens to be a warm, dry summer after planting. It is attacked by the same insects and fungi as the Scots pine. It is often said that rabbits do not eat Corsican pine, but the statement is incorrect.

The timber is of about the same value as that of the Scots pine, and on similar land will yield far higher volume.

The Cluster or Maritime Pine (*Pinus Pinaster*).

A native of the south of Europe, it was introduced into Great Britain in 1596. It is a fairly hardy tree when grown on a warm coast, but is not suitable for high inland exposed places. It is a very useful tree to grow along the coast as it withstands the salt winds excellently, and is of great use in forming shelter-belts behind which other species may be grown. It is a light-demander and must be given plenty of space. It does best on a deep dry sand or a light loam. It does not succeed on limy soils. The timber is used in France for boards, packing-cases, &c., and large quantities of pit-wood are exported to England, but home-grown timber is inferior and of much less value than that of Scots pine.

The Weymouth Pine (*Pinus Strobus*).

A native of Canada and the United States, it was introduced into Great Britain in 1705. It is very hardy, but to do well it requires a sheltered situation. It stands about half-way between light-demanders and shade-bearers. It has a deep-going root system and is storm-firm. It will produce good timber on any aspect. It prefers a deep, fresh, loamy sand, but is very accommodating and can be grown on almost any soil provided it is not very dry. It is a quick grower and will produce a much larger volume of timber per acre than the Scots pine. It can be grown in pure woods, but does very well when mixed with other conifers or beech. It thrives best when fully exposed to light, but it can be used for underplanting larch or Scots pine, as it improves the soil; it is useful for filling in blanks in existing woods. It can be cut on a rotation of sixty to eighty years. The timber is largely imported under the name of 'yellow pine', though it is called 'white pine' in America, and is used for house-building. Home-grown timber is, however, not very durable and is more suitable for paper manufacture and for packing-cases and other purposes where a light, soft wood is wanted. It is a very ornamental tree, but it is not valuable enough to plant as a forest tree except on a small scale.

Weymouth pine suffers from much the same kinds of insects and fungi as the Scots pine. *Peridermium strobi*, the Weymouth pine bark blister, causes much damage to young trees, and *Chermes corticalis*, an insect forming a woolly covering on the stem, does serious harm in many localities, and therefore this tree is seldom planted.

Many other pines are grown as ornamental trees, but none of them is of much sylvicultural interest. Possibly Banks's pine (*Pinus Banksiana*) and the Remarkable pine (*Pinus radiata*) may be of use in certain localities to fix shifting sands on the sea coast, while the dwarf mountain pine (*Pinus montana*) is useful for providing cover for game at high elevations above the limit of ordinary forest tree growth and for the outer rows of a shelter-belt. The Cembran pine (*Pinus Cembra*) is very hardy in exposed situations and may be used as a shelter-belt, but it is of slow growth.

None of these species will produce paying timber, except possibly *Pinus radiata*, and *Pinus contorta* var. *Murrayana*.

The Common or Norway Spruce (Picea Abies).

A native of Europe, it was introduced into Great Britain about 1548. In Europe it is a tree of the mountains, requiring but little warmth, and in England it seems to succeed well in high-lying exposed places, north and east aspects being the best. It grows better in Scotland and Wales than in England. It is fairly frost-hardy, but is very sensitive to drought, and doe. best where both the air and soil are moist. It is easily blowi. over by gales, and is the least storm-firm of all British fores' crees when grown in woods, but trees grown in the open have roots which spread to a great distance and are fairly storm-firm. It bears a light shade, but to do well it must be grown fully exposed to light; it does not appear to bear as much shade in Great Britain as it does on the Continent. It is fairly accommodating as to soil provided that there is sufficient moisture, and it will succeed on shallow soils as it has not got deep-going roots. It does best on fresh or moist loams, and on such a soil produces the best class of timber, but it will succeed fairly well on moist sands, clayey soils, or peats.

It is a slow grower for the first few years, but when once it starts growing, at about the tenth year, it continues to grow at a very rapid rate. It should be mound-planted on wet soils.

It is suitable for pure woods as it is a soil-improving species, but it is sometimes grown in mixture as a subordinate species with more valuable trees such as larch or Scots pine in groups. It is not very suitable for underplanting, though it can be used in the more open spaces for this purpose. It should be planted closely, at a not greater distance than $4\frac{1}{2}$ feet by $4\frac{1}{2}$ feet, and thinnings should be very lightly conducted, because clean timber will never be obtained if the trees are grown in anything approaching an open state. It is mature at from sixty to eighty years of age. The timber is largely imported from the Baltic under the names of 'white deal' or 'white fir'. Home-grown

PLATE XII

MATURE SPRUCE AT WALCOT

Photograph by M.C. DUCHESNE. *From the* QUARTERLY JOURNAL OF FORESTRY

timber is usually full of knots, but this is due to the fact that it has mostly been grown in woods of too open a character.

Spruce does not usually pay well in Britain when grown on small areas, but large woods of this tree would probably be very profitable.

Spruce is attacked by several insects and fungi. The pine weevil and several bark beetles do much damage, and the spruce gall aphis (*Chermes viridis*) injures young plants. Of fungi, the honey fungus (*Armillarea mellea*) and *Fomes annosus* do much harm, while *Pestalozzia Hartigii* causes young plants to turn yellow and die.

The Sitka Spruce (*Picea sitchensis*).

A native of America, it was introduced into Great Britain in 1831. It is rather frost-tender but otherwise hardy and accommodating. It is a moderate shade-bearer and can be used for underplanting. The timber is of a better class than that of the common spruce, and the tree is now very extensively planted throughout the country in place of the latter. It will succeed on all fairly deep soils except dry sandy ones, and it is a useful tree for stiff clays. It can be treated sylviculturally like the common spruce. The needles being very prickly it escapes damage from animals to a great extent.

Unfortunately, the honey fungus attacks it very badly and *Mysaphis abietina* causes defoliation.

It withstands fumes and is one of the best species in the South Wales colliery districts. It should be mound-planted on wet soils.

The Yew (*Taxus baccata*).

A native of Great Britain. This is a common tree in our woods and is widely distributed, but it is in no sense a tree which is grown for profit. It usually only attains a height of 30 to 40 feet, and is a very slow grower, but lives to a great age. It is ornamental, and a few specimens in the woods are not out of place. It is hardy and will grow on most situations, and is a great shade-bearer. It will grow on all soils except dry, sandy ones, but it does best where there is plenty of lime. The timber is hard and very durable, takes a fine polish, and makes excellent furniture. Any yew that may happen to be cut can be used for fencing-posts, as it is extremely durable and will outlast iron provided that it is used in the round and is not squared up.

Where there are yew trees in a wood or park care should be taken to prevent cattle obtaining access to them. Cattle readily eat the leaves, which are very poisonous, and occasionally valuable cattle are killed in this way.

CHAPTER XIII

FENCING AND DRAINING

IT is usually necessary to enclose all woods and plantations with an efficient fence of some kind to keep out cattle. For this purpose a hedge, wire fence, or stone wall is required.

HEDGES

A hedge forms a very effective fence so long as it is kept in good condition, and, in addition to keeping out cattle, it also gives some shelter to young plantations. It has the disadvantage of not forming a fence for some years after it has been planted, and during these years it has to be itself protected by a temporary fence of some kind. Hedges are therefore expensive to form, but once made they will, if well cared for, last a century and more. In the great majority of cases the best plant to use is whitethorn, or quick, as it flourishes in a great variety of soils and situations. It is, however, an unsatisfactory hedge at very high elevations, and the young plants in such places are difficult to establish. Whitethorn lives for a long period, and, if kept well trimmed, animals will seldom be able to force their way through it. It is a light-demanding species, and therefore plantations should be formed at such a distance away from the hedge that it is not likely to be overshadowed when the woods grow up. This is a disadvantage, as it necessitates the loss of a good deal of area. The branches of trees which overhang a hedge should be pruned off, and around woods no trees should be grown *in* the hedge.

Formation of a new hedge. Hedges may be formed on a flat surface or on a bank. The advantage of using a bank is that an effective fence is obtained within a few years, but for all other reasons planting on the flat is best, as a hedge thus formed lasts longer. The bed should be prepared with care; it should be dug to a width of $4\frac{1}{2}$ feet, of which the middle $1\frac{1}{2}$ feet should be 2 feet deep, and the rest 1 foot. This work should be finished at least a month before planting begins, at any time in open weather, from November to March. Three-year-old plants may be used, and these can be placed in single or double rows. Some estates plant two rows of quick, 4 inches apart, with the plants 8 inches apart in the rows, the plants in one row being opposite the spaces in the other row. There are thus about 190 plants to the chain. On other estates the plants are placed in single rows with the quicks 4 inches apart, the number of plants to the chain being the same as above. Others prefer to place the plants 8 inches apart in two rows with 8 inches between the rows, as it is easier to weed the bed with a hoe. As all the above systems give excellent hedges, if afterwards managed properly, it is a matter of small importance which method is used. When planted, the quicks are cut off to a uniform height, about 2 or 3 inches above the ground, and this may be done at once or in the first April after planting. They are then left to grow on.

When a new hedge is to be formed on the site of an old one it is essential to renew the soil. This may be done by making a wide deep trench which is then filled up with soil from the adjoining field or wood. The soil may be obtained by digging another trench within the wood at a spade's throw away from the hedge, the soil from the first trench being thrown back into the second one to fill it up.

As soon as the hedge is planted it must be protected from cattle by a temporary post-and-rail fence.

After-management. The bed must be kept clean of weeds, and during the first few years a hoe or Dutch hoe may be used between the plants. Later on the weeds must be persistently cut back with a hook.

There are two ways of obtaining a good hedge, and either may be adopted. The first method is to trim the hedge into the shape desired by annual trimmings, the first of which is made in the third year after planting. In the course of a few years a good dense hedge is thus obtained. This annual trimming may be done at any time in autumn or winter, while a second trimming in summer between hay time and harvest is of great advantage. Another system is to allow the young quicks to grow up to a height of 6 or 8 feet without any trimmings; they are then *layered* or *laid*, an efficient fence being obtained as soon as this is done. Live stakes are left 2 feet apart; the rest of the rods are partially cut through at the base and are bent down and wattled between the stakes at an angle of about forty degrees with the ground. Young shoots arise from the cut surface and fill up the bottom of the hedge. In future years the hedge is trimmed annually to the desired shape.

Ditch and Bank. Where it is desirable to have a ditch along the fence to prevent cattle breasting the hedge a bank may be formed as is done in Leicestershire.

A ditch is cut 3 feet wide and 2 feet deep, the soil taken out being formed into a bank about 1 foot high with a flat surface. The quicks are planted in the centre of the bank, the future management being the same as on flat ground. The ditch should be sufficiently near the bank to prevent cattle from placing their feet on it, as they are then unable to apply their weight to the temporary post-and-rail fence which is made on the top edge of the bank. The quicks should be placed well away from the ditch, as otherwise soil falling off the bank may expose the roots.

Preservation and restoration of old hedges. A hedge once formed should be trimmed annually, and if this is done it can be kept in good condition for thirty or forty years and more. When this has not been done it will usually become gappy and useless, and must be restored. Often such a hedge is cut down to the ground to coppice, but this is a bad method as there is then no effective fence for some years. When it is short and gappy it must be allowed to grow for some years till it is tall enough to be laid; this can be done immediately with high rough hedges. First, all decaying stumps should be cut off level with the ground, and rods for wattling should be chosen from the most vigorous stools, the straightest being preserved and all others not wanted being cut out. Honeysuckle, clematis, brambles, rose, and elder should be got rid of as they do great harm. The bank, if there is one, should be repaired. Stakes, cut if possible from material in the hedge, are placed at 2 feet apart, and the rods are then half cut through a few inches from the ground with, whenever possible, an upward cut; these are bent downwards and are wattled between the stakes. The brush should be trimmed off nearest the hedger, so as to leave a straight side, as this facilitates his work. Care must be taken not to put in too much material as otherwise there is insufficient room for young growth. The hedge may be laid, where there is no bank, to a height of 4 feet, but on a bank it may be less than this. After the rods are laid the brush is trimmed and a header or binder, which consists of a number of thin hazel rods, is interwoven about the tops of the stakes. This keeps the brush down and increases the strength of the hedge. In future years the hedges should be kept in good condition by annual trimmings.

The repairing of old hedges is a work which urgently requires to be done throughout the country, not only along the boundaries of woods but also on farm land. Everywhere one sees overgrown and gappy hedges, and unless these are repaired they will shortly become useless as fences and a large expenditure will have to be undertaken in erecting wire fences instead. This will spoil the beauty of the countryside and the valued shelter will be lost.

Other plants used for hedges.

Blackthorn. A good hedge plant on strong loams, but it often spreads into the neighbouring fields by suckers. It should only be substituted for whitethorn on strong wet soils.

Myrobella or Cherry Plum. A good plant on soils suitable for plums. It produces stout thorns and forms an efficient fence very rapidly. It will stand sea breezes.

Beech makes a good hedge in exposed situations, and is useful when shelter is wanted. It does not, however, make a strong fence against cattle. The plants should not be closer than 18 inches and should not be cut back when planting. It may be trimmed after the second year.

Hornbeam is a shade-bearer, and makes a good hedge under the shade of other trees. Its dead leaves remain on in winter and it therefore gives good shelter.

Holly makes a strong fence and gives good shelter. It grows slowly, but lasts a long time. It does well in thin sandy soils, and will grow under hedgerow trees, as it is a shade-bearer.

Gorse makes a good fence if grown on a bank, and can be used on barren sand and in exposed places where other plants will not grow. *Yew*, *Box*, and *Privet* do not make strong enough fences for forest purposes.

WIRE FENCES

A wire fence has the advantage over a hedge in that it keeps out cattle immediately it is made, and is usually cheaper to erect; on the other hand it will only last some twenty years, and it gives no shelter. Nevertheless, wherever hedges do not exist already it will usually be best for the present owner to put up a wire fence round his plantations in order to obtain immediate effect, and because a wire fence requires very little repairs in future years.

There is a great variety of fences which can be erected, but it is not necessary to enumerate or describe them in this book. For the purpose of forestry it is usually best to form a fence with wooden posts, if possible of oak or larch cut from the woods on the estate. Their durability may be increased by charring and tarring the parts which go below ground, and for a few inches above the ground level. To protect plantations against cattle and sheep an efficient fence is as follows: Strong posts of oak or larch, roughly squared with the axe to 7 inches square on the part above the ground, and left rough on the part to go below ground, are cut 7 or 7½ feet in length. These are used as straining posts, and are placed at all corners of the fence and at intervals of about 200 yards in all straight parts. They are let into the ground to a depth of 3 feet, leaving 4 or $4\frac{1}{2}$ feet above ground. They are supported with stays about $7\frac{1}{2}$ feet long placed in the line of the fence to prevent the straining posts being pulled out of position. At intervals of 50 or 60 yards intermediate posts about 5 inches square may be placed.

At every 6 feet piles or standards are driven into the ground. These may be made of split oak or of sawn larch, and are 6 feet long, and about $3\frac{1}{2}$ inches by 3 inches, and are pointed. If round stakes are used they should be $3\frac{1}{2}$ inches diameter at the small end. These are driven in after the lowest wire has been stretched to give the line, and are best erected with a slight lean outwards.

To make a good fence on the flat it is usually necessary to use 8 wires, the lowest being 5 inches from the ground and the others 5, $5\frac{1}{2}$, $5\frac{1}{2}$, 6, 7, 8, and 9 inches from the one below, the top wire being 3 inches below the top of the posts. This gives a fence 4 feet 3 inches high. On banks 5 wires will be usually sufficient to form a fence 2 feet 6 inches high. Wires should be of the best galvanized drawn wire, and the two top ones should be No. 6 gauge, of which about 390 yards go to the cwt., while the others can be No. 8, giving about 570 yards to a cwt. They should be fixed to the posts with $1\frac{1}{2}$ inch galvanized staples, which should not be driven tightly on to the wire except at the straining posts. Any form of straining machine can be used to tighten the wires; screwed eye bolts are good, as when these are used the wires can be tightened or loosened when necessary without trouble. Winder brackets are also good. The top of the posts should be sawn off at an angle to prevent water lodging on them. The cost of the fence should be kept as low as possible by putting in as few wires as will serve the purpose.

There is no difficulty in obtaining plenty of timber for making fencing posts on any existing woodland estate, but where the afforestation of waste lands is being carried out it may be difficult and costly to get. In such a case it is worth considering whether concrete posts, locally made, will serve the purpose.

Where rabbits alone are to be kept out the following makes an efficient fence:

Use posts cut from the woods, of larch, oak, ash, or chestnut, 4 feet 9 inches long, about as thick as a man's arm; set these 12 feet apart, driving them 1 foot 6 inches into the ground, and have stronger posts at the corners. Put up one top wire, No. 8 gauge, at 3 feet from the ground. To this tie galvanized wire-netting 42 inches wide, $1\frac{1}{4}$ inch mesh, and No. 17 gauge. Turn 6 inches of this under the turf towards the outside of the plantation, or if the soil is very sandy, drop 6 inches vertically into the ground, to prevent rabbits burrowing under. Erect this fence two or three months before planting the area and during this period exterminate the rabbits within the fence. This can be done quite well by persistent trapping, ferreting, and shooting. The fence must be periodically inspected throughout its length to repair any holes.

Where a wire fence already exists it can be made rabbit-proof by attaching wire-netting to it, care being taken to take the above-mentioned measures to prevent the rabbits burrowing. Netting must also be put on all gates and across drains running under the fence.

In order to reduce the cost *per acre* it is important to enclose as large an area as possible at one time, as small enclosures cost more per acre than large ones. Thus, in square plantations, an area of one acre requires 280 yards of fence, and four acres requires 560 yards. If the fencing costs 2s. per yard the one-acre plot costs 560s., while the four-acre plot costs 280s. per acre, and so on, halving the cost per acre every time the area is quadrupled.

WALLS

These give good shelter, but nowadays they are seldom made, as it is usually considerably cheaper to use wire fences. Even if wooden posts cannot be obtained in the neighbourhood iron ones can be erected, and the fence will not usually cost as much as a stone wall. Where stone is very plentiful a wall may possibly be desirable, and if so it should be built to a height of about 3 feet 9 inches without lime or mortar, except that the top stones should be bedded in lime to keep the wall from falling.

DRAINAGE

Swampy ground is unsuitable for the growth of trees because the roots cannot get a good hold of the soil, and the trees may afterwards be blown down by gales; moreover, as the soil contains no air, growth is stunted and the roots decay. Wherever possible, however, it is better to plant some species such as poplar, willow, alder, and (especially if planted on turfs) spruce, or Sitka spruce, which will grow to a certain size on swampy land, than to go to the expense of draining in order to grow a more valuable species. In many cases one or two shallow drains, dug to remove the surface water, will enable the area to be planted up with these species.

Before draining a large area the consequences must be carefully considered, as otherwise unlooked-for results may be obtained. For instance, the drainage of an extensive swamp at a high elevation may reduce the water level of a large tract of lower-lying country, and may thus do damage to agricultural land, and brooks and streams may dry up. For these reasons the woodman should only drain small local swamps unless expert advice is first obtained. Drainage should be done while land is bare of trees, as if it is carried out in existing woods, the water level being reduced, the standing trees may die. The best time to drain land used for forest purposes is about three years before planting, as the ground then settles, and the new water level finds its place, before the trees are planted.

In forestry, open ditches are used, because pipes would soon be choked up by the roots, and ditches are cheaper. Where drainage has been decided on, ditches are dug at from 16 to 22 yards apart according to the soil; the stiffer this is the nearer must be the drains. The depth may vary from 4 feet on very stiff soil down to about 2 feet on lighter land. The width depends on depth, the general rule on the lighter soils being to make the width of the top of the drain one-third wider than the depth; thus a drain 3 feet deep should be 4 feet wide at the top, the sides being given a suitable slope to prevent the soil falling in. On stiff soil the width may be about equal to the depth, and the sides can be almost vertical. The bottom of the smallest drain made should be a little wider than a spade, so as to enable it to be easily cleaned out.

In laying out a drainage system a main drain should be made along the line of lowest level, and this should terminate in a stream or existing large ditch. From this, other large drains, called leaders, are made along the lowest depressions to all parts of the area, and from these the feeder drains are laid out. All ditches should fall into the larger drains in such a way that the water will not scour away the sides. The feeders need not be so large as the main drain or leaders, and are usually about 2 feet deep, and $2\frac{1}{2}$ feet wide at the top; these run to all parts of the area. A fall of about 1 foot in every 100 feet should be given to all drains, with rather more on very stiff soils.

The ditches should be dug in the driest part of the year, and the earth taken out should be thrown over the surrounding land, as if left on the side of the drain it may fall in again. Wherever the drain has to pass under a ride or road a culvert must be made, or a pipe can be used.

Care must be taken to clean out periodically all ditches or they will get filled up with dead leaves, &c., and will be useless.

The above remarks apply chiefly to drainage of wet land on mineral soil. The lay-out of the drainage system in a really boggy area requires considerable foresight. The method of straight leaders with a herring-bone formation of feeder drains is often not satisfactory on such land. Exploration of the area will usually disclose a fairly definite seepage line along which the water is entering. A drain just under this line and running almost directly along the contour, but with just sufficient fall to give the necessary flow, will give better results with considerably less digging. Similarly for the drainage of a sloping area of peat wherein the water is mainly held up, as by a sponge, on the surface, the best results will be obtained from a series of ditches running nearly parallel with one another at a slight angle to the contour of the slope. Definite springs are trapped and led away in open ditches in the ordinary way, but even here the whole volume of the water will be better caught by a wide 'Y'-shaped ditch just below the outfall.

After draining the bog in this way, turf-drains should be made in addition, as described under turf-planting on page 69.

CHAPTER XIV

FELLING AND MEASUREMENT OF TIMBER

ON a large estate it is best to have a staff of woodcutters who are given permanent employment, as temporary men may not take the same interest in their work, and are then not likely to do it so well as the home staff. On small estates, where permanent work cannot be given, only experienced woodcutters should be employed. Whether the timber is sold standing or felled it should be cut by men employed by the owner, except perhaps where the area is to be clear cut, in which case the purchaser may be allowed to employ his own men, as they do not have much chance of doing harm.

Woodcutters should be paid by piecework for all ordinary work, but when they are cutting standards over natural regeneration or are thinning young woods, where special care is required, payment should be made by the day, as otherwise sufficient care will not be taken to prevent damage to standing trees.

Fellings in uneven-aged woods, such as those managed under the selection method, where the trees are of different height, are always more difficult to carry out without damage than in woods of even age.

Fellings should take place in winter, as timber felled at this period is more durable than that felled in summer. The work is usually done with axe and saw combined, there being much less wastage than when the axe alone is used.

No amount of reading will enable the young woodman to cut a tree, and no description will therefore be attempted here as to the method of felling. Practical experience must be gained by working with an expert woodcutter, and it is satisfactory to know that a good British woodcutter is as good as any in the world. There are, however, a few general rules to which the woodcutter should pay attention. These are as follows:

1. An endeavour should be made to throw every tree in such

a way as to do the least amount of damage to surrounding stand-ing trees and young growth. If the tree to be felled has a large crown, and is surrounded by natural regeneration, it may be necessary to lop off all large branches before felling it, though if the young growth is close under the tree this is not necessary, as the crown would fall beyond it. Lopping is dangerous work, and should be avoided if possible.

2. Each tree should be thrown in the direction where the least damage will be done to itself. On steep slopes trees should be thrown along the contour line, as the crown has then only a small distance to fall, and the tree is less apt to be broken than when it is thrown downhill. A tree thrown directly uphill may shoot backwards, and is therefore dangerous to the woodcutters. Trees should not be thrown across rocks or felled logs, as they may break, and for the same reason they should not be felled across depressions in the ground. Trees felled in frosty weather are more likely to break than those cut on damp days, as they are less flexible.

3. In felling trees, attention should be paid to easy removal of the logs. They should not therefore be thrown into ravines or ditches. On slight slopes they should be felled uphill, as they are more easily dragged out when the butts lie down-wards.

4. During heavy wind felling should be stopped. This is specially important when felling amongst young growth. It is dangerous to the woodcutter to fell in a strong wind if there are other gangs near him, as the noise of the wind prevents him hearing what is going on. The safest place, as the tree falls, is near the stump at right angles to the direction in which the tree is falling. When felling uphill the most dangerous place is behind the stump.

5. Trees must be felled in such a way as to reduce wastage to the minimum. They must therefore be cut as close to the ground as possible, and the saw should be used in preference to the axe, the latter only being used to trim the butt in readiness

for the saw, and to cut a notch in the side on which the tree is to fall.

6. Where coppice is cut with the intention of obtaining a further crop of coppice shoots the surface of the cut should be left as smooth as possible. The value of coppice in most parts of England is now, however, so low, that too much time should not be spent on trimming the stools.

Each tree, when felled, must be converted into the most valuable material obtainable. Thus, if logs and pit-wood are saleable no tree should be cut up into pit-wood if it is possible to sell it as a log, as the price per cubic foot is much less when it is sold as pit-wood. Logs of broad-leaved trees should ordinarily be cut off at the point where they are 6 inches in diameter, while conifers are usually run out to 3 inches, but the sizes vary in different localities. The woodcutter should be given instructions as to what are the proper sizes of the various classes of produce.

When the cutting is completed all produce should be ranked up according to its quality and size, and should be sold as early as possible, so as to get the ground clear for replanting without more delay than is necessary.

Measurement of felled timber.

The *true* volume of a log is found by taking its girth, or diameter, in the middle; calculating the sectional area of this place; and then multiplying the sectional area by the length. The sectional area means the number of square feet or inches on a section cut in the middle of the log. This may be found from the girth by the formula:

$$\text{Sectional area} = (\text{girth})^2 \times 0.0796$$

the expression $(\text{girth})^2$ being read as 'girth squared', and meaning girth multiplied by girth.

The volume is therefore:

$$(\text{girth})^2 \times 0.0796 \times \text{length}.$$

Thus if a log has a girth in the middle of 6 feet, and is 20 feet long, the volume is

$$6 \times 6 \times 0.0796 \times 20 = 57.31 \text{ cubic feet.}$$

To make the working-out of the sum shorter one can use the figure 0.08 instead of 0.0796, in which case the cubic contents of the above log would come to

$$6 \times 6 \times 0.08 \times 20 = 57.6 \text{ cubic feet.}$$

If the *diameter* in the middle of the log is measured with callipers, the sectional area is found by the formula:

Sectional area = (diameter)$^2 \times 0.785$, and the volume is therefore: (diameter)$^2 \times 0.785 \times$ length.

Thus if a log has a diameter in the middle of 2 feet and length 20 feet, its volume will be:

$$2 \times 2 \times 0.785 \times 20 = 62.8 \text{ cubic feet.}$$

The above methods give the *true* cubic contents of the log, but the woodman will hardly ever be called upon to make these calculations in England, as timber is measured here by a system called the *square-of-quarter-girth measurement*, which makes an allowance of $21\frac{1}{2}$ per cent. for wastage in conversion. By this system the volume is found by the formula:

$$\text{Volume} = \left(\frac{\text{girth}}{4}\right)^2 \times \text{length.}$$

Thus if a log has a girth of 8 feet and length of 20 feet, its volume is:

$$\tfrac{8}{4} \times \tfrac{8}{4} \times 20 = 2 \times 2 \times 20 = 80 \text{ cubic feet,}$$

whereas its true volume would be:

$$8 \times 8 \times 0.0796 \times 20 = 101.8 \text{ cubic feet.}$$

If the quarter-girth is taken in inches and the length in feet, then the result must be divided by 144.

Thus if a log has a girth of 3 feet 4 inches and length of 20 feet, its quarter-girth will be 10 inches and its volume:

$$\frac{10 \times 10 \times 20}{144} = 13 \text{ feet 10 inches,}$$

an inch being $\frac{1}{12}$th part of a cubic foot, and *not* a cubic inch, which is $\frac{1}{1728}$th part of a cubic foot. An inch in timber measurement is therefore a block of timber equal to 144 cubic inches.

The *true* cubic contents can also be obtained approximately by this method, dividing by 113 instead of by 144, thus the true contents of this log will be:

$$\frac{10 \times 10 \times 20}{113} = 17\cdot7 \text{ cubic feet.}$$

A woodman who does not happen to be well acquainted with arithmetic will find this method to be the easiest one with which to work out the true volume of any log. It is sometimes used in England by railway companies to calculate the volume of logs upon which carriage charges are paid. True measure should be used in all measurements taken for scientific purposes.

It is sometimes useful to be able to turn true measure into quarter-girth measure rapidly. To do this deduct $21\frac{1}{2}$ per cent. from the true volume. Thus a log which is 200 cubic feet by true measure will be $200 - (21\frac{1}{2}$ per cent. of $200) = 200 - 43 = 157$ cubic feet by quarter-girth measure over bark. To make a bark allowance deduct 16 per cent. of this; thus volume by quarter-girth measure under bark is $157 - (16$ per cent. of $157) = 157 - 25 = 132$ cubic feet. In the same way the true volume of a log over bark is obtained from the volume by quarter-girth under bark, by adding 53 per cent.; thus a log whose volume by quarter-girth under bark is 100 cubic feet has a true volume over bark of 153 cubic feet.

For ordinary work by the square-of-quarter-girth method it is not necessary to work out the figures, because prepared tables, such as those compiled by Hoppus, are used.

No tables are given in this book because useful cards, in convenient form for the pocket, are obtainable for a few pence.

If the tree is measured over bark it is usual to make an allowance for this, but the amount varies in different parts of the country. The most usual is half an inch for any quarter-girth up to 12 inches, with an extra half-inch for every additional 6 inches of quarter-girth for oak and other rough-barked trees. Thus if a log has a quarter-girth of 10 inches over bark, its quarter-girth under bark will be taken as $9\frac{1}{2}$ inches, while if it is 16 inches over bark it will be taken as 15 inches under bark, and then the calculation of volume will be made as before. This allowance is equal to a reduction of 16 per cent. on the total volume of wood and bark, and in many cases is too much. In measuring beech in Buckinghamshire no allowance is made.

In actual practical work the measurement of felled timber proceeds as follows:

First the length of the log is taken, odd inches being neglected, a 5 foot stick being the most convenient measuring instrument. The length is noted in the woodman's notebook, and the half-length is calculated and marked on the log. The girth is taken at this point with a piece of whip-cord attached to a bent wire by the aid of which it can be easily pushed under the tree. The string is withdrawn and is twice folded so that its length is then equal to $\frac{1}{4}$ of the girth. It is held up against a foot rule and its length is read off to the nearest $\frac{1}{4}$ inch below the actual length. Bark allowance is deducted from this, and the quarter-girth under bark thus obtained is entered in the notebook. Prepared tables are now used to obtain the volume, the cubic contents being looked out under the heading for the given quarter-girth and opposite the given length of the log.

If the log is not symmetrical but is irregular, each part of it is measured separately as if it was a different log, and the volumes of the different parts are added together to get the volume of the whole tree.

Care must be taken in taking the girth to pull the string tight, though not stretching it, and to see that it goes straight round the log, as a half-inch more or less on the quarter-girth makes a considerable difference to the measurement of a long log. A tape with quarter-girth marked on the back can be used, but the string is more convenient and is even more accurate; moreover, tapes soon get worn out if large numbers of logs are measured. Whatever method is used, all timber on the estate should be measured on the same system, as timber merchants can then rely on the figures and can fix their prices accordingly.

Branch wood and small stuff is usually measured by the cord of 128 stacked cubic feet. The converted wood is ranked up, and the number of stacked cubic feet is ascertained by multiplying together the length, width, and height of the stack. Thus in some parts of the country firewood is cut into lengths of 2 feet 2 inches and is ranked up into stacks 2 feet 2 inches wide, 2 feet 2 inches high, and 27 feet 4 inches long. Such a stack contains:

$2\frac{1}{6} \times 2\frac{1}{6} \times 27\frac{1}{3} = 128$ cubic feet stacked, that is, including air.

Such a stack would contain between 60 and 75 cubic feet of solid wood, according to the size of the sticks and closeness of stacking.

When selling felled timber it is more satisfactory to measure it with the purchaser's measurer, as any difference can then be settled on the spot. Where the logs are irregular two men will seldom get the cubic contents exactly the same, and it saves future disputes if representatives of both seller and buyer measure it together.

With regard to whether it is best to sell timber felled or standing, the chief advantage of selling it felled is that there is no difficulty in deciding the correct number of cubic feet; but the seller is rather in the hands of the timber merchants, as they know that the timber must be sold. Where the trees are sold standing the seller can postpone the sale for a year or two if the price offered is not suitable, though this should not be done more often than is absolutely necessary as the regularity of the yield is interfered with.

On the whole the method of selling the trees standing at so much per load or per cubic foot, the trees being measured when they are felled, is satisfactory. If standing trees are sold for a lump sum it is essential that the woodman should estimate their cubic contents very carefully beforehand, so that he may know that the price offered is not outrageously low. Timber merchants have been known to offer a good price per cubic foot, having previously underestimated the number of cubic feet by a very large amount.

Measurement of single standing trees.

The volume of a standing tree can only be accurately measured by taking the height to timber point with an instrument, and by climbing the tree to take the quarter-girth at half this height. This, of course, can only be done for special reasons.

Under ordinary circumstances the best procedure is as follows:

The tree is viewed from all sides, and the height of the spot up to which it is measurable is determined with a height measurer. There are several excellent instruments for taking heights now obtainable, and every head forester or woodman should be in possession of one. The author prefers Weise's hypsometer, obtainable from William Spoerhase, Giessen, Hessen, Germany. It is difficult to get this instrument in England, but other types are obtainable from W. F. Stanley & Co., High Holborn, London.

The instrument consists of a tube, T, with cross wires at O, and an eye-piece, E. A toothed scale, H, is fixed to the tube. D is a movable scale with a plumb-line, P, attached to it. To take the height, stand at any point where the top and bottom of the tree can be seen. Then measure the horizontal distance to the tree. Fix the scale D in such a way that it indicates, at the level of the scale H, the same number of units as there are in the distance between the observer and the tree. Thus, if the distance is 40 feet, set the scale at 40. Look at the top of the tree through the tube, allowing the plumb-line to swing clear; on getting the cross wires to coincide with the top of the tree, turn the tube gently to the right so that the plumb-line is caught in the teeth. Read off the number at this point on the scale H. This gives the height above the level of the observer's eye. Repeat the operation looking at the bottom of the tree. If the plumb-line is now caught on the *O* side of the scale *D*, add the result to the previous one; if it is caught on the *E* side of the scale, subtract the second reading from the first. The total given is the height of the tree in feet, if the unit is 1 foot. Where the tree is very high, or the distance great, the unit may be taken as 2 feet or a yard.

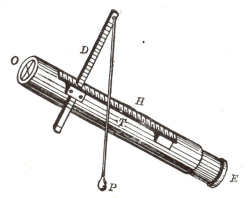

Fig. 14. Weise's Hypsometer.

Thus, if the observer is standing 90 feet away this may be taken as 30 yards, and the scale is set at 30. The height is then obtained in yards, but as the scale is marked to show half units, the result is correct to within 18 inches.

The instrument is simple and easy to use.

The height having been obtained, the place where the half height would be on the tree is noted. An assistant takes the quarter-girth with a tape as high as he can reach, and the wood-man estimates the fall-off in quarter-girth from this place up to half height. This is difficult to do accurately, especially on irregular trees. If the woodman has the opportunity of measuring this fall-off on large numbers of felled trees he will, however, soon be able to estimate correctly to within half an inch of quarter-girth. As a general rule, on normally shaped trees, the fall-off is about 1 inch in quarter-girth for every 10 feet in height for conifers, and about 1½ inches in 10 feet with broad-leaved trees. Taking these figures as a basis the woodman must add or deduct from them according to the shape of the tree.

Having thus measured the length and estimated the quarter-girth at half height, the cubic contents are worked out as for felled trees, using tables, and making the usual bark allowance if the volume under bark is required.

When large numbers of trees are to be measured singly it would be tedious to take the height of each tree with an instrument; the work can be hastened without losing much accuracy by using a pole, say 20 feet long, with feet marked on it. This should be propped against the tree, and the woodman can then estimate the length of timber above the top of the pole. Such a pole will be quite sufficient for short trees, but with tall ones the estimate should be checked periodically with the height measurer. After a little practice the length will be obtained with a very fair degree of accuracy. Beginners, when using a pole, usually underestimate the height.

Having found the volume of each tree, the volume of the wood is obtained by adding all the volumes together.

The calculation of the volume of woods by estimating each tree singly is a very difficult piece of work, and any great degree of accuracy can only be obtained by constant practice, and by comparing the estimates continually with the actual measurement when felled. This method should only be adopted where the method described on pages 195 to 200 is impossible; that is, in woods where the trees are of all sizes, and are branched and irregular, as we find the standards over coppice or trees in very open woods of any kind.

Branch wood is seldom estimated, but if there are very large branches, an estimate may be made of those on one side of the tree. All should not be included, as some are likely to be broken in the fall of the tree:

For small branches the most satisfactory procedure is to cut a small area and to ascertain the out-turn per acre, or this may be obtained from the results of previous fellings. Thus, if an acre of oak wood is cut and gives an out-turn of 600 feet of timber, 12 cords of pit-wood, and 9 cords of fuel, it may be assumed that in similar woods the same out-turn of pit-wood and fuel will be obtained per acre.

Measurement of standing woods.

Wherever woods which have grown up fairly densely, so that all the trees are more or less of the same height and shape, are to be measured, the work can be done far more quickly than by estimating the volume of each tree separately. Nearly all middle-aged plantations, especially of conifers, can be measured as follows.

The method is based on the proved fact that all trees, in a well-grown fairly dense wood, which have the same diameter at breast height, and the same height, will have about the same volume.

The diameters at breast height, 4 feet 3 inches from the ground, are found by using callipers made of wood, which are marked with inches and decimals of an inch. These can be easily prepared by any estate carpenter at a small cost. The instrument consists of a rule with two arms at right angles to it, one placed at the end being fixed, while the other is movable. The movable arm is pushed towards the end of the rule till the tree to be measured can be clasped between it and the fixed arm. The diameter can then be read off to a tenth of an inch. Where large numbers of trees are to be measured the work can be done far quicker by taking the diameter with callipers than by taking the girth with a tape. Where a single tree is measured two diameters at right angles should be taken, and the average between the two is the diameter of the tree. This is necessary, as trees may be, and often are, larger in diameter in one direction than they are in another. Where large numbers of trees are measured the average is obtained by measuring each tree in a different direction, the first being taken say north and south, the next east and west, and so on. By doing this, about half the trees will be taken on the long diameter and the other half on the short diameter, and no great inaccuracy will be obtained in the total volume of the wood.

When measuring whole woods it is not necessary to take the diameter accurately to the tenth part of an inch. All trees

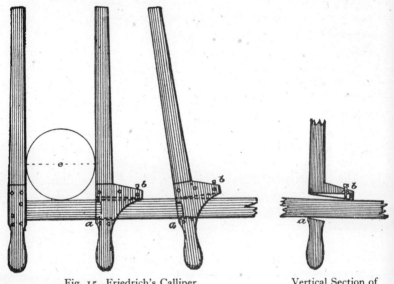

Fig. 15. Friedrich's Calliper.   Vertical Section of
Movable Arm.

between $7\frac{1}{2}$ and $8\frac{1}{2}$ inches diameter are taken as 8 inches; all between $8\frac{1}{2}$ and $9\frac{1}{2}$ as 9 inches, and so on; this reduces the work, and it is found in practice that doing this makes no perceptible difference to the volume of the wood, as there will be about as many trees from $8\frac{1}{2}$ to 9 inches as there are from 9 to $9\frac{1}{2}$, and the average diameter of all the trees from $8\frac{1}{2}$ to $9\frac{1}{2}$ will in fact be practically 9 inches. There are several slightly different ways of measuring a wood when using callipers, but the most convenient for the woodman for all ordinary purposes is as follows.

A party of three or more men work up and down the wood, taking narrow strips at a time. One man books the measurement, the others take the diameters of all the trees, with callipers, calling out the result to the booker. The calliper men should place a chalk mark on each tree as it is measured to prevent its being taken again, all chalk marks being made on the side of the tree which will be visible when they return on the next strip. The booker enters the trees in his note-book, as they are called out, as follows:

Diameter at 4′3″ in inches	Larch	Oak	Total Larch	Total Oak
6	IHH IHH II	III	12	3
7	IHH IHH IHH II	IIII	17	4
8	IHH IHH IHH III	IHH I	18	6
9	IHH IHH II	IHH III	12	8
10	IHH II	IHH	7	5
11	III	II	3	2
			69	28

A separate column is provided for each species which is to be measured. The totals are filled in when the whole wood is finished.

The calliper men must take care to keep their callipers up to breast height and should read off the diameter while the calliper is on the tree. The booker should repeat the figure as he enters it, to prevent mistakes. The work can be done with only one calliper man, but the booker can keep up with two men and sometimes with three or four. If an extra man is available he can keep a general look-out to see that no trees are omitted.

Each diameter class is called an *inch-class*. When the totals for each inch-class have been made out, a sample tree of exactly the right diameter is found for each inch-class. This should be a tree of average height, and of good shape. It is sometimes difficult to find a tree of exactly the size of the inch-class if this is left to the end, and the author has found it preferable to choose these sample trees while the callipering is going on. When the calliper man finds a tree whose diameter is exactly 6, 7, 8, or 9 inches, or whatever the diameter of the inch-class may be, he calls out to the booker, who examines the tree, and if it seems a good average one it can be marked at once, so that it will be easily found again. A good way to mark it is to pin a large piece of white paper to it. When a sample tree has thus been found, the booker places a cross in his note-book against that inch-class to indicate that no further sample tree is required for that class. By doing this carefully, sample trees will have been found for each inch-class by the time that all the trees have been measured. If this method is carried out it is necessary to ascertain the average height of the inch-classes beforehand with an instrument. Then as each sample tree is found its height is taken and compared with the average. If very different in height the tree is not chosen.

The sample trees are cut down and each is carefully measured by the ordinary square-of-quarter-girth method as already described. Bark allowance can be made at the same time. The volume of each inch-class is now worked out by multiplying the volume of the sample tree by the number of trees in the inch-class, and the volume of the whole wood is ascertained by adding together the volume of all the inch-classes.

The following example illustrates the method. The figures are those obtained on one acre of larch wood aged sixty-five years in the Tintern woods; the trees were measured by the School of Forestry, Forest of Dean. The wood was afterwards cut and the measured felled timber came to practically the same amount.

The following are the details of the sample trees felled, and measured by square-of-quarter-girth with the usual bark allowance. The trees were measured down to 3 inches diameter at the thin end.

It will be noticed that the trees were somewhat thin, but were of great length.

Diameter at 4′ 3″ in inches.	Length of measurable timber.	Quarter-girth under bark in middle, in inches.	Volume of tree in cubic feet and inches.
			ft. in.
6	40	3¼	2 11
7	54	3¾	5 3
8	60	4¼	6 8
9	*55	4¾	8 7
10	60	5½	12 7
11	62	6	15 6
12	68	6½	19 11
13	70	7	23 9

* This tree was evidently not a good sample tree, as its length of useful timber is less than it should be.

The following figures show how the volume of the wood was ascertained.

Diameter at 4′ 3″ in inches.	Number of trees.	Volume of the sample tree as above.	Volume of the inch-class.
		ft. in.	cubic feet.
6	23	2 11	67
7	48	5 3	252
8	52	6 8	346
9	63	8 7	540
10	57	12 7	717
11	44	15 6	682
12	23	19 11	458
13	6	23 9	142
	316		3,204

Total number of trees per acre = 316.
Total volume under bark = 3,204 cubic feet.
Average volume per tree = 10 cubic feet.

If it is impossible to find a sample tree of exactly the size of the inch-class, one as near as possible must be chosen and cut. In this case a slight allowance must be made in the volume of the sample tree. Thus, if a 9-inch tree cannot be found, but one 9·2 or 9·3 inches is found and cut, its volume may be reduced by 1 cubic foot before the calculation of the volume of the inch-class is made. In the same way, if a tree 8·8 or 8·7 is found, its measured volume may be increased by from a half to one cubic foot. The inaccuracy thus introduced will not be great.

Should the true measure be required, then it is only necessary to measure the sample tree by true measure instead of by the square-of-quarter-girth. Again, if the timber is only saleable down to 6 inches diameter at the thin end, the sample tree should be measured down to this point.

The accuracy of the method depends on finding sample trees of average height and of exactly the same diameter at breast height as the inch-class, and in careful measurement of their volume. There are other methods of measuring whole woods in which it is not so necessary to find sample trees of exact size, but as these methods involve a good deal of mathematics usually beyond the knowledge of the ordinary woodman, they are not described here. They will be found fully explained in Schlich's *Manual of Forestry*, Volume III.

The following figures abstracted from the Forestry Commission's Bulletin No. 10 show the volumes in cubic feet quarter-girth measure under bark which are found in well-stocked British woods under *average* conditions. Unfortunately no accurate figures, based on the measurement of British woods, are yet available for other species.

Age.	Larch. c. ft.	Douglas fir. c. ft.	Spruce. c. ft.	Sitka Spruce. c. ft.	Corsican pine. c. ft.	Scots pine. England. c. ft.	Scotland. c. ft.
30	1,460	4,450	2,140	4,860	2,250	1,130	1,300
35	1,890	5,240	2,950	5,800	2,840	1,650	1,920
40	2,290	5,930	3,680	6,660	3,360	2,110	2,480
45	2,640	6,570	4,360	7,460	3,870	2,520	3,000
50	2,910	7,160	4,930	8,200	4,330	2,890	3,450
55	3,200		5,440			3,270	3,910
60	3,440		5,910			3,550	4,250
65	3,700		6,340			3,820	4,600
70	3,910		6,730			4,060	4,880
75	4,130					4,300	5,170
80	4,300					4,470	5,400

CHAPTER XV

WORKING PLANS

In order to do away with all haphazard working, and to arrange for a regular out-turn so that an approximately equal revenue will be obtained year after year, the general lines of treatment must be decided for a long period, usually one rotation of the crop. The compiler of the working plan decides the method of treatment which will be most suitable, and lays this down in a working plan report in such a way as to enable the forester in charge to know exactly what work is to be done each year; the report is accompanied by maps which show the present state of the crop, the division of the forest, and the proposed arrangement of the fellings.

Although the general lines of treatment are determined for a rotation, the actual details are laid down only for a short period, generally ten years. At the end of this period the plan is revised and the details for the next ten years are then decided.

A very small area cannot be managed so as to give an equal annual revenue, and hence no working plan is necessary for such a wood. It is managed solely according to sylvicultural rules, the woodman carrying out each year, or at regular intervals, the work which should be done to improve the crop.

All large woods should be worked according to the prescriptions of a plan; otherwise there will be no continuity in working and no system; there will be no assurance that the woods are not being either over- or under-felled, and the out-turn, and coincidently the revenue, will rise and fall irregularly. It is obvious that the main axiom of forestry—not to remove annually from a wood more than that wood can annually produce—cannot with certainty be adhered to unless it is ascertained what this figure of production is. Moreover, since most woods are not normal or in their best possible condition of production, the working plan must arrange to bring about a condition of normality and this will almost certainly lead to an increased out-turn and to a revenue higher than that obtained at the present time. A *normal forest* is one fully stocked and consisting of a complete series of growths of all ages from the seedling to the mature tree, each age class having equal yield capacity, and in which the growth is proportionate to the fertility of the soil.

The annual production of a normal forest depends on a large variety of circumstances and it can only be approximately ascertained, but at any rate a working plan can guarantee that there shall be neither excessive nor greatly deficient felling.

As the whole future of the forest depends on the compiler of the plan, an expert must prepare it. A woodman will not be called upon to do this work, but he ought to know what a working plan means, and he may at times be called upon to collect the data, and to assist the expert.

A working plan is divided into two parts, the first being an account of past and present conditions, the second containing the prescriptions for future working. These parts are divided into a number of heads such as are given below, but all of them will not be required in every case, while occasionally other additional heads may be necessary.

PART I. PAST AND PRESENT CONDITIONS

1. *Description of the Area.*
   Configuration and situation.
   Underlying rock and soil.
   Climate.

2. *Composition and Condition of the Woods.*
   Distribution and area.
   Boundaries.
   General description of the forest growth.
   Injuries to which the crops are liable.

3. *Management and Utilization.*

> Past and present system of management.
> Past revenues and expenditure.
> Markets and lines of export.
> Prices obtainable for produce.
> Cost of extraction and supply of labour.
> The staff employed.

4. *Miscellaneous.*

> The legal position; rights and privileges.
> Data as to growth and out-turn.

PART II. FUTURE MANAGEMENT

1. *Objects of management.*
2. *Considerations upon which the plan is based.*
3. *The method of treatment.*

> Choice of species.
> Rotation and felling cycles.
> Sylvicultural system.

4. *Allocation of working circles, felling series, and annual felling areas.*
5. *The Felling Prescriptions.*

> Main fellings.
> Thinnings.
> Cleanings.

6. *Sowing and Planting.*
7. *The Yield.*
8. *Supplementary Prescriptions.*

> Roads and rides.
> Buildings and wells.
> Saw mills and mechanical means of transport.
> Alterations in the forest staff.
> Provisions for collection of statistics.

9. *Financial Forecast.*

1. Maps: small scale to show working circles or stock or both; large scale to show annual felling areas or stock or both.

2. Detailed description of the woods.

Part I can mostly be prepared from records in the estate office or elsewhere, and from a careful inspection of the woods. The results of this inspection are placed in an appendix where they will constitute a useful record of the state of the woods as they were at the time the working plan was prepared. This field work may very likely be allotted to the woodman. The woods are taken in detail and are divided up for the purpose of description into moderate-sized areas, each such area being called a *compartment*. These compartments, it should be understood, have nothing directly to do with the working circles or with the felling areas eventually prescribed; they are purely for purposes of description. There is no necessity to mark the boundaries of compartments on the gound, provided they can be picked up from the map, but it is often useful eventually so to mark them by erecting small squared wooden pillars at all corners, the number of the compartment facing each side of the pillar being painted on it. When this is done it enables any one having work in the woods to find any particular spot. Compartments should usually be of moderate size, from 10 to 40 acres, but this depends on the local conditions.

The boundaries are, if possible, fixed on natural features, separate woods, ridges, roads, rides, and so forth, the main point being convenience of description. In some parts of the forest the condition of the crop, the soil, the aspect, or other factor may vary within quite restricted areas and this will necessitate small compartments. In another part there may be a large area of 100 or 200 acres covered with exactly the same type of forest, and the whole can then be placed within one compartment. Thus the compartments need not be equal in size. They are numbered from 1 upwards, one series running through the whole forest, and proceeding in succession across the ground, compartment 20 being next to compartment 21 and so on.

The description itself, besides being a record, is also referred to by the compiler of the plan when allocating the felling areas, as to do this he must know exactly what the stock and conditions are like at all points of the area dealt with. The description must, in fact, present a complete picture of the area, and notes should be made on the following points.

1. *Climate*. Elevation above the sea, aspect, slope, exposure to strong or dry winds, the degree of exposure to frost.

2. *Soil*. The underlying rock, mineral composition, depth, degree of porosity, degree of moisture, surface covering.

3. *Growing stock*. Method of treatment in the past, species, density, age, height, volume estimated or measured, quality.

In addition notes regarding future treatment may be useful, the following points being taken into consideration. Whether the wood requires underplanting; any cleaning, pruning, or thinning required; whether the wood should be finally felled, and if so, what species should be grown and whether it should be sown, planted, or naturally regenerated. Any special measures necessary for protection against fire or other dangers; any roads or draining necessary; any improvement of the boundaries possible.

These notes are usually made by the compiler as a guide, though the future treatment can only be decided after the full description of the area has been completed.

For the field work the note-book should be divided up as on pp. 206–7, and by way of explanation sample descriptions are given.

Under Part I is a head for data of growth and out-turn. In most woods such figures will not be available when a plan is first prepared, but the plan may provide for the collection of such statistics, which would be of great value when it is revised in the future; the woodman may be entrusted with the work.

Name of block.	No. of compartment.	Area.	Situation and climate.
Copes	12	30	On a slope with westerly aspect. Elevation 300 to 500 feet. Rather exposed to westerly gales.
Beechenhurst	13	25	On a slope with north-west aspect. Elevation 400 to 500 feet. Sheltered from gales and not frosty, except in the lower part.

The rate of growth in cubic contents per acre is roughly ascertained from the results of a number of measurements made, in the way already described in Chapter XIV, at intervals of five years, throughout specially marked off areas known as 'growth measurement' or 'sample' plots. If such measurements are made at regular intervals in woods of different ages, the compiler will be able to judge approximately what amount of timber will be added to a wood in any given number of years, and he will also get some idea of the 'possibility' of the forest. The *possibility* is the maximum quantity of material which may, for the time being, be annually removed from a forest consistently with such treatment as shall tend to bring the forest as near as possible to the normal state, and maintain a constant yield.

In some plans the compiler fixes the out-turn by volume only,

COMPARTMENTS

Soil and surface covering.	Description of crop.	Notes regarding future treatment, and remarks.
Deep good sandy loam over Millstone grit. Surface clean in most parts with brambles and fern in the more open places.	Fine growth of oak standards 100–140 years old, 70 to 80 feet high, about 40 trees to the acre with good clean stems. Estimated volume 3,000 cubic feet per acre. Pure beech coppice about 25 feet high, dense. Young oak and ash here and there in the coppice.	Cut away beech where endangering the young oaks or ash. Otherwise leave the wood alone to grow on. Right of way from X to Y as marked on the map.
Fairly good sandy loam over Coal measures. Surface covered with fern and brambles.	Poor growth of oak about 100 years old, 50 trees to the acre, height 50 feet; estimated volume 800 cubic feet per acre. Here and there in the more open spaces are groups of larch 12 years old, 15 feet high.	Clear cut all the oaks leaving the larch. Plant up with groups of larch, Douglas fir, and Scots pine, in order to obtain a crop which can be cut for pit-wood in 50 years.

laying down that so many cubic feet are to be cut every year, and in this case he must ascertain the possibility in cubic feet. The first estimate can be constantly corrected as time passes, and experience is gained from results. In other plans the above detail is not entered into, and the possibility is merely one by area governed by sylvicultural conditions. This will usually be the case at present in British working plans, the area to be cut each year being laid down; the possibility in this case is the annual yield, or the volume which can be obtained from the area cut annually. This is ascertained by measuring the standing crop in the compartments to be felled, or from the results of previous cuttings in similar woods.

The woodman will find no difficulty in understanding all that is written in a plan under the remaining heads in Part I.

Part II is the plan proper. It may be extremely complex, but it will be prepared by the compiler, and only a few points need be considered here in order to enable the woodman to understand the reasons of the prescriptions laid down.

In the first place it has to be considered what is the object aimed at. For example, it might be that the woods were required to supply pit-props, or to meet some special industry—such as that of the wheelwright, the chair-maker, or the clog-maker—or large timber may be aimed at, or a part may be required for shooting-coverts, and so forth.

Next the special circumstances of the property have to be considered, for example, the presence or absence of a saw-mill, a line of rail, a wharf, a canal, these affecting the disposal of the produce. Again, the woods may be unusually exposed, or at a very high altitude. In short, a hundred different circumstances may have to be taken into consideration when deciding the form the plan shall take and the method of treatment to be prescribed.

The aim and circumstances being known, the species to maintain or to introduce can be settled, and the sylvicultural method of treatment decided. With this are naturally connected the rotation and felling cycles. This is usually the most important part of the plan.

Then the compiler considers where the markets lie, and decides how many *working circles* are required. Each working circle is divided into the number of felling areas, sometimes called 'coupes', corresponding to the years of the felling cycle, and the compiler decides upon the arrangement of these felling areas, possibly forming several *felling series*. When settled, the working circles and felling areas have to be plotted on the large-scale map and the acreage worked out.

Some further explanation appears desirable regarding this division of the forest into working circles and felling series.

Working circles.

A working circle is a wood, or part of a wood, which, at the end of the rotation, will contain a complete series of age classes.

Thus, in a wood with a total area of 500 acres, and a rotation of 50 years, if an equal area is cut each year there will be, at the end of the rotation, 50 ten-acre blocks covered with woods varying in age from 50 down to 1 year old, as shown in the following diagram.

Wind direction.

46	41	36	31	26	21	16	11	6	1
47	42	37	32	27	22	17	12	7	2
48	43	38	33	28	23	18	13	8	3
49	44	39	34	29	24	19	14	9	4
50	45	40	35	30	25	20	15	10	5

The area marked 1 is the first area cut, and at the end of the rotation it will have 50-year-old trees upon it. Such a wood forms one working circle. The total area of 500 acres need not form a compact block; blocks say of 100, 200, and 200 acres respectively can be included in one working circle.

One circle is usually sufficient where the area is not large, and where the crop is of such a character that the whole forest can be managed on one system.

In the following cases, especially in large woods, it will be necessary to divide the forest into two or more circles.

1. If the woods contain two species with different rotations, growing in pure woods; for instance, if part contains conifers on a 50-year rotation, and the rest broad-leaved trees on a rotation of 120 years.

2. If two or more parts of a wood are to be managed on different systems; for instance, if part is coppice-with-standards and the rest is high forest with clear cutting.

3. If it is necessary to have cuttings in two or more parts of the forest at the same time. This will usually be the case in extensive woods; for instance, there may be a regular demand for timber at two ends of an estate, and two cutting areas will

be necessary each year, so as to supply the purchasers without forcing them to go long distances.

4. Even if the whole forest can be managed on one system and rotation, it may be necessary to have two or more circles, so as to reduce the cutting area in one spot to a workable size. Thus, if 50 acres are to be cut each year, it may be better to cut 25 acres in one place and 25 in another than to have the whole 50 acres cut in one large block. This arrangement also facilitates supervision, as the whole work will not be in the charge of one woodman. The workmen also may not have to go so far to their work.

5. In conifer woods it is desirable to have small felling areas in order to reduce danger from insects. This is ensured by having several working circles.

Where there are two circles, both worked on a 50-year rotation, the arrangement of the cutting is somewhat as follows:

Working Circle B.   Working Circle A.

46	41	36	31	26	21	16	11	6	1	46	41	36	31	26	21	16	11	6	1
47	42	37	32	27	22	17	12	7	2	47	42	37	32	27	22	17	12	7	2
48	43	38	33	28	23	18	13	8	3	48	43	38	33	28	23	18	13	8	3
49	44	39	34	29	24	19	14	9	4	49	44	39	34	29	24	19	14	9	4
50	45	40	35	30	25	20	15	10	5	50	45	40	35	30	25	20	15	10	5

→

Wind direction.

In each year both the areas with the same number will be cut. At the end of the rotation each circle will have a complete series of age classes.

Each circle need not form a compact block as in the diagram; for instance, all the existing conifer woods on an estate, wherever they are situated, may be placed together into one circle, and all the broad-leaved woods into another.

Very few high forests in England have anything approaching

a proper series of age classes, and it is often the main object of the compiler to obtain it as soon as possible.

Felling Series.

Where the woods consist wholly of broad-leaved trees, or of a mixture of conifers and broad-leaved trees, the working circle need not be divided. But in extensive pure conifer woods there is danger of serious damage by insects if a felling is made adjoining an area cut within the last three or four years, which is stocked with a young plantation. To avoid this the working circle is divided into several *felling series*, and a felling is made in a different one each year, so that the crops in a series vary by a fixed number of years. Thus, if it is decided that three full years should elapse before a cutting is made next to a previous one, the working circle is divided into four series *A B C D*, and the fellings proceed as indicated in the following diagram.

Felling Series *C*.　Felling Series *A*.

15	11	7	3	13	9	5	1
31	27	23	19	29 / 45	25	21	17
47	43	39	35	49	41	37	33
16	12	8	4	14	10	6	2
32	28	24	20	30 / 46	26	22	18
48	44	40	36	50	42	38	34

Felling Series *D*.　Felling Series *B*.

Wind direction. ⟶

It will be seen that the working circle will contain, at the end of the rotation, a complete series of age classes as before, but these will not follow each other regularly over the area. The felling series need not be marked on the ground, but, in order that there may be no danger of windfall, each series should be separated from the next by a broad ride, as the ride-side trees then become storm-firm and are not so easily blown down when the wood lying to the windward is cut. If the woods happen to be in several isolated blocks, each may form a separate series, or two or more small blocks may be included in one series.

After deciding upon the working circles and felling series the compiler lays down the felling prescriptions, which will follow the sylvicultural method of treatment adopted. There may also be special prescriptions not directly following the lines of a well-known method of treatment, and such would be given in full detail. In locating the annual felling areas the compiler takes into consideration the direction in which the felling should proceed. This is usually from the north-east or east of each block towards the south-west or west, as this is in the opposite direction to the prevailing winds. By proceeding thus, danger from windfall is reduced and young plantations are formed behind the shelter of standing woods. Directly following the felling prescriptions come the instructions for sowing and planting. The yield will be estimated from such data as are available, and into this matter will come questions of possibility by area, possibility by volume, possibility by number of stems, and so on, which are connected with the method of treatment adopted. Without going into this subject it will be sufficient to say that the compiler of the plan must arrange that the yield is so checked that excessive felling is impossible, while insufficient cutting is avoided, for this too would be an error.

The supplementary provisions are instructions concerning roads, buildings, staff, or any such matter. Finally, it is desirable to form an estimate of the future revenue and expenditure.

CHAPTER XVI

THE FORESTRY ACT AND FORESTRY COMMISSION

BEFORE the war the approximate area of woods in the United Kingdom was 3,043,300 acres, or only 4 per cent. of the total area of the country as compared with 26 per cent. in Germany, 18 per cent. in France, and 18 per cent. in Belgium. The United Kingdom was, in fact, the least wooded country in Europe with the one exception of Portugal. The urgent need for afforestation was well recognized before the war, but nothing was done by the Government which led in any way to increased planting, though a certain amount of land was acquired and a good deal was also done to encourage forestry education and to give expert advice to landowners. The Crown woods had also during the period 1905 to 1914 been brought under systematic and scientific management, and a very great deal of good work had been done in them. The Forest of Dean and Tintern woods, with a total area of over 17,000 acres, were fast becoming an ideal training-ground for British foresters. Nevertheless, the general position of British forestry was bad, and it was urgently necessary both to improve the condition of existing woods and to add largely to the total area.

Then during the war the position rapidly became worse; owing to the scarcity of shipping, timber could only be imported with difficulty, while at the same time the demand for timber increased enormously owing to the huge consumption at the front. It became necessary for the Government to form the Timber Supply Department to purchase and fell very large areas of woods, and from 1915 to 1918 about the only work done in the woods was the felling of as much timber as could be obtained. Altogether, out of our scanty supply, it is estimated— as no precise figures are available—that about 500,000 acres were felled during the war. Moreover, the areas cut contained

the best of our coniferous woods, and the areas left consisted
largely of coppice, inferior oak woods of little value, and im-
mature plantations.

In July 1916 the position had become so serious that a Committee was appointed, under the chairmanship of The Right
Hon. F. D. Acland, M.P., with Mr. R. L. Robinson as secretary,
'to consider and report upon the best methods of conserving and
developing the woodland and forestry resources of the United
Kingdom, having regard to the experience gained during the
war'. This Committee issued a report in 1918, and the following
summary of their conclusions is taken from page 4 of the report:

1. 'The total area under woodland in the United Kingdom
before the war was estimated at three million acres, the annual
yield from which is believed to have been forty-five million
cubic feet, or about one-third of what it should have been under
correct sylvicultural management. These figures indicate the
unsatisfactory condition of British and Irish woods as at present
managed, and prove the urgency of remedial measures in the
interests of national economy.'

2. 'During the five years preceding the war the average
annual imports of timber similar in character to that produced
in the British Isles were equivalent to five hundred and fifty
million cubic feet of standing timber. The home production
was therefore less than eight per cent. of the consumption. The
imports of timbers of all kinds during the years 1915 and 1916
were respectively three-quarters and two-thirds of the normal
pre-war imports, and their cost for the two years was seventy-
four million pounds, or thirty-seven millions in excess of their
pre-war value. These imports absorbed seven million net tons
of shipping, equivalent to approximately fourteen million tons
dead weight.'

3. 'The area of land utilized for rough grazing, but capable
of growing first-class coniferous timber of the same character
as that imported, is not less than three and probably more than
five million acres. Two million acres could be devoted to timber

production without decreasing the home production of meat by more than 0·7 per cent., and if so used would ultimately afford employment to at least ten times the number of men now engaged on that area.'

4. 'Dependence on imported timber has proved a serious handicap in the conduct of the war. The United Kingdom cannot run the risk of future wars without safeguarding its supplies of timber as every other Power that counts has already done.'

5. 'In order to render the United Kingdom independent of imported timber for three years in an emergency, it is necessary, while making due allowance for an improved yield from existing woods, to afforest 1,770,000 acres. Taking eighty years as the average rotation, we advise that two-thirds of the whole should be planted in the first forty years. We consider that the quota to be planted in the first ten years should, in view of the initial difficulties, be limited to 200,000 acres, of which we advise 150,000 acres should be planted by the State and 50,000 acres by public bodies and private individuals assisted by grants, or by co-operation between them and the State. The area to be planted by the State in subsequent years may be reduced in the same degree as private individuals come forward to undertake the work.'

6. 'It is not proposed to plant arable land, but a limited area of arable land should be acquired with the forest sites, wherever possible, in order to provide small-holdings for forest workers. Our proposals carry with them the important contingent advantage that they will cause large areas of the United Kingdom, now almost waste, to be put to their best economic use. They will also, if provision is made in time, afford the means for settling discharged soldiers on the land under healthy conditions.'

7. 'Forestry demands long views, but the first-fruits are not so long delayed as many imagine. The policy of State afforestation which we recommend will begin to provide pit-wood from the quicker-growing species on the better kinds of mountain land from the fifteenth year onwards; by the fortieth year the plantations made in the first ten years alone will contain sufficient

timber to keep our pits supplied, in emergency, for two years on the scale of present consumption.'

8. 'The first essential is a Forest Authority equipped with funds and powers to survey, purchase, lease, and plant land, and generally to administer the areas acquired, with compulsory powers to be exercised, when needed, after due inquiry and the award of fair compensation. The care of forestry, now divided among several departments, should be centralized in this body.'

9. 'We recommend that the Authority should be authorized to make limited grants for every acre replanted or newly afforested during the first ten years after the war by public bodies or private individuals; such plantations to be made in accordance with approved plans and conditions.'

10. 'We estimate the cost for the first ten years at £3,425,000. It may be necessary to invest £15,000,000 altogether in this enterprise during the first 40 years. After that time the scheme should be self-supporting. The financial return depends on prices, wages, bank rates, &c., which are difficult to forecast. Forests are a national necessity; the country must have them even though they yield less than the current rate of interest on capital invested. The whole sum involved is less than half the direct loss incurred during the years 1915 and 1916 through dependence on imported timber.'

11. 'The above proposals are framed in the interest of national safety, which requires that more timber should be grown in the British Isles. There remains a further question. The United Kingdom derives more than half its imported timber from virgin forests in foreign countries, which are steadily being depleted. Canada contains the only large reserves within the empire. Unless arrangements can be made with the Dominion Government for the effectual conservation of these reserves, it is inevitable that provision should be made within the British Isles on a far larger scale than is here proposed for purposes of defence. We consider that this question should be taken up at once with the Dominion Government.'

As a result of this report the Forestry Act 1919 was passed and the Forestry Commission was appointed in November, 1919, thus for the first time setting up a properly constituted authority to deal with forestry in the United Kingdom. The Forestry Act provides for the appointment of Forestry Commissioners, who have full power to appoint and employ such officers as they think necessary. They are charged with the general duty of promoting the interests of forestry and the development of afforestation. They are given power to purchase or lease land suitable for afforestation, to grant loans to persons desiring to afforest their own land, to give advice to owners of woods, to carry on woodland industries, to collect statistics, to promote forestry education, and have many other powers and responsibilities.

A copy of the Act can be obtained through any bookseller or from H.M. Stationery Office, Imperial House, Kingsway, London, W.C. 2, price 2d.

To give some idea of the work which has been done by the Commission since November 1919 the following figures have been taken from 'The Thirteenth Annual Report of the Forestry Commissioners for the year ending September 30, 1932'. The figures given refer to work done in England, Wales, and Scotland. Certain additional work was done in Ireland before March 31, 1922, after which date the Commission ceased to be responsible for forestry work in Ireland.

The total area of plantable land acquired by purchase, lease, or feu was 439,885 acres. The area planted was 211,674 acres, of which 198,759 acres were conifers and 12,915 acres were broad-leaved species.

In addition to the above, 90,575 acres were planted by public authorities or by private persons with the aid of grants given by the Commission.

The plantations are scattered over the country in areas some of which are large and some small, the total number of 'State forests' being 96 in England and Wales, and 83 in Scotland.

There were, at the end of 1932, 914 acres of nurseries stocked with 83 million transplants and 216 million seedlings.

The total number of persons employed in the Commission's forests varied from 2,720 in summer to 3,985 in winter.

In addition to forestry work proper, the Commission has done considerable building of houses for their workmen, having, since 1924, formed 1,156 forest-workers' holdings, each of which consists of a house with a few acres of land.

There are two Schools of Forestry for working men, at Parkend in Gloucestershire and at Benmore in Argyllshire. The Commission gives grants to assist forestry education at various Universities and Colleges, and also does a large amount of research work.

These figures show that the Commission has made an excellent start and has a good record for its first thirteen years' work. It has come through difficult times caused by uncertainty in respect of funds, which are provided by Government, and which have twice had to be reduced owing to national emergency. Although in 1931, for financial reasons, a reduction in the planting programme had to be made, the Commission is now planting at the rate of a minimum of 20,000 acres a year.

In 1924 the Commission carried out a census of woodlands in England, Wales, and Scotland, and the results are of great interest. The following figures are taken from the *Report on Census of Woodlands, 1924*, which can be obtained (price 1s. 9d. net) from H.M. Stationery Office or through any bookseller.

High forest. Conifers	671,841	acres
,, Hardwoods . . .	443,354	,,
,, Mixed	301,695	,,
Coppice and coppice-with-standards . .	528,680	,,
Scrub	330,703	,,
Felled or devastated	478,106	,,
Uneconomic. (Amenity or shelter woods) .	204,293	,,
Total	2,958,672	,,

This total is 5·3 per cent. of the land area of Great Britain. It will be noticed that scrub and felled woodlands together total 808,809 acres; this area is producing nothing whatever of value. There is great scope here for improvement and it is to be hoped that everything possible will be done to put this large area into an economic state.

Applications to the Commission for planting grants, leaflets, &c., should be addressed to the Secretary, Forestry Commission, 9 Savile Row, London, W.1.

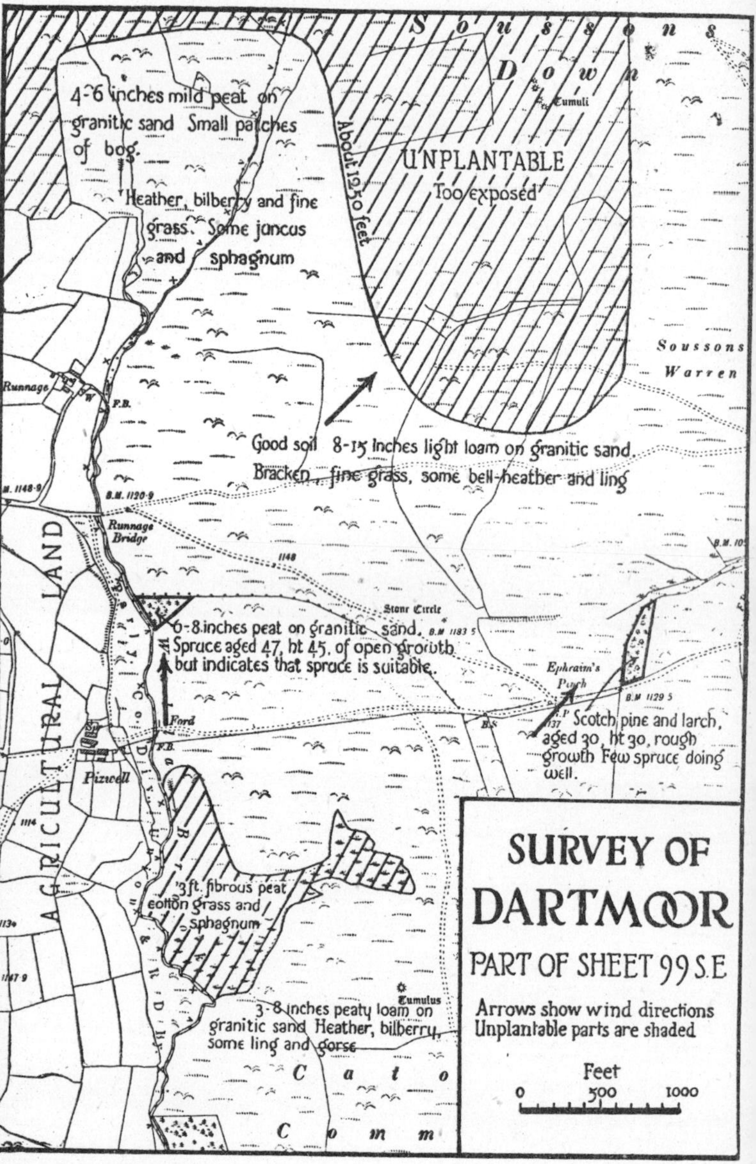

Survey of Dartmoor map. Text visible within the map:

S o u s s o n s   D o w n

Cumuli

UNPLANTABLE
Too exposed

4-6 inches mild peat on granitic sand. Small patches of bog.

Heather, bilberry and fine grass. Some juncus and sphagnum

About 1350 feet

Soussons Warren

Runnage

Good soil 8-15 inches light loam on granitic sand. Bracken, fine grass, some bell-heather and ling

B.M. 1148·9

B.M. 1120·9

Runnage Bridge

1148

Stone Circle   B.M. 1183·5

Ephraim's Pinch   B.M. 1129·5

6-8 inches peat on granitic sand. Spruce aged 47, ht. 45, of open growth but indicates that spruce is suitable.

Ford

Scotch pine and larch, aged 30, ht 30, rough growth Few spruce doing well.

Pizwell

3 ft. fibrous peat cotton grass and sphagnum

3-8 inches peaty loam on granitic sand. Heather, bilberry, some ling and gorse

Tumulus

C a t o

C o m m

AGRICULTURAL LAND

SURVEY OF DARTMOOR
PART OF SHEET 99 S.E.

Arrows show wind directions
Unplantable parts are shaded

Feet
0   500   1000

Based upon the Ordnance Survey Map with the sanction of H.M. Stationery Office

CHAPTER XVII

THE AFFORESTATION OF WASTE LANDS

UNDER the scheme of the Forestry Commission a large area of waste land is likely to be planted annually for many years, and it appears desirable to add a few notes upon this special work, although, of course, the choice of species, details of planting operations, &c., have been dealt with in previous chapters.

Survey.

Before any planting scheme over an extensive area of waste land is decided upon, it is desirable to inspect thoroughly every part of the land to make sure that it is in every respect suitable for afforestation. With a six-inch map the officer making the survey walks over the area and makes notes upon the map. If the land is at a high elevation he should first walk up-hill until he reaches an elevation above which he considers planting should not be done. He then walks along the contour and marks upon the map this line or 'planting limit'. He decides this upon the spot, and does not settle beforehand the elevation above which he will not plant. It is a mistake to go out with a fixed line, say 1,500 feet, in one's mind as the limit. It is far better to fix the line after considerable scrutiny from all sides, and after getting a really good idea of the exposure. In places the planting limit can go farther up the hill because the heights beyond it are higher, and give good shelter; in other places the line must descend, because possibly there is a gap in the hills, and a strong current of wind runs between them. Perhaps, though the exposure is not too great, the soil is too peaty above a certain point. When fixing this planting limit it is as well to be on the safe side, and when in doubt to show the land as unplantable.

Having walked along and marked on the map the planting limit, the officer traverses the area below it and notes on his map the depth and character of soil, the vegetation, and the growth of any trees or woods he may come across; he also sketches in any swamps or rocky areas which are unplantable, and shows by arrows the direction of the prevailing wind, this being often well indicated by the bending of the tops and branches of isolated trees or shrubs.

When traversing the area, care should be taken to examine thoroughly the soil by making holes with a spade at reasonable distances apart. A soil-borer is not very reliable. A special lookout should be kept for deep peat and for the presence of a 'pan', or hard layer of impermeable matter which may lie at varying depths from the surface. If a pan is found within 2 feet of the surface it will have to be broken through before planting, and this is expensive. A pan is often found on sandy soils, the clay being washed out of the sand and forming a hard layer at some depth beneath the surface.

It is also necessary to make full notes on the vegetation. Many indications are given by the nature of the vegetation as regards the suitability of the soil and the most suitable species to be planted. This subject has not yet been fully worked up, and more information is required before one can lay down rules, but sphagnum moss, cotton grasses, and bog-asphodel are plants which indicate ground where planting is unsuitable. Land covered with bell-heather and ling mixed with any of the above plants is of the very poorest quality, while bell-heather and ling on dry land, and mixed plentifully with good pasture grasses, is of fairly good planting value. Bracken and ferns indicate good, well aerated planting-ground, and gorse or bell-heather with plenty of pasture grass is also good. When ling and grass are found, especially if the ling is stunted, the land is usually of poorer quality than where bell-heather and grass occur, but is plantable. The best land is usually that which has had a crop of scrub or coppice, or where there is a luxuriant growth of bracken, or good pasture grass. On peat land where rushes and bog myrtle are found, the ground may usually be planted on turfs or mounds after draining.

Having surveyed the whole area, a brief report should be drawn up under the following headings:

1. Ordnance sheets. (Give numbers of 6″ maps covering the area.)

2. Area statement. (Example):

Rough pasture. Plantable .	.	.	2,123	acres
,,　　　,,　　Unplantable	.	.	240	,,
Woods .	.	.	.	.	10	,,
Agricultural land	.	.	.	.	40	,,
		Total		2,413	,,

3. Topography.

4. Soil and geology.

5. Aspect, slope, and exposure.

6. Vegetation.

7. Forest growth.

8. Planting limit. (Reasons for fixing the limit as shown on map.)

9. General remarks. (Species to be chosen, drainage required, facilities for transport, &c.)

The survey and preparation of the report will be of great value, and ensures that the whole scheme is well thought out before any planting is undertaken.

Clearing the land.

The survey being completed and a decision to plant having been made, it will be necessary to clear the surface to prepare it for planting. On waste lands there will usually be a growth of bracken, gorse, heather or ling, bilberry and grasses, and there may be also patches of scrub or thorn, or possibly some growth of trees in places, probably of a scrubby nature. Remembering the necessity to take advantage of all available shelter, it may be best to leave the scrubby trees or thorns standing, if they are sufficiently dense to give any real shelter. Otherwise they may be cut away. The clearance of fern, gorse, or heather will seldom give trouble on this class of land. If a decision to plant has been made early enough, the best method is to burn it off in the summer before planting. Bracken is most easily burnt in March, while heather, ling, and gorse can be burnt after any spell of dry weather. The fire should be kept well in hand, and very dry weather should be avoided as there is a danger of the fire getting hold of the peat and burning for a long time. If conditions are such that the area cannot be cleared by fire as it stands, the area to be planted that year should be cut over with long-handled hooks, the vegetation being collected into heaps and burnt. No attempt should be made to plant until the vegetation is cut or burnt, as the plants would have little chance to thrive, and a good fire over the area leaves a clear surface and the plants get a one or two years' start before the vegetation is thick enough to do damage. Where, however, the heather or bracken is not too thick or too high it may be best to leave it untouched as it gives useful shelter.

Draining.

This is necessary on all wet or boggy parts of the area, as an insufficiently drained plantation will never succeed. Where there is a good deal of marshy land, as is likely to be the case on extensive waste lands, a good system of drainage should be carried out, especially draining the wetter places as early as possible so as to give at least a year's time before the area is planted. In many places surface drains will be sufficient, afterwards turf-planting with spruce or Sitka spruce, or some species which will stand rather wet soil. Very bad bogs should be left unplanted, as they are not worth the expense of draining.

Fencing.

This is very expensive and must be dispensed with as far as possible. It is better to stand the damage done by a few stray animals rather than to fence, but if there is a chance of trespass by large numbers of sheep or cattle a stock fence must be erected.

Rabbits should be exterminated if possible, otherwise the area must be fenced with rabbit netting. On really large areas bordered by woods and fields it may be sufficient to erect a fence along the dangerous boundary, leaving the farther side, especially at the higher elevation in hilly land, open. If a rabbit catcher is employed it will often be found possible to keep down the rabbits and gradually to exterminate them, and to dispense with a completely closed fence. If the forest staff is given permission to set wire snares and to retain the rabbits for their own use, it is wonderful how quickly the rabbits disappear, now that they are of considerable value, and if this can be accomplished it saves the owner a very large sum in fencing. Still, of course, where rabbits are really numerous, netting must be erected, care being taken to exterminate all those inside the fence. Fencing against deer is seldom necessary, it being better to stand the damage done and to fill up gaps than to spend the large sum required for fencing. This applies, however, only to English areas; in Scotland it is usually essential to fence.

Laying out of rides and roads.

Before planting commences it is essential to lay out on the ground the system of rides. No roads need be made to start with, but the line along which they will eventually be required for transport should form a ride. It may be possible in fairly flat land to lay out these rides by eye, but in hilly land it will be necessary to make a proper survey and to take levels. In doing this work thought should be given to the future transport of timber, to fire-lines, and to the division of the plantations into compartments and future felling series. Much trouble will be saved in the future if this work is done with care before planting begins.

Species to plant.

On the type of waste land likely to be taken up for afforestation the best species to plant are one or more of the following:

Japanese larch, larch, spruce, Sitka spruce, Douglas fir, Corsican and Scots pines, with beech or sycamore as a mixture, or for protection belts. Only a small proportion of waste land is likely to be good enough for Douglas fir, and this should ordinarily be planted in the more sheltered places on the better and bracken-covered land; larch is best on the better land at higher elevations than the Douglas, but not on wind-swept ridges or plateaux, and it should be mixed with beech. Japanese larch is a specially useful tree for a first crop and has the advantage of standing fumes in colliery districts; spruce and Sitka spruce are best for the wetter land and peaty areas at all elevations and should be turf- or mound-planted. Corsican pine is a very valuable tree for the afforestation of the drier types of waste land, and Scots pine also, but the latter tree must not be used too extensively on the higher elevations subject to much snow. It succeeds best in the warmer climates on sandy soils at low elevations. Beech, and perhaps sycamore, are useful for shelter-belts round plantations and along ride-sides and for fire-belts, as well as for admixture with the other species to improve the soil.

Planting operations.

When the area is extensive it is best to start planting on that side of the area where labour will be most easily obtained and arrangements for supply of plants most easily made. Though the eventual fellings will have to take place in a direction contrary to the prevailing wind, it is not absolutely essential to plant in this order unless the planting is to be carried on over many years. Nevertheless, as far as possible planting should proceed against the wind direction. Planting on waste lands should ordinarily be done by notching, or with the mattock, as described in Chapter V. Where the land is flat enough it will be a great advantage if a plough can be used to loosen the soil in furrows at the proper distance apart. The distance apart should be kept as small as possible consistent with expense, so as to get a cover over the ground at the earliest possible date. The transport of plants will be a heavy item of expense, and it will be economical to form a nursery on the area at an early date, so as to supply plants as cheaply as possible. It is cheaper and better to use a piece of land already used for agriculture than to prepare a nursery on uncultivated land, and it is often possible to find a piece of suitable land on a farm near by.

Filling in blanks or beating up.

However carefully the planting has been done there are always a certain number of failures, and even when the plants have been closely spaced the death of three or four plants in a place will lead to a big gap. For the first two years after planting, therefore, it is essential that all blanks and failures be filled up. They may be filled with the same species as before, but, in larch plantations especially, this is a good opportunity to bring in an admixture of beech, by filling up all failures with this species.

Weeding.

All plantations should be looked at annually, and the necessary weeding must be done. As long as the weeds are doing no real harm, expense should be saved; but when it is found that the plants are beginning to get smothered, weeding is essential. It is a mere waste of money to plant and then to try to save expense by not carrying out necessary weeding. Nevertheless, the tendency to do unnecessary weeding after the crop is well established should be guarded against.

CHAPTER XVIII

THE USES OF BRITISH TIMBER

BROAD-LEAVED TREES

Alder. Cigar-boxes, clog-soles, barrel-staves, broom-heads, toys; the charcoal is used for making gunpowder. It is well suited for use underground and in water.

Ash. Coach-building, furniture, stamping-hammers, wheelwright's work, joinery implements, tool- and whip-handles, billiard cues, racquets, hurdles, barrel-hoops, gymnastic apparatus, lance-shafts, rudders and oars, thatchwood for stacks, bobbins, sieve-rims, aeroplane construction, and for any purpose where toughness and elasticity are required.

Beech. Chair-making, bent-wood furniture, for floors and staircases, stamping-hammers, railway-sleepers, street paving-blocks, pianofortes, carpenters' benches, wheelwright's work, agricultural implements, calico-mill rollers, packing-cases, sieve-frames, wooden shoes, gun-stocks, broom-heads, brush-backs, handles of planes and other tools, bobbins, boot-trees, pit-wood.

Birch. Joinery, cabinet-making, furniture, wheelwright's work, barrel-staves, crates, turnery, wagon-making, carving, brush-backs, clogs, brooms, spools and bobbins.

Elm. Furniture, coffins, coach- and wagon-building, turnery, wheelwright's work, butchers' blocks, inner lining of ships, keels of boats, tin-plate boxes, sieve-frames.

Common elm timber is more valuable than that of wych elm.

False Acacia. Wheelwright's work, especially spokes, and for rungs, tree-nails, tool-handles, gate- and fence-posts, turnery.

Hazel. Hoops, sieve-frames, walking-sticks, rods for hurdle-making.

Hornbeam. Wheelwright's work, cogged wheels and other woodwork in machinery, turnery, shoemakers' pegs and lasts, plane-boxes, carpenters' benches, tool-handles, agricultural implements, pulley-blocks, and all small articles where great toughness is required.

Horse-chestnut. Sides and bottoms of carts, cabinet-making, turnery, reels and bobbins.

Lime. Carving, founders' models, used under veneer, wooden basket-work, pianofortes and organs, wooden shoes. There is not much demand for lime timber.

Oak. Superstructures, hydraulic works, bridges, ship- and boat-building, house-building and interior decorations, gate-posts, mill-wheels, railway-sleepers, mining timber, pit-wood, joiner's work, cabinet-making, carriage-building, wheelwright's work, blocks, staves, bungs, sieve-frames, shingles, tree-nails, wood-carving, pianoforte making, turnery, window-frames, park palings, hurdles, rungs for ladders, cask-staves.

The timber of sessile oak is softer and more easily worked than that of pedunculate oak, and is preferred where great strength is not essential. Pedunculate oak is the best for all work of construction.

Poplar. Framework for veneered furniture, wheelwright's work, packing-cases, bottoms and sides of carts and stone-wagons, brake-blocks for railway carriages, cigar-boxes, matches, pulp for paper. Aspen is preferred for matches and for pulp for paper.

Sweet Chestnut. Interior work in house-building, furniture, gate-posts, park palings, fences and hurdles, staves, hop-poles, hoops, pit-wood.

Sycamore and Maple. Furniture, turnery, carving, reels and bobbins, churns and other dairy utensils, box-making, musical instruments, gun-stocks, whip-handles, bread-platters, wooden spoons, clog-soles, blocks of pulleys, calico-mill rollers.

Walnut. Cabinet-making, gun-stocks, veneer, wood-carving, turnery.

Willow. Framework for veneered furniture, packing-cases, hurdles, bottoms and sides of carts, bread-platters, knife-boards, cricket-bats, basket-work, clothes-pegs, withies.

Service Tree, *Apple*, *Pear*, *and Cherry*. Cabinet-making, turnery, carving, printers' tools, veneers.

CONIFERS

Austrian and Corsican Pine. Used for the same purposes as Scots pine, but the wood of both is coarser and less durable.

Douglas Fir. Used for the same purposes as larch, but the timber is not of the same quality.

Larch. Telegraph and telephone posts, railway-sleepers, bridges, boats, cart-making, masts, fencing, pit-wood. Larch of all sizes is useful, and is one of the most durable of British timbers. It is much used for all estate work.

Scots Pine or 'Red Deal'. Used for similar purposes as larch, but it is not so durable: it is also used for scaffolding, and house-building.

Spruce or 'White Deal'. House-building, for rafters and boarding, furniture, masts, telegraph posts, scaffolding and ladders, packing-cases, boxes, toys, cask-staves, musical instruments, pit-wood, wood pulp, fencing.

Silver Fir or 'White Pine'. Used for similar purposes as spruce.

Weymouth Pine or 'Yellow Pine'. House-building, especially in roofs, packing-cases, cabinet-making. It is very light in weight.

Yew. Bows, cabinet-making, wood-carving, turnery.

INDEX

Abies alba, 20.
  Nordmanniana, 165.
Acacia, notes on, 146.
  uses of, 228.
Accommodating species, 34.
Acer platanoides, 20, 158.
  pseudo-platanus, 20, 157.
Acland Committee report, 214.
Address of Forestry Commission, 219.
  of Stationery Office, 217.
Aesculus hippocastanum, 152.
Afforestation of waste land, 221.
Age class, 202.
  to ascertain, 15.
Alder, notes on, 146.
  uses of, 228.
Alnus glutinosa, 20, 146.
  incana, 20, 147.
Animals, protection against, 106.
Annual rings, 14.
Anther, 16.
Aphis abietina, 122.
  on beech, 122.
  on larch, 122, 167.
  on spruce, 120.
Apple timber, uses of, 230.
Arboriculture, definition of, 9.
Area of woods cut during war, 213.
  of woods in United Kingdom, 213.
Argyresthia atmoriella, 167.
Armillarea mellea, 127, 168, 173.
Ash, natural regeneration of, 93.
  notes on, 147.
  uses of, 228.
Aspect, influence of, 22, 24.
Aspen, notes on, 156.
Austrian pine, notes on, 169.
  uses of, 230.

Banks's pine, 171.
Bark allowance, 189.
  structure of, 14.
Bast, 14.
Beating up blanks, 68, 71, 227.
Beech, for hedges, 178.
  natural regeneration of, 92.
  notes on, 148.
  seedling mildew, 134.

Beech (*cont.*)
  uses of, 228.
  woolly aphis, 122.
Beetles, 112.
Betula pubescens, 20, 149.
Birch, natural regeneration of, 93.
  notes on, 149.
  uses of, 228.
Birds, classification of, 109.
  protection against, 108.
Black Italian poplar, 156.
  mauls, 161.
  poplar, 155.
  thorn for hedges, 178.
Blanks, beating up, 68, 71, 227.
Bole, 9.
Bordeaux mixture, 135.
Box for hedges, 179.
Bracken, damage by, 123.
Bramble, 123-5.
Broad-leaved tree, definition of, 18.
  trees, notes on, 146.
Brown oak, 155.

Callipers, 195.
Calyx, 16.
Cambium, 13.
Canary wood, 159.
Canker of broad-leaved trees, 134.
  of larch, 131.
  of silver fir, 130.
Carbohydrates, 10.
Carbon, 11.
  dioxide, 10, 11.
Carpel, 16.
Carpinus Betulus, 20, 152.
Castanea sativa, 20, 157.
Cells, 13.
Cembran pine, 171.
Census of woodlands, 218.
Chermes Cooleyi, 121, 164.
  corticalis, 171.
  nüsslini, 121.
  strobilobius, 120.
  viridis, 120, 167, 173.
Cherry, notes on, 150.
  uses of, 230.
Chestnut, horse, notes on, 152.

Chestnut (*cont.*)
  horse, uses of, 229.
  sweet, notes on, 157.
  sweet, uses of, 229.
Chlorophyll, 10.
Choice of species, 21, 33.
Clay soil, 30.
Cleaning, 73.
Clear cutting method, 85.
Climate, effect of, 19.
Cluster pine, 170.
Cockchafer, 112, 164.
Coleophora laricella, 117, 167.
Coleoptera, 112.
Colorado Douglas fir, 163.
Commission, Forestry, 213.
  address of, 219.
Compartment, 204.
  description of, 208.
  method of treatment, 87.
Conifer, definition of, 18.
Conversion of coppice woods, 103.
Coppice, definition of, 83.
  shoots, 17.
  system, 97.
Coppice-with-standards, conversion
  of, 103.
  definition of, 83.
  improvement of, 100.
  system, 99.
Cord of firewood, 191.
Cork cambium, 13.
Corolla, 16.
Corsican pine, notes on, 169.
  uses of, 230.
Corylus avellana, 151.
Counterfiring, 144.
Coupe, 208.
Crack willow, 160.
Cricket-bat willow, 160.
Crown of a tree, 9.
Cryptococcus fagi, 122, 149.
Cupressus macrocarpa, 162.
Cuttings, final, 91.
  preparatory, 90.
  seeding, 90.
Cypress, large-coned, 162.
  Lawson's, 162.

Dartmoor, survey of, 220.
Dasyscypha calycina, 131, 167.
Death duty, 72.

Depth of soil, 31.
Dicotyledons, 15.
Dioecious species, 17.
Disease, prevention of, 126.
Distances to plant, 65.
Ditches, 182.
Dominated trees, 74.
Dominating trees, 74.
Douglas fir, notes on, 163.
  uses of, 230.
Drainage, 182, 224.
Drought, protection against, 137.
Durmast oak, 154.
Dutch elm disease, 135, 151.

Elevation, effect of, 22.
Elm disease, 135.
  notes on, 150.
  uses of, 228.
Exacting species, 34.

Fagus sylvatica, 20, 148.
False acacia, 146.
Felling of timber, 185.
  series, 208, 211.
Fellings during the war, 213.
Fences, wire, 179.
Fencing, 175.
  against cattle, 179.
  against rabbits, 181.
  of waste land, 224.
Fertilization, 17.
Field book for description of com-
  partments, 206.
  for measuring timber, 197.
Filling up blanks, 68, 71, 227.
Final cuttings, 91.
Fires, protection against, 141.
Firewood, cord, 191.
Flowers, 15.
Fomes annosus, 129, 167, 168, 173.
Food of a tree, 9.
Forest of Dean, 22.
Forestry Act, 213, 217.
Forestry Commission, 213.
  address of, 219.
  grants by, 72.
  leaflets, 112.
  work of, 217.
Forestry schools, 218.
Forests, State, 217.
Formation of mixed woods, 40.

Foxy trees, 130.
Fraser River Douglas fir, 163.
Fraxinus americana, 148.
    excelsior, 20, 147.
Frost crack, 136.
    danger from, 24.
    effect of, 24.
    hardy trees, 25.
    holes, 25.
    lifting, 136.
    protection against, 26, 136.
    rib, 136.
    tender trees, 25.
Fructification of fungi, 126.
Fruit, 17.
Fungi, 125.
    protection against, 126.

Game coverts, 102.
Gean, 150.
Girdling, 11.
Glibskins, 161.
Goat moth, 156.
Goat willow, 159.
Gorse for hedges, 179.
Grants for planting, 72.
Graphium ulmi, 135, 151.
Grease bands, 111.
Green sucklings, 161.
Grey alder, 147.
    poplar, 156.
Group method of treatment, 94.
Growth in height, 39.
    in thickness, 13.
    of a tree, 13.
Gymnosperms, 15.

Hardwood, definition of, 18.
Hares, 106.
Hazel, notes on, 151.
    uses of, 228.
Heart-rot, 129, 167.
    wood, 14.
Heather, 123.
Hedges, formation of, 175.
    layering, 177.
    management of, 176.
    plants for, 178.
    trimming of, 177.
Heeling in plants, 49.
Height growth, 39.
    measurer, 192.

Hemiptera, 120.
High forest, 83, 85.
    two-storied, 87.
Holly for hedges, 179.
    notes on, 151.
Honey fungus, 127, 168.
Honeysuckle, 123.
Hoppus's tables, 189.
Hornbeam for hedges, 179.
    notes on, 152.
    uses of, 228.
Horse-chestnut, notes on, 152.
    uses of, 229.
Humus, 34, 35.
Hylobius abietis, 114, 164, 168.
Hymenoptera, 118.
Hyphae, 126.
Hypsometer, 192.

Ilex aquifolium, 151.
Imago, 109.
Improvement of soil, 34.
Inch class, 197.
    of timber, 189.
Insects, life-history of, 109.
    prevention of attack by, 110.
    remedial measures against, 111.
Ivy, 123.

Japanese larch, 167.
Juglans regia, 159.

Keithia thujina, 163.

Laburnum, 153.
Larch aphis, 120, 167.
    canker, 131, 167.
    Japanese, 167.
    Kurile, 167.
    miner moth, 117, 167.
    notes on, 166.
    sawfly, 119.
    shoot moth, 167.
    Siberian, 167.
    uses of, 230.
    Western, 167.
Larix decidua, 20, 166.
    Kaempferi, 20, 167.
Larva, 109.
Latitude, effect of, 22.
Lawson's cypress, 162.
Leaf canopy, 9.
    cast of Douglas fir, 135.

Leaflets issued by Forestry Commission, 112.
Lenticels, 12.
Lepidoptera, 116.
Lifting by frost, 136.
 plants, 58, 63.
Light, 10.
 demanding species, 28, 29.
 effect of, 28.
 necessity for, 28.
Lime tree, notes on, 153.
 uses of, 229.
Linden, 153.
Liriodendron tulipifera, 158.
Liverpool virus, 108.
Loam, 30.
Locust tree, 146.
Lombardy poplar, 156.
Longicorn beetle, 156.
Lophyrus pini, 118, 168.
 rufus, 119.

Manure for nursery, 52.
Maple, great, 157.
 Norway, 158.
 uses of, 229.
Maritime pine, 170.
Marl, 30.
Mattock-planting, 68.
Measurement of branch wood, 191.
 of felled timber, 187.
 of standing trees, 192.
 of whole woods, 195.
Medullary rays, 11, 15.
Megastigmus spermotrophus, 164.
Melampsorella, 130, 165.
Melolontha vulgaris, 112.
Meria Laricis, 167.
Methods of planting, 66.
 of treatment, 83.
Mice, 107.
Mineral composition of soil, 30.
Mixed woods, 37.
Moisture in the soil, 32.
Monocotyledons, 15.
Monoecious species, 17.
Moss on stems, 123.
Mother trees, 87.
Moths, 116.
Mound planting, 69.
Mountain ash, 153.
 pine, 171.

Mycelium, 126.
Myelophilus piniperda, 115, 168.
Myrobella plum, 178.
Mysaphis abietina, 173.

Names of trees, 20.
Natural orders, 20.
 regeneration, 88.
 regeneration by groups, 95.
Nectary, 16.
Nectria cinnabarina, 152.
 ditissima, 134, 148, 154.
Nematus Erichsoni, 119, 167.
Nordmann's fir, 165.
Normal forest, 202.
Norway maple, notes on, 158.
 spruce, notes on, 172.
Notch-planting, 67.
Number of plants per acre, 66.
 of trees per acre, 78.
Nurseries, 48.
 area of, 51.
 choice of site for, 50.
 density of sowing in, 53, 54.
 formation of, 51.
 laying out of, 52.
 manuring of, 52.
 pricking out seedlings in, 57, 59.
 quality of seed for, 56.
 season for sowing in, 55, 56.
 sowing seed beds in, 53.
 temporary, 49.
 tending of, 59.
 transplanting in, 58.
Nursery management, 48.
Nurses in plantations, 46, 78.

Oak, brown, 155.
 leaf-roller moth, 116.
 natural regeneration of, 92.
 pedunculate, notes on, 154.
 sessile, notes on, 154.
 Turkey, notes on, 155.
 uses of, 229.
Objects of the owner, 21.
Occlusion, 80.
Oregon pine, 164.
Osier holts, 98.
 notes on, 160.
Ovary, 16.
Ovules, 16.
Oxygen, 11.

Pan, 222.
Paraffin emulsion, 112.
Parasite, 126.
Partial clearance, 78.
Pear tree, uses of, 230.
Peat, 30.
  choice of species on, 33.
Peg-planting, 69.
Peridermium pini, 130, 169.
  strobi, 171.
Pestalozzia Hartigii, 173.
Petals, 16.
Phomopsis pseudotsugae, 135, 164.
Photosynthesis, 10, 12.
Phytophthora omnivora, 134.
Picea Abies, 20, 172.
  sitchensis, 20, 173.
Pine, Austrian, 169.
  Banks's, 171.
  beetle, 115, 168.
  blister, 130, 169.
  Cembran, 171.
  Cluster, 170.
  Corsican, 169.
  Maritime, 170.
  Mountain, 173.
  Remarkable, 171.
  sawfly, 118, 168.
  Scots, 167.
  shoot moth, 168.
  weevil, 168.
  Weymouth, 170.
Pinus Banksiana, 171.
  Cembra, 171.
  contorta, 171.
  montana, 171.
  nigra, 20, 169.
  pinaster, 170.
  radiata, 171.
  Strobus, 20, 170.
  sylvestris, 20, 167.
Pistil, 16.
Pith, 15.
Pit-planting, 66.
Plane, 155.
Plans, working, 201.
Planting, 61.
  density of, 64, 65.
  grants, 72.
  methods of, 66.
  notes on, 71.
  season for, 62.

Planting (*cont.*)
  triangle, 66.
Plant lice, 120.
Plants, age and size of, 61.
  distribution of, 63.
  lifting of, 62.
  number per acre, 66.
  pruning of, 58, 71.
  purchase of, 48.
  raising of, 49.
Platanus, 155.
Plots, sample, 206.
Poison for mice, 108.
Pollen, 16.
Polyporus sulphureus, 133.
Poplar longicorn beetle, 156.
Poplars, notes on, 156.
  uses of, 229.
Populus, 20, 155.
Porosity of the soil, 32.
Possibility, 206.
Prays curtisella, 148.
Preparatory cuttings, 90.
Privet, 179.
Protection against animals, 106.
  against birds, 108.
  against fire, 141.
  against frost, 26, 136.
  against fungi, 126.
  against insects, 110.
  against storms, 139.
  against weeds, 123.
Protoplasm, 13.
Pruning of plants, 58, 71.
  of trees, 80.
Prunus Avium, 150.
Pseudotsuga taxifolia, 20, 163.
Pumped trees, 129.
Pupa, 109.
Purchase of plants, 48.
Pure woods, 37, 46.
Pyrus aucuparia, 153.

Quercus cerris, 155.
  ilex, 18.
  pedunculata, 20.
  Robur, 20, 154.
  sessiliflora, 20, 154.

Rabbits, 106.
  fencing against, 181.
Rates on woodlands, 72.

Rays, medullary, 11, 15.
Red cedar, 162.
  deal, 168, 230.
  fir, 168.
  lead, 56.
  rot, 133.
Remarkable pine, 171.
Report of Acland Committee, 214.
Reproduction, 15.
Respiration, 11, 12.
Retinia buoliana, 168.
Rhabdocline pseudotsugae, 135, 164.
Rhizomorphs, 127.
Rhytisma acerina, 158.
Rings, annual, 14.
Robinia pseudacacia, 20, 146.
Root, 9.
  hairs, 10.
Rotation, 83, 84.

Salix, 20, 98, 159.
Sallow, notes on, 159.
Sample plots, 206.
Sandy soil, 30.
Saperda populnea, 156.
Saprophytes, 126.
Sapwood, 14.
Saugh, 159.
Sawflies, 118.
Scale insects, 120.
Schlich's spade, 68.
Schools of forestry, 218.
Scientific names of trees, 20.
Scolytus Geoffroyi, 150.
Scots pine, natural regeneration of,
  93.
  notes on, 167.
  uses of, 230.
Screefing, 68.
Sectional area, 187.
Seed, age at which produced, 94.
  beds, 53.
  depth to cover, 55.
  dispersal of, 17.
  number per lb. of, 54.
  percentage of germination, 54.
  production of, 15.
  quality of, 56.
  season for collecting, 54.
  sowing, 53.
  testing of, 56.
  thickness to sow, 55.

Seeding cutting, 90.
Selection method, 96.
Sepals, 16.
Sequoia sempervirens, 18.
Service tree, uses of, 230.
Shade bearers, 28, 29.
  demanders, 30.
  effect of, 28.
Shelter belts, 27.
Silver fir canker, 130.
  notes on, 165.
  uses of, 230.
Silver grain, 11, 15.
Softwoods, definition of, 18.
Soil, depth of, 31.
  effect of, 30.
  examination of, 36.
  fertility of, 34.
  improving species, 35.
  porosity of, 32.
  mineral composition of, 30.
  moisture in, 32.
Soils, choice of species on various,
  33.
  classification of, 30.
Sowing in the nursery, 53.
  in the forest, 60.
  in strips, 60.
  season for, 55, 56, 60.
Spanish chestnut, 157.
Spawn, 126.
Species, choice of, 21, 225.
  list of, 20.
  most important, 19.
  most paying, 21.
  names of, 20.
Spores, 126.
Spraying, 112, 135.
Spruce gall-aphis, 120, 173.
  green fly, 122.
  Norway, notes on, 172.
  Sitka, notes on, 173.
  uses of, 230.
Squirrels, 107.
Stagheadedness, 43.
Stamens, 16.
Standards, number of, 99.
Starch, 10.
State forests, 217.
Stationery Office, address of, 217.
Stem, 9.
Stigma, 16.

Stomata, 12.
Stool shoots, 17.
Storms, protection against, 138.
Struggle for existence, 73.
Style, 16.
Suckers, 17.
Sugar, formation of, 10.
Suppressed trees, 75.
Survey of Dartmoor, 220.
  of waste lands, 221.
Swamp cypress, 18.
Sweet chestnut, notes on, 157.
  uses of, 229.
Sycamore, natural regeneration of,
  93.
  notes on, 157.
  uses of, 229.
Sylvicultural notes on broad-leaved
  trees, 146.
  notes on conifers, 162.
  systems, 83.
Sylviculture, definition of, 9.
Synthesis, 10.

Taxation, remission of, 72.
Taxodium distichum, 18.
Taxus baccata, 173.
Tending of woods, 73.
Thaws, effect of, 23.
Thinning, 73.
  degree of, 78.
  necessity for, 74.
Thuya plicata, 162.
Tilea europaea, 153.
Timber, felling of, 185.
  measurement of, 187.
  uses of British, 228.
Toadstools, 128.
Tortrix viridana, 116.
Transpiration, 12.
Transplanting board, 58.
Transport of plants, 62.
Treatment, methods of, 83.
Tree, breathing of, 11.
  food of, 9.
  growth of, 13.
  life-history of, 9.
  structure of, 9.
Trees, names of, 20.
Trunk, 9.
Tulip tree, 158.
Turf-planting, 69.

Turkey oak, 155.
Twigs, growth of, 13.
Two-storied high forest, 87.

Ulmus campestris, 20, 150.
  glabra, 20, 151.
  montana, 20.
Underplanting, 44.
Uses of British timber, 228.

Vegetation as soil indicator, 222.
Voles, 107.
Volume statement, 200.

Walls, 181.
Walnut, notes on, 159.
  uses of, 229.
Waste land, afforestation of, 221.
  species to plant on, 225.
  survey of, 221.
Weeds, protection against, 123.
Weymouth pine, notes on, 170.
  uses of, 230.
White alder, 147.
  ash, 148.
  deal, 230.
  pine, 230.
  poplar, 156.
  thorn, 175.
  willow, 159.
  wood, 159.
Willow, notes on, 159.
  uses of, 229.
Wind, 27.
  protection against, 138.
Winged seeds and fruits, 17.
Wire fences, 179.
Witches' broom, 130, 165.
Wood, structure of, 14.
Woodlands, census of, 218.
Woods, tending of, 73.
Working circle, 208.
  plans, 201.
Wych elm, notes on, 151.

Yellow pine, 230.
  poplar, 159.
Yew, for hedges, 179.
  notes on, 173.
  uses of, 230.
Yield table, 200.